The Great Illusion a Study of the Relation of Military Power in Nations to Their Economic and Social Advantage

Norman Angell, Simeon Eben Baldwin

INTO CITY London

U17009

The Making of Modern Law collection of legal archives constitutes a genuine revolution in historical legal research because it opens up a wealth of rare and previously inaccessible sources in legal, constitutional, administrative, political, cultural, intellectual, and social history. This unique collection consists of three extensive archives that provide insight into more than 300 years of American and British history. These collections include:

Legal Treatises, 1800-1926: over 20,000 legal treatises provide a comprehensive collection in legal history, business and economics, politics and government.

Trials, 1600-1926: nearly 10,000 titles reveal the drama of famous, infamous, and obscure courtroom cases in America and the British Empire across three centuries.

Primary Sources, 1620-1926: includes reports, statutes and regulations in American history, including early state codes, municipal ordinances, constitutional conventions and compilations, and law dictionaries.

These archives provide a unique research tool for tracking the development of our modern legal system and how it has affected our culture, government, business – nearly every aspect of our everyday life. For the first time, these high-quality digital scans of original works are available via print-on-demand, making them readily accessible to libraries, students, independent scholars, and readers of all ages.

The BiblioLife Network

This project was made possible in part by the BiblioLife Network (BLN), a project aimed at addressing some of the huge challenges facing book preservationists around the world. The BLN includes libraries, library networks, archives, subject matter experts, online communities and library service providers. We believe every book ever published should be available as a high-quality print reproduction; printed on-demand anywhere in the world. This insures the ongoing accessibility of the content and helps generate sustainable revenue for the libraries and organizations that work to preserve these important materials.

The following book is in the "public domain" and represents an authentic reproduction of the text as printed by the original publisher. While we have attempted to accurately maintain the integrity of the original work, there are sometimes problems with the original work or the micro-film from which the books were digitized. This can result in minor errors in reproduction. Possible imperfections include missing and blurred pages, poor pictures, markings and other reproduction issues beyond our control. Because this work is culturally important, we have made it available as part of our commitment to protecting, preserving, and promoting the world's literature.

GUIDE TO FOLD-OUTS MAPS and OVERSIZED IMAGES

The book you are reading was digitized from microfilm captured over the past thirty to forty years. Years after the creation of the original microfilm, the book was converted to digital files and made available in an online database.

In an online database, page images do not need to conform to the size restrictions found in a printed book. When converting these images back into a printed bound book, the page sizes are standardized in ways that maintain the detail of the original. For large images, such as fold-out maps, the original page image is split into two or more pages

Guidelines used to determine how to split the page image follows:

• Some images are split vertically; large images require vertical and horizontal splits.
• For horizontal splits, the content is split left to right.
• For vertical splits, the content is split from top to bottom.
• For both vertical and horizontal splits, the image is processed from top left to bottom right.

N. M. W.

Simeon E. Baldwin

from

Elizabeth W. Whitney

Dec. 25 1911

The Great Illusion

The Great Illusion

A Study of the Relation of Military Power
in Nations to their Economic
and Social Advantage

By

Norman Angell

Third Revised and Enlarged Edition

G. P. Putnam's Sons
New York and London
The Knickerbocker Press
1911

The Knickerbocker Press, New York

Editions of *The Great Illusion* appeared simultaneously in the following publishing centres:

London	Borgä (Finland)
New York	Leyden
Paris	Turin
Leipsic	Stockholm
Copenhagen	Tokio
Madrid	

PREFACE

THE present volume is the outcome of a large pamphlet published in Europe at the end of last year entitled *Europe's Optical Illusion.* The interest that the pamphlet created and the character of the discussion provoked throughout Europe persuaded me that its subject-matter was worth fuller and more detailed treatment than then given it. Herewith the result of that conviction. The thesis on its economic side is discussed in the terms of the gravest problem which now faces European statesmanship, but these terms are also the living symbols of a principle of universal application, as true with reference to American conditions as to European. If I have not "localized" the discussion by using illustrations drawn from purely American cases, it is because these problems have not at present in the United States reached the acute stage that they have in Europe, and illustrations drawn from the conditions of an actual and pressing problem give to any discussion a reality which to some extent it might lose if discussed on the basis of more suppositious cases.

It so happens, however, that in the more abstract

section of the discussion embraced in the second part, which I have termed the "Human Nature of the Case," I have gone mainly to American authors for the statement of cases based on those illusions with which the book deals.

To the hurried reader (the vanity of authorship would like to believe that he is non-existent) I may hint that the "key" chapter of the first part is Chapter III; of the second part, Chapter II; of the third part, Chapter II. Though this method of treatment—the summarization within one chapter of the whole scope of the argument dealt with in the section—involves some small repetition of fact and illustration, such repetition is trifling in bulk (it does not amount in all to the value of two pages) and I have been more concerned to make the matter in hand clear to the reader than to observe all the literary canons. I may add that apart from this the process of condensation has been carried to its extreme limit in view of the character of the data dealt with, and that those who desire to understand thoroughly the significance of the thesis with which the book deals—it is worth understanding—had really better read every line of it.

One personal word may perhaps be excused as explaining certain phraseology which would seem to indicate that the author is of English nationality. He happens to be of English birth, but to have passed his youth and early manhood in the United

States, having acquired American citizenship there. This I hope entitles him to use the collective "we" on both sides of the Atlantic. I may add that the last twelve years have been passed mainly in Europe studying at first hand the problems here dealt with.

N. A.

PARIS, August, 1910.

SYNOPSIS

WHAT are the real motives prompting international rivalry in armaments, particularly Anglo-German rivalry? Each nation pleads that its armaments are purely for defence, but such plea necessarily implies that other nations have some interest in attack. What is this interest or supposed interest?

The supposed interest has its origin in the universally accepted theory that military and political power give a nation commercial and social advantages, that the wealth and prosperity of the defenceless nation are at the mercy of stronger nations, who may be tempted by such defencelessness to commit aggression, so that each nation is compelled to protect itself against the possible cupidity of neighbours.

The author boldly challenges this universal theory, and declares it to be based upon a pure optical illusion. He sets out to prove that military and political power give a nation no commercial advantage; that it is an economic impossibility for one nation to seize or destroy the wealth of another, or for one nation to enrich itself by subjecting another.

He establishes this apparent paradox by showing that wealth in the economically civilized world is founded upon credit and commercial contract. If these are tampered with in an attempt at confiscation by a conqueror, the credit-dependent wealth not only vanishes, thus giving the conqueror nothing for his conquest, but in its collapse involves the conqueror; so that if conquest is not to injure the conqueror, he must scrupulously respect the enemy's property, in which case conquest becomes economically futile.

Thus it comes that the credit of the small and virtually unprotected States stands higher than that of the Great Powers of Europe, Belgian three per cents standing at 96 and German at 82; Norwegian three and a half per cents at 102; and Russian three and a half per cents at 81.

For allied reasons the idea that addition of territory adds to a nation's wealth is an optical illusion of like nature, since the wealth of conquered territory remains in the hands of the population of such territory.

For a modern nation to add to its territory no more adds to the wealth of the people of such nation than it would add to the wealth of Londoners if the City of London were to annex the county of Hertford. It is a change of administration which may be good or bad; but as tribute has become under modern economic conditions impossible (which means that taxes collected from a given territory must directly or indirectly be spent on that territory), the fiscal situation of the people concerned is unchanged by conquest.

When Germany annexed Alsace, no individual German secured a single mark's worth of Alsatian property as the spoils of war.

The author also shows that international finance has become so independent and so interwoven with trade and industry that the intangibility of an enemy's property extends to his trade. It results that political and military power can in reality do nothing for trade, since the individual merchants and manufacturers of small nations exercising no such power compete successfully with those of the great. Swiss and Belgian merchants are driving English from the Canadian market; Norway has, relatively to population, a much greater mercantile marine than Great Britain.

The author urges that these little-recognized facts, mainly the outcome of purely modern conditions (rapidity of communication creating a greater complication and delicacy of the credit system), have rendered the problems of modern international politics profoundly and essentially different from the ancient; yet our ideas are still dominated by the principles and axioms and phraseology of the old.

In the second part—"The Human Nature of the Case"—the author asks, What is the basis, the scientific justification of the plea that man's natural pugnacity will indefinitely stand in the way of international agreement? It is based on the alleged unchangeability of human nature, on the plea that the warlike nations inherit the earth that warlike qualities alone can give the virile energy necessary for nations to win in the struggle for life.

The author shows that human nature is not unchanging; that the warlike nations do not inherit the earth; that warfare does not make for the survival of the fittest or virile; that the struggle between nations is no part of the evolutionary law of man's advance, and that that idea resides on a profound misreading of the biological law that physical force is a constantly diminishing factor in human affairs, and that this diminution carries with it profound psychological modifications; that society is classifying itself by interests rather than by State divisions; that the modern State is losing its homogeneity; and that all these multiple factors are making rapidly for the disappearances of State rivalries. He shows how these tendencies, like the economic facts dealt with in the first part, are very largely of recent growth, and may be utilised for the solution of the armament difficulty, not by inviting the invader, through defencelessness to come in, but by showing the invader that he has no interest in going; in other words, by so modifying current ideas on statecraft that aggression will be deprived of its main motive, and the risk of war and necessity for armament by that much lessened.

PART I

THE ECONOMICS OF THE CASE

PART II

THE HUMAN NATURE OF THE CASE

PART III

THE PRACTICAL OUTCOME

CONTENTS

Contents

CHAPTER IV

THE IMPOSSIBILITY OF CONFISCATION

CHAPTER V

FOREIGN TRADE AND MILITARY POWER

Contents

PART II

THE HUMAN NATURE OF THE CASE

CHAPTER I

THE PSYCHOLOGICAL CASE FOR WAR

"You cannot leave human nature out of the account"
—Nations too good to fight; also too bad—Material
comfort not the main motive in many human activities
—Military rivalry needs long preparation—Such rivalry
does not arise from "hot fit," therefore, but actual

Contents

CHAPTER II

OUTLINE OF THE PSYCHOLOGICAL CASE FOR PEACE

CHAPTER III

UNCHANGING HUMAN NATURE

CHAPTER IV

DO THE WARLIKE NATIONS INHERIT THE EARTH?

CHAPTER V

THE DIMINISHING FACTOR OF PHYSICAL FORCE: PSYCHOLOGICAL RESULTS

CHAPTER VI

THE STATE AS A PERSON: A FALSE ANALOGY AND ITS CONSEQUENCES

Contents

PART III

THE PRACTICAL OUTCOME

CHAPTER I

ARMAMENT, BUT NOT ALONE ARMAMENT

CHAPTER II

THE RELATION OF DEFENCE TO AGGRESSION

CHAPTER III

METHODS

PART I
The Economics of the Case

The Great Illusion

CHAPTER I

STATEMENT OF THE ECONOMIC CASE FOR WAR

Where can the Anglo-German rivalry of armaments end?—
Why peace advocacy fails—Why it deserves to fail—
The attitude of the peace advocate—The presumption that
the prosperity of nations depends upon their political
power, and consequent necessity of protection against
aggression of other nations who would diminish our power
to their advantage—These the universal axioms of international politics.

IT is pretty generally admitted that the present
rivalry in armaments with Germany cannot
go on in its present form indefinitely. The net
result of each side meeting the efforts of the
other with similar effort is that at the end of a
given period the relative position of both is
what it was originally, and the enormous sacrifices of both have gone for nothing. If it is
claimed that England is in a position to maintain
the lead because she has the money, Germany

can retort that she is in a position to maintain
the lead because she has the population, which
in the end must mean money. Meanwhile,
neither side can yield to the other, as the one so
doing would, it is felt, be placed at the mercy of
the other, a situation which neither will accept.
There are two current solutions which are offered
as a means of egress from this *impasse*. There
is that of the smaller party, regarded in both
countries for the most part as dreamers and
doctrinaires, who hope to solve the problem
by a resort to general disarmament, or, at least,
a limitation of armament by agreement. And
there is that of the larger and more practical
party who are quite persuaded that the present
state of rivalry and recurrent irritation is bound
to culminate in an armed conflict, which, by
definitely reducing one or other of the parties
to a position of manifest inferiority, will settle
the thing for at least some time, until after a
longer or shorter period a state of relative
equilibrium is established, and the whole process
will be recommenced *da capo*.

This second solution is, on the whole, accepted
as one of the laws of life: one of the hard facts
of existence which men of ordinary courage take
as all in the day's work. Most of what the
nineteenth century has taught us of the evolution of life on the planet is pressed into the
service of this struggle-for-life philosophy. We

are reminded of the survival of the fittest, that the weakest go to the wall, and that all life, sentient and non-sentient, is but a life of battle. The sacrifice involved in armament is the price which nations pay for their safety and for their political power. And the power of England has been regarded as the main condition of her past industrial success: her trade has been extensive and her merchants rich, because she has been able to make her political and military force felt and to exercise her influence among all the nations of the world. If she has dominated the commerce of the world in the past, it is because her unconquered navy has dominated, and continues to dominate, all the avenues of commerce. Such is the currently accepted argument.

And the fact that Germany has of late come to the front as an industrial nation, making giant strides in general prosperity and well-being, is deemed also to be the result of her military successes and the increasing political power which she is coming to exercise in Continental Europe. These things, alike in England and in Germany, are accepted as the axioms of the problem. I am not aware that a single authority of note, at least in the world of workaday politics, has ever challenged or disputed them. Even those who have occupied prominent positions in the propaganda of peace are at one with the veriest fire-eaters on this point. Mr. W. T. Stead is one of the leaders of the big navy party in England. Mr. Frederic Harrison, who all his life had been known as the philosopher protagonist of peace, declares that, if England allow Germany to get ahead of her in the race for armaments, "famine, social anarchy, incalculable chaos in the industrial and financial world would be the inevitable result. Britain may live on . . . but before she began to live freely again she would have to lose half her population, which she could not feed, and all her overseas Empire which she could not defend. . . . How idle are fine words about retrenchment, peace, and brotherhood, whilst we lie open to the risk of unutterable ruin, to a deadly fight for national existence, to war in its most destructive and cruel form." On the other side we have friendly critics of England, like Professor von Schulze-Gaevernitz, writing: "We want our [*i. e.* Germany's] Navy in order to confine the commercial rivalry of England within innocuous limits and to deter the sober sense of the English people from the extremely threatening thought of attack upon us. . . . The German Navy is a condition of our bare existence and independence, like the daily bread on which we depend, not only for ourselves but for our children."

Confronted by a situation of this sort, one is bound to feel that the ordinary argument of the pacifist entirely breaks down; and it breaks down for a very simple reason. He himself

accepts the premise which has just been indicated
—viz., that the victorious party in the struggle
for political predominance gains some material
advantage over the party which is conquered.
The proposition even to the pacifist seems so
self-evident that he makes no effort to combat
it. He pleads his case otherwise. "It cannot
be denied, of course," says one peace advocate, "that the thief *does* secure some material
advantage by his theft. What we plead is that
if the two parties were to devote to honest labour
the time and energy devoted to preying upon each
other, the permanent gain would more than offset
the occasional booty."

Some pacifists go farther and take the ground
that there is conflict between the natural law and
the moral law, and that we must choose the
moral even to our hurt. Thus Mr. Edward
Grubb writes:

Self-preservation is not the final law for nations any more than for individuals. . . . The
progress of humanity may demand the extinction
(in this world) of the individual, and it may
demand also the example and the inspiration of
a martyr nation. So long as the Divine provi-
dence has need of us, Christian faith requires that
we shall trust for our safety to the unseen but
real forces of right dealing, truthfulness, and love;
but, should the will of God demand it, we must be
prepared, as Jeremiah taught his nation long ago, to

give up even our national life for furthering those great ends to which the whole creation moves. This may be "fanaticism," but, if so, it is the fanaticism of Christ and of the prophets, and we are willing to take our places along with them.[1]

The foregoing is really the keynote of much pacifist propaganda. In our own day Count Tolstoi has even expressed anger at the suggestion that any but religious reaction against militarism can be efficacious.

The peace advocate pleads for "altruism" in international relationships, and in so doing admits that successful war may be the interest, though the immoral interest, of the victorious party. That is why the "inhumanity" of war bulks so largely in his advocacy, and why he dwells so much upon its horrors and cruelties.

It thus results that the workaday world and those engaged in the rough and tumble of practical politics have come to look upon the peace ideal as a counsel of perfection which may one day be attained when human nature, as the common phrase is, has been improved out of existence, but not while human nature remains what it is, and while it remains possible to seize a tangible ad-

[1] *The True Way of Life*, p. 29. I am aware that many modern pacifists are more objective in their advocacy than Mr. Grubb, but in the eyes of the "average sensual man pacifism is still deeply tainted with this self-sacrificing altruism." See Chap. III, Part III.

vantage by a man's strong right arm. So long as that is the case the strong right arm will seize the advantage, and woe betide the man who cannot defend himself.

Nor is this philosophy of force either as conscienceless, as brutal, or as ruthless as its common statement would make it appear. We know that in the world as it exists to-day, in spheres other than those of international rivalry, the race is to the strong, and the weak get scant consideration. Industrialism, commercialism, is as full of cruelties as war itself—cruelties, indeed, that are more long drawn out, more refined, though less apparent, and, it may be, appealing less to the common imagination. With whatever reticence we may put the philosophy into words, we all feel that conflict of interests in this world is inevitable, and that what is an incident of our daily lives we do not feel should be shirked as a condition of those occasional titanic conflicts which mould the history of the world.

The virile man doubts whether he ought to be moved by the plea of the "inhumanity" of war. The masculine mind accepts suffering, death itself, as a risk which we are all prepared to run even in the most unheroic forms of money-making; none of us refuses to use the railway train because of the occasional smash, to travel because of the occasional shipwreck, and so on. Indeed, peaceful industry demands a heavier toll even in blood than does war, a fact which the casualty statistics in railroading, fishing, mining, seamanship, eloquently attest. The cod-fisheries of Europe have been the cause of as much suffering within the last quarter of a century, of the loss of as many lives; such peaceful industries as fishing and shipping are the cause of as much brutality.[1] Our peaceful administration of the tropics takes as heavy a toll in the health and lives of good men, and much of it, as in the West of Africa, involves, unhappily, a moral deterioration of human character as great as that which can be put to the account of war.

Beside these peace sacrifices the "price of war" is trivial, and it is felt that the trustees of a nation's interests ought not to shrink from paying that price should the efficient protection of those interests demand it. If the common man is prepared, as we know he is, to risk his life in a dozen dangerous trades and professions for no object higher than that of improving his position or increasing his income, why should the statesman shrink from such sacrifices as the average war

[1] The newspaper *Le Matin* recently made a series of revelations, in which it was shown that the master of a French cod-fishing vessel had, for some trivial insubordinations, disembowelled his cabin-boy alive, and put salt into his intestines, and then thrown the quivering body into the hold with the cod-fish. So inured were the crew to brutality that they did not effectively protest, and the incident was only brought to light months later by wine-shop chatter. The *Matin* quotes this as the sort of brutality that marks the Newfoundland cod-fishing industry in French ships.

demands if thereby the great interests which have been confided to him can be advanced? If it be true, as even the pacifist admits that it may be true, that the tangible material interests of a nation may be advanced by warfare; if, in other words, warfare can play some large part in the protection of the interests of humanity, the rulers of a courageous people are justified in disregarding the suffering and the sacrifice that it may involve.

Of course the pacifist falls back upon the moral plea: we have no right to take by force. But here again the "common" sense of ordinary humanity does not follow the peace advocate. If the individual manufacturer is entitled to use all the advantages which great financial and industrial resources may give him against a less powerful competitor, if he is entitled, as under our present industrial scheme he is entitled, to overcome competition by a costly and perfected organization, of manufacture, of advertisement, of salesmanship, in a trade in which poorer men gain their livelihood, why should not the nation be entitled to overcome the rivalry of other nations by utilizing the force of its public bodies? It is a commonplace of industrial competition that the "big man" takes advantage of *all* the weaknesses of the small man—narrow means, his ill-health even—to undermine and to undersell. If it were true that industrial competition were always merciful, and national or political competition always cruel, the plea of the peace man might be unanswerable; but we know, as a matter of fact, that this is not the case, and returning to our starting-point, the common man feels that he is obliged to accept the world as he finds it, that struggle and warfare in one form or another are one of the conditions of life, conditions which he did not make. And he is not at all sure that the warfare of arms is necessarily either the hardest or the most cruel form of that struggle which exists throughout the universe. In any case, he is willing to take the risks, because he feels that military predominance gives him a real and tangible advantage, a material advantage translatable into terms of general social well-being, by enlarged commercial opportunities, wider markets, protection against the aggression of commercial rivals, and so on. He faces the risk of war in the same spirit that a sailor or a fisherman faces the risk of drowning, or a miner that of the choke-damp, or a doctor that of a fatal disease, because he would rather take the supreme risk than accept for himself and his dependants a lower situation, a narrower and meaner existence, with complete safety. And also he asks whether the lower path is altogether free from risks. If he knows much of life he knows that in so very many circumstances the bolder way is the safer way.

And that is why it is that the peace propaganda has so signally failed, and why the public opinion of the countries of Europe, far from restraining the tendencies of their governments to increase armaments, is pushing them into enlarged instead of into reduced expenditure. They find it universally assumed that national power means national wealth, national advantage; that expanding territory means increased opportunity for industry; that the strong nation can guarantee opportunities for its citizens that the weak nation cannot. The Englishman believes that his wealth is largely the result of his political power, of his political domination, mainly of his sea power; that Germany with her expanding population must feel cramped; that she must fight for elbow room; and that if he does not defend himself he will illustrate that universal law which makes of every stomach a graveyard. And he has a natural preference for being the diner rather than the dinner. As it is universally admitted that wealth and prosperity and well-being go with strength and power and national greatness, he intends so long as he is able to maintain that strength, and power, and greatness, that he will not yield it even in the name of altruism until he is forced to. And he will not yield it, because should he do so, it would be simply to replace British power and greatness by the power and greatness of some other nation, which he feels sure would do no more for the well-being of civilization as a whole than he is prepared to do. He is persuaded that he can no more yield in the competition of nations than as a business man or as a manufacturer he could yield in commercial competition to his rival; that he must fight out his salvation under conditions as he finds them, since he did not make them, and since he cannot change them.

And admitting his premises—and these premises are the universally accepted axioms of international politics the world over—who shall say that he is wrong?

CHAPTER II

THE AXIOMS OF MODERN STATECRAFT

Are the foregoing axioms unchallengeable?—Some typical
statements of them—German dreams of conquest—Mr.
Frederic Harrison on results of defeat of British arms and
invasion of England—Forty millions starving.

BUT are these universal axioms unchallengeable?

Is it true that wealth and prosperity and well-
being depend on the political power of nations, or,
indeed, that the one has anything whatever to do
with the other?

Is it true that one nation can gain a solid,
tangible advantage by the conquest of another?

Does the political or military victory of a
nation give any advantage to the individuals of
that nation which is not still possessed by the
individuals of the defeated nation?

Is it possible for one nation to take by force
anything in the way of material wealth from
another?

Is it possible for a nation in any real sense

15

to "own" the territory of another—to own it, that is, in any way which can benefit the individual citizens of the owning country?

If England could conquer Germany to-morrow, completely conquer her, reduce her nationality to so much dust, would the ordinary British subject be the better for it?

If Germany could conquer England would any ordinary German subject be the better for it?

The fact that all these questions have to be answered in the negative, and that a negative answer seems to outrage common sense, shows how much our political axioms are in need of revision.

The trouble in dealing with this problem, at bottom so very simple, is that the terms commonly employed in its discussion are as vague and as lacking in precision as the ideas they embody. All European statesmen talk glibly of the "collapse" of the British Empire or of the German, as the case may be, of the "ruin" of this or that country, of the domination and supremacy of this or that Power, but all these terms may respectively, so it appears, stand for a dozen different things. And in attempting to get at something concrete, and tangible, and definite, one is always exposed to the criticism of taking those terms as meaning something which the authors never intended.

I have, however, taken at random certain solemn and impressive statements of policy, typical of many, made by responsible papers and responsible public men. These seem quite definite and unmistakable in their meaning. They are from current papers and magazines which lie at my hand, and can consequently be taken as quite normal and ordinary and representative of the point of view universally accepted—the point of view that quite evidently dominates both German and English policy:

It is not Free Trade, but the prowess of our Navy . . . our dominant position at sea . . . which has built up the British Empire and its commerce.—*Times* leading article.

Because her commerce is infinitely vulnerable, and because her people are dependent upon that commerce for food and the wages with which to buy it . . . Britain wants a powerful fleet, a perfect organization behind the fleet, and an army of defence. Until they are provided this country will exist under perpetual menace from the growing fleet of German *Dreadnoughts*, which have made of the North Sea their parade-ground. All security will disappear, and British commerce and industry, when no man knows what the morrow will bring forth, must rapidly decline, thus accentuating British national degeneracy and decadence."—H. W. Wilson in *The National Review*, May, 1909.

Sea-power is the last fact which stands between Germany and the supreme position in international

commerce. At present Germany sends only some fifty million pounds worth, or about a seventh, of her total domestic produce to the markets of the world outside Europe and the United States. . . . Does any man who understands the subject think there is any power in Germany, or, indeed, any power in the world, which can prevent Germany, she having thus accomplished the first stage of her work, from now closing with Great Britain for her ultimate share of this 240 millions of overseas trade? Here it is that we unmask the shadow which looms like a real presence behind all the moves of present-day diplomacy and behind all the colossal armaments that indicate the present preparations for a new struggle for sea-power."
—Mr. Benjamin Kidd, in *The Fortnightly Review*, April 1, 1910.

It is idle to talk of "limitation of armaments" unless the nations of the earth will unanimously consent to lay aside all selfish ambitions. . . . Nations, like individuals, concern themselves chiefly with their own interests, and when these clash with those of others, quarrels are apt to follow. If the aggrieved party is the weaker he usually goes to the wall, though "right" be never so much on his side; and the stronger, whether he be the aggressor or not, usually has his own way. In international politics charity begins at home, and quite properly; the duty of a statesman is to think first of the interests of his own country."—
United Service Magazine, May, 1909.

Why should Germany attack Britain? Because Germany and Britain are commercial and political rivals; because Germany covets the trade, the colonies, and the Empire which Britain now possesses.—Robert Blatchford, *Germany and England*, p. 4.

It is upon their national security (assured by naval supremacy) that their economic future—their food, clothing, and housing—depends.—Admiral Mahan in the *Daily Mail*, July 4, 1910.

Great Britain with her present population exists by virtue of her foreign trade and her control of the carrying trade of the world; defeat in war would mean the transference of both to other hands and consequent starvation for a large percentage of the wage-earners.—T. G. Martin in the *World*.

If the command of the sea could be taken from us for a week or two these islands and their riches would be absolutely open to the plunderer. . . . When a landlord was shot by his parishioners, a Catholic priest asked indignantly from the pulpit, What right had he to tempt the poor people in this district to murder him by going about unarmed? We do not want the Powers of Europe to be tempted after this fashion.—Mr. J. St. Loe Strachey, editor of the *Spectator*, in "A New Way of Life," p. 80.

We offer an enormously rich prize if we are not able to defend our shores; we may be perfectly certain that the prize which we offer will go into the mouth of somebody powerful enough to overcome our resistance and to swallow a considerable portion of us up.—The Speaker of the House of Commons in a speech at Greystoke, reported by the *Times*.

What is good for the beehive is good for the bee. Whatever brings rich lands, new ports, or wealthy industrial areas to a State enriches its treasury, and therefore the nation at large, and therefore the individual.—Mr. Douglas Owen in a letter to the *Economist*, May 28, 1910.

Do not forget that in war there is no such thing as international law, and that undefended wealth will be seized wherever it is exposed, whether through the broken pane of a jeweller's window or owing to the obsession of a humanitarian Celt.—*Referee*, November 14, 1909.

We appear to have forgotten the fundamental truth—confirmed by all history—that the warlike races inherit the earth, and that Nature decrees the survival of the fittest in the never-ending struggle for existence. . . . Our yearning for disarmament, our respect for the tender plant of non-conformist conscience, and the parrot-like repetition of the misleading formula that the "greatest of all British interests is peace" . . . must inevitably give to any people who covet our wealth and our possessions . . . the ambition to strike a swift and deadly blow at the heart of the Empire—undefended London.—*Blackwood's Magazine*, May, 1909.

These are taken mainly from English sources, but there is not a straw to choose between them and current German opinion on the subject. Thus a German Grand Admiral writes:

The steady increase of our population compels us to devote special attention to the growth of our overseas interests. Nothing but the strong fulfilment of our naval programme can create for us that importance upon the free-world-sea which it is incumbent upon us to demand. The steady increase of our population compels us to set ourselves new goals and to grow from a Continental into a world power. Our mighty industry must aspire to new overseas conquests. Our world trade—which has more than doubled in twenty years—which has increased from 500 millions sterling to 800 millions sterling during the ten years which our naval programme was fixed—and 600 millions sterling of which is sea-borne commerce—only can flourish if we continue honourably to bear the burdens of our armaments on land and sea alike. Unless our children are to accuse us of short-sightedness it is now our duty to secure our world power and position among other nations. We can do that only under the protection of a strong German fleet, a fleet which shall guarantee us peace with honour for the distant future. —Grand Admiral von Koester, President of the Navy League, reported in the *Norddeutsche Allgemeine Zeitung*.

One popular German writer sees the possibility of "overthrowing the British Empire" and "wiping it from the map of the world in less than twenty-four hours." (I quote him textually, and I have heard almost the counterpart of it in the mouth of a serious English public man.) The author in question, who, in order to show how the thing could come about, deals with the matter prophetically, and, writing from the standpoint of 1911, admits that:

At the beginning of the twentieth century Great Britain was a free, a rich, and a happy country, in which every citizen, from the Prime Minister to the dock-labourer, was proud to be a member of the world-ruling nation. At the head of the State were men possessing a general mandate to carry out their programme of government, whose actions were subject to the criticism of public opinion, represented by an independent Press. Educated for centuries in self-government, a race had grown up which seemed born to rule. The highest triumphs attended England's skill in the art of government, in her handling of subject peoples. . . . And this immense Empire, which stretched from the Cape to Cairo, over the southern half of Asia, over half of North America and the fifth continent, could be wiped from the map of the world in less than twenty-four hours! This apparently inexplicable fact will be intelligible if we keep in sight the circumstances which rendered possible the building up of England's colonial power. The true basis of her world-supremacy was not her own strength, but the maritime weakness of all the other European nations. Their meagre or complete lack of naval preparations had given the English a position of monopoly which was used by them for the annexation of all those dominions which seemed of value. Had it been in England's power to keep the rest of the world as it was in the nineteenth century the British Empire might have continued for an unlimited time. The awakening of the Continental States to their national possibilities and to political independence introduced quite new factors into *Weltpolitik*, and it was only a question of time as to how long England could maintain her position in the face of the changed circumstances.

And the writer tells how the trick was done, thanks to a fog, efficient espionage, the bursting of the English war balloon, and the success of the German one in dropping shells at the correct tactical moment on to the British ships in the North Sea:

This war, which was decided by a naval battle' lasting a single hour, was of only three weeks' duration—hunger forced England into peace. In her conditions Germany showed a wise moderation. In addition to a war indemnity in accordance with the wealth of the two conquered States, she contented herself with the acquisition of the African Colonies, with the exception of the southern States, which had proclaimed their independence, and these possessions were divided with the other two Powers of the Triple Alliance. Nevertheless, this war was the end of England. A lost battle had sufficed to manifest to the world at large the feet of clay on which the dreaded Colossus had stood. In a night the British Empire had crumbled altogether; the pillars which English diplomacy had erected after years of labour had failed at the first test.

The appearance of a book by Dr. Rudolph Martin, a German Privy Councillor, "whose opinions may be taken as expressing the great bulk of the educated classes of Germany," emphasizes how much the foregoing represents very common aspirations in Germany. Dr. Martin says:

The future of Germany demands the absorption of Austria-Hungary, the Balkan States, and Turkey, with the North Sea ports. Her realms will stretch towards the east from Berlin to Bagdad, and to Antwerp on the west.

For the moment we are assured there is no immediate intention of seizing the countries in question, nor is Germany's hand actually ready yet to clutch Belgium and Holland within the net of the Federated Empire.

"But," he says, "all these changes will happen within our epoch," and he fixes the time when the map of Europe will thus be rearranged as from twenty to thirty years hence.

But Germany, according to the writer, means to fight while she has a penny left and a man to carry arms, for she is, he says, "face to face with a crisis which is more serious even than that of Jena."

And, recognising the positions, she is only waiting for the moment she judges the right one to break in pieces those of her neighbours who work against her. All Germans, declares Dr. Martin, know that this is not far off.

France will be her first victim, and she will not wait to be attacked. She is, indeed, preparing for the moment when the allied Powers attempt to dictate to her.

Germany, it would seem, has already decided

to annex the Grand Duchy of Luxemburg, and Belgium incidentally with, of course, Antwerp, and will add all the northern provinces of France to her possessions, so as to secure Boulogne and Calais.

All this is to come like a thunderbolt, and Russia, Spain, and the rest of the Powers friendly to England will not dare to move a finger to aid her. The possession of the coast of France and Belgium will dispose of England's supremacy for ever.

The necessity for armament is put in other than fictional form by so serious a writer as Dr. Gaevernitz, Pro-Rector of the University of Freiburg. Dr. Schulze-Gaevernitz is not unknown in England, nor is he imbued with inimical feelings towards her. But he takes the view that her commercial prosperity depends upon the political domination of Germany.[1]

After having described in an impressive way the astonishing growth of Germany's trade and commerce, and shown how dangerous a competitor Germany has become for England, he returns to the old question, and asks what might happen if England, unable to keep down the inconvenient upstart by economic means, should, at the eleventh hour, try to knock him down. Quotations from the *National Review*, the *Ob-*

---

[1] See letter to the *Matin*, August 22, 1908, and citations from his article given in Part III. of this book.

server,. the *Outlook,* the *Saturday Review,* etc., facilitate the professor's thesis that this presumption is more than a mere abstract speculation. Granted that they voice only the sentiments of a small minority, they are, according to our author, dangerous for Germany in this—that they point to a feasible and consequently enticing solution. The old peaceful Free Trade, he says, shows signs of senility. A new and rising Imperialism is everywhere inclined to throw means of political warfare into the balance of economic rivalry.

How deeply the danger is felt even by those who can in no sense be considered Jingoes may be judged by the following from the pen of Mr. Frederic Harrison. I make no apology for giving the quotations at some length. In a letter to the *Times* he says:

Whenever our Empire and maritime ascendancy are challenged it will be by such an invasion in force as was once designed by Philip and Parma, and again by Napoleon. It is this certainty which compels me to modify the anti-militarist policy which I have consistently maintained for forty years past. . . . To me now it is no question of loss of prestige—no question of the shrinkage of the Empire; it is our existence as a foremost European Power, and even as a thriving nation. . . . If ever our naval defence were broken through, our Navy overwhelmed or even dispersed for a season, and a military occupation of our arsenals, docks, and capital were effected, the ruin would be such as modern history cannot parallel. It would not be the Empire, but Britain, that would be destroyed. . . . The occupation by a foreign invader of our arsenals, docks, cities, and capital would be to the Empire what the bursting of the boilers would be to a *Dreadnought*. Capital would disappear with the destruction of credit. . . . A catastrophe so appalling cannot be left to chance, even if the probabilities against its occurring were 50 to 1. But the odds are not 50 to 1. No high authority ventures to assert that a successful invasion of our country is absolutely impossible if it were assisted by extraordinary conditions. And a successful invasion would mean to us the total collapse of our Empire, our trade, and, with trade, the means of feeding forty millions in these islands. If it is asked, "Why does invasion threaten more terrible consequences to us than it does to our neighbours?" the answer is that the British Empire is an anomalous structure, without any real parallel in modern history, except in the history of Portugal, Venice, and Holland, and in ancient history Athens and Carthage. Our Empire presents special conditions both for attack and for destruction. And its destruction by an enemy seated on the Thames would have consequences so awful to contemplate that it cannot be left to be safeguarded by one sole line of defence, however good, and for the present hour however adequate. . . . For more than forty years I have raised my voice against every form of aggression, of Imperial expansion, and Continental militarism. Few men have more earnestly protested against postponing social reforms and the well-being of the people to Imperial conquests and Asiatic and African adventures. I do not go back on a word that I have uttered thereon. But how hollow is all talk about industrial reorganization until we have secured our country against a catastrophe that would involve untold destitution and misery on the people in the mass—which would paralyze industry and raise food to famine prices, whilst closing our factories and our yards!

CHAPTER III

THE GREAT ILLUSION

These views founded on a gross and dangerous misconception—What a German victory could and could not accomplish—What an English victory could and could not accomplish—The optical illusion of conquest—There can be no transfer of wealth—The prosperity of the little States in Europe—German Three per Cents at 82 and Belgian at 96—Russian Three and a half per Cents at 81, Norwegian at 102—What this really means—Why security of little States not due to treaty—Military conquest financially futile—If Germany annexed Holland, would any German benefit or any Hollander?

I THINK it will be admitted that there is not much chance of misunderstanding the general idea embodied in the foregoing. Mr. Harrison is especially definite. At the risk of "damnable reiteration" I would again recall the fact that he is merely expressing one of the universally accepted axioms of European politics—namely, that a nation's financial and industrial stability, its security in commercial activity—in short, its prosperity and well-being, depend upon its being able to defend itself against the aggression of other nations, who will, if they are able, be tempted to commit such aggression because in so doing they will increase *their* power and consequently *their* prosperity and well-being, at the cost of the weaker and vanquished.

I have quoted, it is true, largely journalistic authorities because I desired to indicate real public opinion, not merely scholarly opinion. But Mr. Harrison has the support of other scholars of all sorts. Thus Mr. Spenser Wilkinson, Chichele Professor of Military History at Oxford, and a deservedly respected authority on the subject, confirms in almost every point in his various writings the opinions that I have quoted, and gives emphatic confirmation to all that Mr. Frederic Harrison has expressed. In his book, *Britain at Bay*, Professor Wilkinson says: "No one thought when in 1888 the American observer, Captain Mahan, published his volume on the influence of sea-power upon history, that other nations besides the British read from that book the lesson that victory at sea carried with it a prosperity and influence and a greatness obtainable by no other means."

Well, it is the object of these pages to show that this all but universal idea, of which Mr. Harrison's letter is a particularly vivid expression, is a gross and desperately dangerous misconception, partaking at times of the nature of an optical illusion, at times of the nature of a superstition, —a misconception not only gross and universal, but so profoundly mischievous as to misdirect an immense part of the energies of mankind and to misdirect them to such degree that unless we liberate ourselves from this superstition civilization itself will be threatened.

And one of the most extraordinary features of this whole question is that the absolute demonstration of the falsity of this idea, the complete exposure of the illusion which gives it birth, is neither abstruse nor difficult. Such demonstration does not repose upon any elaborately constructed theorem, but upon the simple exposition of the political facts of Europe as they exist to-day. These facts, which are incontrovertible, and which I shall elaborate presently, may be summed up in a few simple propositions, which sufficiently expose the illusion with which we are dealing. These propositions may be stated thus:

1. An extent of devastation, even approximating to that which Mr. Harrison foreshadows as the result of the conquest of Great Britain by another nation, is a physical impossibility. No nation can in our day by military conquest permanently or for any considerable period destroy or greatly damage the trade of another, since trade depends upon the existence of natural wealth and a population capable of working it. So long as the natural wealth of the country and

the population to work it remain, an invader cannot "utterly destroy it." He could only destroy the trade by destroying the population, which is not practicable, and if he could destroy the population he would destroy his own market, actual or potential, which would be commercially suicidal.

2. If an invasion by Germany did involve, as Mr. Harrison and those who think with him say it would, the "total collapse of the Empire, our trade, and the means of feeding forty millions in these islands . . . the disturbance of capital and destruction of credit," German capital would, because of the internationalization and delicate interdependence of our credit-built finance and industry, also disappear in large part, and German credit also collapse, and the only means of restoring it would be for Germany to put an end to the chaos in England by putting an end to the condition which had produced it. Moreover, because also of this delicate interdependence of our credit-built finance the confiscation by an invader of private property, whether stocks, shares, ships, mines, or anything more valuable than jewellery or furniture—anything, in short, which is bound up with the economic life of the people—would so react upon the finance of the invader's country as to make the damage to the invader resulting from the confiscation exceed in value the property confiscated. So that

Germany's success in conquest would be a demonstration of the complete economic futility of conquest.

3. For allied reasons in our day the exaction of tribute from a conquered people has become an economic impossibility; the exaction of a large indemnity of doubtful benefit to the nation receiving it, even when it can be exacted.

4. Damage to even an infinitely less degree than that foreshadowed by Mr. Harrison could only be inflicted by an invader as a means of punishment costly to himself, or as the result of an unselfish and expensive desire to inflict misery for the mere joy of inflicting it. In this self-seeking world it is not practical to assume the existence of an inverted altruism of this kind.

5. For reasons of a like nature to the foregoing it is a physical and economic impossibility to capture the external or carrying trade of another nation by military conquest. Large navies are impotent to create trade for the nations owning them, and can do nothing to "confine the commercial rivalry" of other nations. Nor can a conqueror destroy the competition of a conquered nation by annexation; his competitors would still compete with him—*i. e.*, if Germany conquered Holland, German merchants would still have to meet the competition of Dutch merchants, and on keener terms than originally, because the Dutch merchants would then be

within the German's customs lines. Moreover, Germans would not be able to take a pennypiece from the citizens of Holland to reimburse the cost of conquest, as any special taxation would simply be taxing Germans, since Holland would then be a part of Germany; the notion that the trade competition of rivals can be disposed of by conquering those rivals being one of the illustrations of the curious optical illusion which lies behind the misconception dominating this subject.

6. The wealth, prosperity, and well-being of a nation depend in no way upon its political power. Otherwise we should find the commercial prosperity and social well-being of the smaller nations which exercise no political power, manifestly below that of the great nations which control Europe, whereas this is not the case. The populations of States like Switzerland, Holland, Belgium, Denmark, Sweden are in every way as prosperous as the citizens of States like Germany, Russia, Austria, and France. The trade *per capita* of the small nations is in excess of the trade *per capita* of the great.

7. No nation could gain any advantage by the conquest of the British Colonies, and Great Britain could not suffer material damage by their loss, however much such loss would be regretted on sentimental grounds, and as rendering less easy certain useful social co-operation between kindred peoples. The use, indeed, of the

word "loss" is misleading. Great Britain does
not "own" her Colonies. They are, in fact,
independent nations in alliance with the Mother
Country, to whom they are no source of tribute
or economic profit, their economic relations being
settled, not by the Mother Country, but by the
Colonies. Economically, England would gain
by their formal separation, since she would be
relieved of the cost of their defence. Their
loss, involving, therefore, no change in economic fact (beyond saving the Mother Country
the cost of their defence), could not involve the
ruin of the Empire and the starvation of the
Mother Country, as those who commonly treat
of such a contingency are apt to aver. As England is not able to exact tribute or economic
advantage, it is inconceivable that any other
country necessarily less experienced in Colonial
management would be able to succeed where
England had failed, especially in view of the past
history of the Spanish, Portuguese, French, and
British Colonial Empires. This history also demonstrates that the position of Crown Colonies
in the respect which we are considering is not
sensibly different from that of the self-governing ones. It is not to be presumed, therefore, that any European nation would attempt
the desperately expensive business of the
conquest of England for the purpose of making an experiment with her Colonies which

all Colonial history shows to be doomed to failure.

The foregoing propositions traverse sufficiently the ground covered in the series of those typical statements of policy, both English and German, from which I have quoted. The simple statement of these propositions, based as they are upon the self-evident facts of present-day European politics, sufficiently exposes the nature of those political axioms which I have quoted. But as men even of the calibre of Mr. Harrison normally disregard these self-evident facts, it is necessary to elaborate them at somewhat greater length.

For the purpose of presenting a due parallel to the statement of policy embodied in the quotations made from the *Times* and Mr. Harrison and others, I have divided the propositions which I desire to demonstrate into seven clauses, but such division is quite arbitrary, and made only in order to bring about the parallel in question. The whole seven can be put into one, as follows: That as the only possible policy in our day for a conqueror to pursue is to leave the wealth of a territory in the complete possession of the individuals inhabiting that territory, it is a logical fallacy and an optical illusion in Europe to regard a nation as increasing its wealth when it increases its territory, because when a province or state is annexed, the population, who are the real and

only owners of the wealth therein, are also annexed, and the conqueror gets nothing. The
facts of modern history abundantly demonstrate
this. When Germany annexed Schleswig-Holstein and Alsace not a single ordinary German
citizen was one pfennig the richer. Although
England "owns" Canada, the English merchant
is driven out of the Canadian markets by the
merchant of Switzerland who does not "own"
Canada. Even where territory is not formally
annexed, the conqueror is unable to take the
wealth of a conquered territory owing to the
delicate interdependence of the financial world
(an outcome of our credit and banking systems),
which makes the financial and industrial security
of the victor dependent upon financial and industrial security in all considerable civilized
centres. So that widespread confiscation or
destruction of trade and commerce in conquered
territory would react disastrously upon the conqueror. The conqueror is thus reduced to economic impotence which means that political and
military power is economically futile—that is to
say, can do nothing for the trade and well-being
of the individuals exercising such power. Conversely, armies and navies cannot destroy the
trade of rivals, nor can they capture it. The
great nations of Europe do not destroy the trade
of the small nations to their benefit, because they
cannot; and the Dutch citizen, whose govern-

ment possesses no military power, is just as well off as the German citizen, whose government possesses an army of two million men, and a great deal better off than the Russian, whose government possesses an army of something like four million. Thus the Three per Cents of powerless Belgium are quoted at 96, and the Three per Cents of powerful Germany at 82; the Three and a half per Cents of the Russian Empire, with its hundred and twenty million souls and its four million army, are quoted at 81, while the Three and a half per Cents of Norway, which has not an army at all (or any that need be considered in the discussion), are quoted at 102. All of which carries with it the paradox that the more a nation's wealth is protected the less secure does it become.[1]

It is this last fact, constituting as it does one of the most remarkable of economic-sociological phenomena in Europe, which might be made the text of this book. Here we are told by all the experts that great navies and great armies are necessary to protect our wealth against the

---

[1] This is not the only basis of comparison, of course. Everyone who knows Europe at all is aware of the high standard of comfort in all the small countries: Scandinavia, Holland, Belgium, Switzerland. Dr. Bertillon, the French statistician, has made an elaborate calculation of the relative wealth of the individuals of each country. The middle-aged German possesses (on the established average) nine thousand francs; the Hollander, *sixteen thousand !* (see *Journal*, Paris, Aug. 1, 1910).

aggression of powerful neighbours, whose cupidity and voracity can be controlled by force alone; that treaties avail nothing, and that in international politics might makes right. Yet when the financial genius of Europe, studying the question in its purely financial and material aspect, has to decide between the great States with all their imposing paraphernalia of colossal armies and fabulously costly navies, and the little States (which, if our political pundits are right, could any day have their wealth gobbled up by those voracious big neighbours) possessing relatively no military power whatever, such genius plumps solidly, and with what is in the circumstances a tremendous difference, in favour of the small and helpless. For a difference of twenty points, which we find as between Norwegian and Russian, and fourteen as between Belgian and German securities is the difference between a safe and a speculative one; the difference between an American railroad bond in time of profound security and in time of widespread panic. And what is true of the Government funds is true in an only slightly less degree of the industrial securities, in the national comparison just drawn.

Is it a sort of altruism or quixoticism which thus impels the capitalists of Europe to conclude that the public funds and investments of powerless Holland and Sweden (any day at the mercy of their big neighbours) are 10 to 20 per cent. safer than the greatest Power of Continental Europe? The question is, of course, absurd. The only consideration of the financier is profit and security, and he has decided that the funds of the undefended nation are more secure than the funds of one defended by colossal armaments. How does he arrive at this decision, unless it be through the knowledge that modern wealth requires no defence, because it cannot be confiscated?

Nor can it be replied that I am confusing two things, political and military, as against commercial security. My whole point is that Mr. Harrison, and those who think with him (that is to say, the statesmen of Europe generally) are for ever telling us that military security and commercial security are identical, and that armaments are justified by the necessity for commercial security; that the Navy is an "insurance," and all the other catch phrases which are the commonplace of this discussion.

If Mr. Harrison were right; if, as he implies, England's commerce, her very industrial existence, would disappear did she allow neighbours who envied her that commerce to become her superiors in armament, how does he explain the fact that the great Powers of the Continent are flanked by little nations infinitely weaker than themselves having always a *per capita* trade equal, and in most cases greater than themselves? If the common doctrines be true the Rothschilds, Barings, Morgans, and Sterns would not invest a pound or a dollar in the territories of the undefended nations, and yet, far from that being the case, they consider that a Swiss or a Dutch investment is more secure than a German one; that industrial undertakings in a country like Switzerland, defended by a comic opera army of a few thousand men, are preferable in point of security to enterprises backed by three millions of the most perfectly trained soldiers in the world. The attitude of European finance in this matter is the absolute condemnation of the view commonly taken by the statesman. If a country's trade were really at the mercy of the first successful invader; if armies and navies were really necessary for the protection of trade, the small countries would be in a hopelessly inferior position, and could only exist on the sufferance of what we are told are unscrupulous aggressors. And yet Norway has relatively to population a greater carrying trade than Great Britain,[1] and Dutch, Swiss, and Belgian merchants compete in all the markets of the world successfully with those of Germany and France.

It may be argued that the small States owe

---

[1] The figures given in the *Statesman's Year-Book* show that proportionately to population Norway has nearly three times the carrying trade of England.

their security to the various treaties guaranteeing their neutrality. But such a conclusion of itself would condemn the supporters of the great armaments, because it would imply that international good faith constituted a better defence than armaments. If this were really the case, armaments would indeed be condemned. One defender of the notion of security by treaty puts the case thus:

It would be a strange result of our modern international rivalry if those smaller members of the European family came to occupy a more favourable position than have their neighbours. But things seem working in that direction, for it is a fact that, with no defence worth speaking of, these countries are more secure against invasion, less fearful of it, less preoccupied by it than England, or Germany, or France, each with its gigantic army or navy. Why is this? Only because the moral force of a treaty affords a stronger bulwark than any amount of material strength.

Then, if these smaller countries can enjoy this sense of safety from a merely moral guarantee, why should not the larger ones as well? It seems absurd that they should not. If that recent agreement between England, Germany, France, Denmark, and Holland can so effectively relieve Denmark and Holland from the fear of invasion that Denmark can seriously consider the actual abolition of her army and navy, it seems only one further step to go for all the Powers collectively, great and small, to guarantee the territorial independence of each one of them severally. The North Sea Treaty of 1907 supplies even the very words that would establish such an agreement.

You may say this is Utopian, but it is at least not more than the futile attempt of the last hundred years to try and base territorial independence solely or mainly on material resources. You will hardly deny that the fear in England of actual invasion has not merely kept pace with, but has outstripped, the increase of our expenditure on our Navy. Nor is the case different with any other country. The more armaments have been piled upon armaments the greater has grown the sense of insecurity. May I not fairly argue from this that we have all gone the wrong way to work, and that the more we reduce our armaments and rely upon simple treaties the safer we shall all feel and the less we shall be afraid of aggression?

But I fear that if we had to depend upon the sanctity of treaty rights and international good faith, we should indeed be leaning on a broken reed.[1]

[1] "The principle practically acted on by statesmen, though, of course, not openly admitted, is that frankly enunciated by Machiavelli: 'A prudent ruler ought not to keep faith when by so doing it would be against his interests, and when the reasons which made him bind himself no longer exist.' Prince Bismarck said practically the same thing, only not quite so nakedly. The European waste-paper basket is the place to which all treaties eventually find their way, and a thing which can any day be placed in a waste-paper basket is a poor thing on which

It is but the other day that Austria, by the hand of "his most Catholic Majesty"—a sovereign regarded as one of the most high-minded in Europe—cynically laid aside solemn and sacred engagements, entered into with the other European Powers, and, without so much as a "by-your-leave," made waste paper of them, and took advantage of the struggle for civilization in which the new Turkish Government was engaged to annex Bosnia and Herzegovina, which he had given a solemn undertaking not to do, and I fear that "his most Catholic Majesty" does not even lose caste thereby. For, though but a few months separate us from this double breach of contract (the commercial equivalent of which would have disgraced an ordinary tradesman), Europe seems to have forgotten the whole thing.

The sanctity of treaty rights is a very frail protection to the small State. On what, therefore, does its evident security rest? Once again, *on the simple fact that its conquest would assure to the conqueror no profit.*[1]

---

to hang our national safety. Yet there are plenty of people in this country who quote treaties to us as if we could depend on their never being torn up. Very plausible and very dangerous people they are—idealists too good and innocent for a hard, cruel world, where force is the chief law. Yet there are, some such innocent people in Parliament even at present. It is to be hoped that we shall see none of them there in future " (Major Stewart Murray, *Future Peace of the Anglo-Saxons*).

[1] On the occasion of the first anniversary of the annexation

Let us put this matter as concretely and as practically, with our feet as close to the earth as possible, and take an actual example. There is possibly no party in Europe so convinced of the general truth of the common axioms that at present dominate international politics as the Pan-germanists of Germany. This party has set before itself the object of grouping into one great power all the peoples of the Germanic race or language in Europe. Were this aim achieved, Germany would become the dominating Power of the Continent, and might become the dominating Power of the world. And according to the commonly accepted view such an achievement would, from the point of view of Germany, be worth any sacrifice that Germans could make. It would be an object so great, so desirable, that German citizens should not hesitate for an instant to give everything, life itself, in its accomplishment. Very good. Let us assume that at the cost of great sacrifice, the greatest sacrifice which it is possible to imagine a modern civilized nation making, this has been accomplished; and that Belgium and Holland and Germany, Switzerland, and Austria, have all become part of the great

---

the Austrian Press dealt with the disillusion the Act involved. One paper says: "The annexation has cost us millions, was a great disturbance to our trade, and it is impossible to point to one single benefit that has resulted." There was not even a pretence of economic interest in the annexation which was prompted by pure political vanity.

German hegemony: *is there one ordinary German citizen who would be able to say that his well-being had increased by such a change?* Germany would then "own" Holland. *But would a single German citizen be the richer for the ownership?* The Hollander, from having been the citizen of a small and insignificant State, would become the citizen of a very great one. *Would the individual Hollander be any the richer or any the better?* We know that, as a matter of fact, neither the German nor the Hollander would be one whit the better, and we know also, as a matter of fact, that in all human probability they would be a great deal worse. We may, indeed, say that the Hollander would be certainly the worse in that he would have exchanged the relatively light taxation and light military service of Holland for the much heavier taxation and the much longer military service of the "great" German Empire.

The following correspondence, provoked by the first edition of this book, throws some further light on the points elaborated in this chapter. Mr. Douglas Owen, writing to the *Economist*, May 28, 1910, says:

Whatever brings rich lands, new ports, or wealthy industrial areas to a State enriches its treasury, and therefore the nation at large, and therefore the individual.

To which another correspondent replied:

Mr. Owen here outlines with admirable brevity the very optical illusion from which the book takes its title. In every civilized State revenues which are drawn from "rich lands, new ports," etc., are expended on the administration of these rich lands, and new ports, and the citizens of the enlarged administrative area are exactly where they were before; and the notion that in some mysterious way wealth may first be drawn from a territory into the treasury, and then be redistributed with a profit to the individuals who have contributed it or to others, is merely a vulgar error due to inattention as to the real methods of modern political administration. It would be just as reasonable to say that the citizens of London are richer than the citizens of Birmingham because London has a richer treasury, or that Londoners would become richer if the London County Council were to "annex" the county of Hertfordshire; or to say that people's wealth varies according to the size of the administrative areas which they inhabit. The whole thing is, of course, what Mr. Angell calls it, an optical illusion. Just as poverty may be greater in the great city than in the small one and taxation heavier, so the citizens of a great State may be poorer than the citizens of a small one—as they very often are. Modern government is mainly, and tends to become entirely, a matter simply of administration, and mere jugglery with the administrative entities, the absorption of small States into large ones, or the breaking up of large States into small ones is not of itself going to affect the matter one way or another.

The letter of another critic provoked the following reply:

While it is true, of course, that if Germany annexed Holland the German Government revenue would be increased by the amount of the Dutch taxes, German expenditure would be charged with the cost of Dutch administration, and any taxes collected in Holland would simply be absorbed by the increased expenditure incurred in the administration and defence of Holland, so that the German Government and German people would be exactly where they were before. If an attempt were made to exact from the newly acquired province some special tribute to be distributed in some way among the other States of the Empire, Dutch discontent would be so great that the cost of administration, policing, repression, defence, etc., would be so increased as certainly to offset the advantages of such tribute. But there is no reason to suppose that Germany would even attempt this. She has not done so in the case of Schleswig-Holstein or Alsace Lorraine—*i.e.*, she has never taken from those provinces a tribute which she has attempted to distribute among the other States of the Empire, so that the individual German is not one pfennig richer because those States have been incorporated in the Empire.

CHAPTER IV

THE IMPOSSIBILITY OF CONFISCATION

Our present vocabulary of international politics an historical
survival—Why modern conditions differ from ancient—
The profound change effected by credit—The delicate
interdependence of international finance—Attila and the
Kaiser—What would happen if a German invader looted
the Bank of England—German trade dependent upon
English credit—Confiscation of an enemy's property an
economic impossibility under modern conditions.

DURING the Jubilee procession an English
beggar was heard to say:

I own Australia, Canada, New Zealand, India,
Burmah, and the Islands of the Far Pacific; and I
am starving for want of a crust of bread. I am a
citizen of the greatest Power of the modern world,
and all people should bow to my greatness. And
yesterday I cringed for alms to a negro savage, who
repulsed me with disgust.

What is the meaning of this?
The meaning is that, as most frequently
happens in the history of ideas, our vocabulary
is a survival of conditions no longer existing,

4   49

and our mental conceptions follow at the tail of our vocabulary. International politics are still dominated by terms applicable to conditions which the processes of modern life have altogether abolished.

In the Roman times—indeed, in all the ancient world—it *was* true that the conquest of a territory meant a tangible advantage to the conqueror; it meant the exploitation of the conquered territory by the conquering State itself to the advantage of that State and its citizens. It not infrequently meant the enslavement of the conquered people and the acquisition of wealth in the form of slaves as a direct result of the conquering war. In mediæval times a war of conquest meant at least immediate tangible booty in the shape of movable property, actual gold and silver, land parcelled out among the chiefs of the conquering nation, as took place at the Norman Conquest, and so forth.

At a later period conquest at least involved an advantage to the reigning house of the conquering nation, and it was mainly the squabbles of rival sovereigns for prestige and power which precipitated the wars of such period.

At a still later period civilization, as a whole— not necessarily the conquering nation—gained (sometimes) by the conquest of savage peoples, in that order was substituted for disorder. In the period of the colonization of newly-discovered land the pre-emption of such territory by one particular nation secured an advantage for the citizens of that nation in that its overflowing population found homes in conditions that were preferable to the social or political conditions imposed by alien nations. *But none of these conditions is part of the problem that we are considering.* We are concerned with the case of fully civilized rival nations in fully occupied territory, and the fact of conquering such territory gives to the conqueror no material advantage which he could not have had without conquest. And in these conditions—the realities of the political world as we find it to-day—"domination," or "predominance of armament," or the "command of the sea," can do nothing for commerce and industry or general well-being; we may build fifty *Dreadnoughts* and not sell so much as a penknife the more in consequence. We might conquer Germany to-morrow, and we should find that we could not, because of that fact, make a single Englishman a shilling's worth the richer in consequence, the war indemnity notwithstanding.

How have conditions so changed that terms which were applicable to the ancient world—in one sense at least to the mediæval world, and, in another sense still to the world of that political renaissance which gave to Great Britain its Empire—are no longer applicable in *any* sense to the conditions of the world as we find them to-day? How has it become impossible for one nation to take by conquest the wealth of another for the benefit of the people of the conqueror? How is it that we are confronted by the absurdity (which the facts of our own Empire go to prove) of the conquering people being able to exact from conquered territory rather less than more advantage than it was able to do before the conquest took place?

The cause of this profound change, largely the work of the last thirty years, is due mainly to the complex financial interdependence of the capitals of the world, a condition in which disturbance in New York involves financial and commercial disturbance in London, and, if sufficiently grave, compels financiers of London to co-operate with those of New York to put an end to the crisis, not as a matter of altruism, but as a matter of commercial self-protection. The complexity of modern finance makes New York dependent on London, London upon Paris, Paris upon Berlin, to a greater degree than has ever yet been the case in history. This interdependence is the result of the daily use of those contrivances of civilization which date from yesterday—the rapid post, the instantaneous dissemination of financial and commercial information by means of telegraphy, and generally the incredible progress of rapidity in communication which has put the half-dozen chief capitals of Christendom in closer contact financially, and has rendered them more dependent the one upon the other than were the chief cities of Great Britain less than a hundred years ago.

A well-known French authority, writing recently in a financial publication, makes this reflection:

The very rapid development of industry has given rise to the active intervention therein of finance, which has become its *nervus rerum*, and has come to play a dominating *rôle*. Under the influence of finance, industry is beginning to lose its exclusively national character to take on a character more and more international. The animosity of rival nationalities seems to be in process of attenuation as the result of this increasing international solidarity. This solidarity was manifested in a striking fashion in the last industrial and monetary crisis. This crisis, which appeared in its most serious form in the United States and Germany, far from being any profit to rival nations, has been injurious to them. The nations competing with America and Germany, such as England and France, have suffered only less than the countries directly affected. It must not be forgotten that, quite apart from the financial interests involved directly or indirectly in the industry of other countries, every producing country is at one and the same time, as well as being a competitor and a rival, a client and a market. Financial and commercial solidarity is increasing every day at the expense of commercial and industrial competition. This was certainly one of the principal causes which a year or two ago prevented the outbreak of war between Germany and France *à propos* of Morocco, and which led to the understanding of Algeciras. There can be no doubt for those who have studied the question that the influence of this international economic solidarity is increasing despite ourselves. It has not resulted from the conscious action on the part of any of us, and it certainly cannot be arrested by any conscious action on our part.[1]

A fiery patriot sent to a London paper the following letter:

When the German Army is looting the cellars of the Bank of England, and carrying off the foundations of our whole national fortune, perhaps the twaddlers who are now screaming about the wastefulness of building four more *Dreadnoughts* will understand why sane men are regarding this opposition as treasonable nonsense.

What would be the result of such an action on the part of a German Army in London? The first effect, of course, would be that, as the Bank of England is the banker of all other banks, there would be a run on every bank in England, and all would suspend payment. But, simultaneously, German bankers, many with credit in London, would feel the effect; merchants the

[1] *L'Information*, August 22, 1909.

world over threatened with ruin by the effect of the collapse in London would immediately call in all their credits in Germany, and German finance would present a condition of chaos hardly less terrible than that in England. The German Generalissimo in London might be no more civilized than Attila himself, but he would soon find the difference between himself and Attila. Attila, luckily for him, did not have to worry about a bank rate and such like complications; but the German general, while trying to sack the Bank of England, would find that his own balance in the Bank of Berlin would have vanished into thin air and the value of even the best of his investments dwindled as though by a miracle; and that for the sake of loot, amounting to a few sovereigns apiece among his soldiery, he would have sacrificed the greater part of his own personal fortune. It is as certain as anything can be that were the German Army guilty of such economic vandalism there is no considerable institution in Germany that would escape grave damage—a damage in credit and security so serious as to constitute a loss immensely greater[1] than the value of the loot obtained. It is not putting the case too strongly to say that for every pound taken from the Bank of England German trade would suffer a thousand. The influence of the whole finance

---

[1] Very many times greater, because the bullion reserve in the Bank of England is relatively small.

of Germany would be brought to bear on the German Government to put an end to a situation ruinous to German trade, and German finance would only be saved from utter collapse by an undertaking on the part of the German Government scrupulously to respect private property, and especially bank reserves. It is true the German Jingoes might wonder what they had made war for, and an elementary lesson in international finance which the occasion afforded would do more than the greatness of the British Navy to cool their blood. For it is a fact in human nature that men will fight more readily than they will pay, and that they will take personal risks much more readily than they will disgorge money, or for that matter earn it. "Man," in the language of Bacon, "loves danger better than travail."

Events which are still fresh in the memory of business men show the extraordinary interdependence of the modern financial world. A financial crisis in New York sends up the English bank rate to 7 per cent., thus involving the ruin of many English businesses which might otherwise have weathered a difficult period. It thus happens that one section of the financial world is against its will compelled to come to the rescue of any other considerable section which may be in distress.

From one of the very latest treatises on international finance,[1] I make the following very suggestive quotations:

Banking in all countries hangs together so closely that the strength of the best may easily be that of the weakest if scandal arises owing to the mistakes of the worst. . . . Just as a man cycling down a crowded street depends for his life, not only on his skill, but more on the course of the traffic there. . . . Banks in Berlin were obliged, from motives of self-protection (on the occasion of the Wall Street crisis), to let some of their gold go to assuage the American craving for it. . . . If the crisis became so severe that London had to restrict its facilities in this respect, other centres, which habitually keep balances in London which they regard as so much gold, because a draft on London is as good as gold, would find themselves very seriously inconvenienced; and it thus follows that it is to the interest of all other centres, which trade on those facilities which London alone gives, to take care that London's task is not made too difficult. This is especially so in the case of foreigners who keep a balance in London which is borrowed. In fact, London drew in the gold required for New York from seventeen other countries. . . .

Incidentally it may be mentioned in this connection that German commerce is in a special sense interested in the maintenance of English credit. The authority just quoted says:

[1] Hartley Withers, *The Meaning of Money*.

It is even contended that the rapid expansion of German trade, which pushed itself largely by its elasticity and adaptability to the wishes of its customers, could never have been achieved if it had not been assisted by the large credit furnished in London. . . . No one can quarrel with the Germans for making use of the credit we offered for the expansion of the German trade, although their over-extension of credit facilities has had results which fall on others besides themselves. . . .

Let us hope that our German friends are duly grateful, and let us avoid the mistake of supposing that we have done ourselves any permanent harm by giving this assistance. It is to the economic interests of humanity at large that production should be stimulated, and the economic interests of humanity at large is the interest of England, with its mighty world-wide trade. Germany has quickened production with the help of English credit, and so has every other economically civilized country in the world. It is a fact that all of them, including our own Colonies, develop their resources with the help of British capital and credit, and then do their utmost to keep out our productions by means of tariffs, which makes it appear to superficial observers that England provides capital for the destruction of its own business. But in practice the system works quite otherwise, for all these countries that develop their resources with our money aim at developing an export trade and selling goods to us, and, as they have not yet reached the point of economic altruism at which they are prepared to sell goods for nothing, the increase in their production means an increasing demand for our commodities and our services. And in the meantime the interest on our capital and credit and the profits of working the machinery of exchange are a comfortable addition to our national income.

But what is a further corollary of this situation? It is that Germany is to-day in a larger sense than she ever was before England's debtor, and that her industrial success is bound up with England's financial security.

What would be the situation in Britain, therefore, on the morrow of a conflict in which she were successful?

I have seen mentioned the possibility of the conquest and annexation of the free port of Hamburg by a victorious British fleet. Let us assume that the British Government has done this and is proceeding to turn the annexed and confiscated property to account.

Now, the property was originally of two kinds: part was private property, and part was German government, or rather Hamburg government, property. The income of the latter was earmarked for the payment of interest of certain government stock, and the action of the British Government, therefore, renders it all but valueless, and in the case of the shares of the private companies entirely so. The paper becomes unsaleable. But it is held in various forms—as collateral and otherwise—by many important banking concerns, insurance companies, and so on, and this sudden collapse of value shatters their solvency. Their collapse not only involves many credit institutions in Germany, but, as these in their turn are considerable debtors of London, English institutions are also involved. London is also involved in another way. As explained previously, many foreign concerns keep balances in London, and the action of the British Government having precipitated a monetary crisis in Germany, there is a run on London to withdraw all balances. In a double sense London is feeling the pinch, and it would be a miracle if already at this point the whole influence of British finance were not thrown against the action of the British Government. Assume, however, that the Government, making the best of a bad job, continues its administration of the property, and proceeds to arrange for loans for the purpose of putting it once more in good condition after the ravage of war. The banks, however, finding that the original titles have, through the action of the British Government become waste paper, and British financiers having already burned their fingers with that particular class of property, withhold support, and money is only procurable at extortionate rates of interest, so extortionate that it becomes quite evident that as a governmental enterprise the thing could not be made to pay. An attempt is made to sell the property to British and German concerns. But the same paralyzing sense of insecurity hangs over the whole business. Neither German nor British financiers can forget that the bonds and shares of this property have already been turned into waste paper by the action of the British Government. The British Government finds, in fact, that it can do nothing with the financial world unless precedently it confirms the title of the original owners to the property, and gives an assurance that titles to all property, throughout the conquered territory shall be respected. In other words, confiscation has been a failure.

It would really be interesting to know how those who talk as though confiscation were still an economic possibility would proceed to effect it. As material property in the form of that booty which used to constitute the spoils of victory in ancient times, the gold and silver goblets, etc., would be quite inconsiderable, and as we cannot carry away sections of Berlin and Hamburg we could only annex the paper tokens of wealth—the shares and bonds. But the value of those tokens depends upon the reliance which can be placed upon the execution of the contracts which they embody. The act of military confiscation upsets all contracts, and the courts of the country from which contracts derive their force are paralyzed because judicial decisions are thrust aside by the sword.

The value of the stocks and shares would collapse, and the credit of all those persons and institutions interested in such property would also be shaken or shattered, and the whole credit system, being thus at the mercy of alien governors only concerned to exact tribute, would collapse like a house of cards. German finance and industry would show a condition of panic and disorder beside which the worst crises of Wall Street would pale into insignificance. Again, what would be the inevitable result? The financial influence of London itself would be thrown into the scale to prevent a panic in which London financiers would be involved. In other words, British financiers would exert their influence upon the British Government to stop the process of confiscation.

CHAPTER V

FOREIGN TRADE AND MILITARY POWER

Why trade cannot be destroyed or captured by a military Power —What the processes of trade really are and how a navy affects them—"Dreadnoughts" and business—While "Dreadnoughts" protect trade from hypothetical German warships, the real German merchant is carrying it off, or the Swiss or the Belgian—The "commercial aggression" of Switzerland—What lies at the bottom of the futility of military conquest—Government brigandage become as profitless as private brigandage—The real basis of commercial honesty on the part of government.

JUST as Mr. Harrison has declared that a "successful invasion would mean to us the total eclipse of our commerce and trade, and with that trade the means of feeding forty millions in these islands," so I have seen it stated in a leading English paper that, "if Germany were extinguished to-morrow, the day after to-morrow there is not an Englishman in the world who would not be the richer. Nations have fought for years over a city or right of succession. Must they not fight for two hundred and fifty million pounds of yearly commerce?"

One almost despairs of ever reaching economic

sanity when it is possible for a responsible English newspaper to print matter which ought to be as offensive to educated folk as a defence of astrology or of witchcraft.

What does the "extinction" of Germany mean? Does it mean that we shall slay in cold blood sixty or seventy millions of men, women, and children? Otherwise, even though the fleet and army were annihilated, the country's sixty million odd of workers still remain, who would be all the more industrious, as they would have undergone great suffering and privation—prepared to exploit their mines and workshops with as much thoroughness and thrift and industry as ever, and consequently just as much our trade rivals as ever, army or no army, navy or no navy.

Even if we could annihilate Germany we should annihilate such an important section of our debtors as to create hopeless panic in London. Such panic would so react on our own trade that it would be in no sort of condition to take the place which Germany had previously occupied in neutral markets, aside from the question that by such annihilation a market equal to that of Canada and South Africa combined would be destroyed.

What does this sort of thing mean? And am I wrong in saying that the whole subject is overlaid and dominated by a jargon which may have had some relation to facts at one time, but from which in our day all meaning has departed?

Our patriot may say that he does not mean permanent destruction, but only temporary "annihilation." (And this, of course, on the other side, would mean not permanent, but only temporary acquisition of that two hundred and fifty millions of trade.)

He might, like Mr. Harrison, put the case conversely,—that if Germany could get command of the sea she could cut us off from our customers and intercept our trade for her benefit. This notion is as absurd as the first. It has already been shown that the "utter destruction of credit" and "incalculable chaos in the financial world," which Mr. Harrison foresees as the result of Germany's invasion, could not possibly leave German finance unaffected. It is a very open question whether her chaos would not be as great as England's. In any case, it would be so great as thoroughly to disorganize her industry, and in that disorganized condition it would be out of the question for her to secure the markets left unsupplied by England's isolation. Moreover, those markets would also be disorganized, because they depend upon England's ability to buy, which Germany would be doing her best to destroy. From the chaos which she herself had created, Germany could derive no possible benefit, and she could only terminate financial disorder, fatal to her own trade, by bringing to an end the condition which had produced it—that is, by bringing to an end the isolation of Great Britain.

With reference to this section of the subject we can with absolute certainty say two things: (1) That Germany can only destroy British trade by destroying the British population; and (2) that if she could destroy that population (which she could not) she would destroy one of her most valuable markets, as at the present time she sells to us more than we sell to her. The whole point of view involves a fundamental misconception of the real nature of commerce and industry.

Commerce is simply and purely the exchange of one product for another. If the British manufacturer can make cloth, or cutlery, or machinery, or pottery, or ships cheaper or better than his rivals he will obtain the trade; if he cannot, if his goods are inferior, or dearer, or appeal less to his customers, his rivals will secure the trade, and the possession of "Dreadnoughts" will make not a whit of difference. Switzerland, without a single "Dreadnought," will drive him out of the market even of his own Colonies, as, indeed, she is driving him out in those cases which I have just referred to. The factors which really constitute prosperity have not the remotest connection with military or naval power, all our political jargon notwithstanding. To destroy the commerce of forty million people Germany would have to destroy their coal and iron mines, to destroy the energy, character, resourcefulness of the population; to destroy, in short, the determination of forty million people to make their living by the work of their hands. Were we not hypnotized by this extraordinary optical illusion we should accept it as a matter of course that the prosperity of a people depends upon such facts as the natural wealth of the country in which they live, their social discipline and industrial character, the result of years, of generations, of centuries, it may be, of tradition and slow, elaborate selective process, and, in addition to all these deep-seated elementary factors, upon countless commercial and financial ramifications—a special technical capacity for such-and-such a manufacture, a special aptitude for meeting the peculiarities of such-and-such a market, the efficient equipment of elaborately constructed workshops, the existence of a population trained to given trades—a training not infrequently involving years, and even generations, of effort. All this, according to Mr. Harrison, is to go for nothing, and Germany is to be able to replace it in the twinkling of an eye, and forty million people are to sit down helplessly because Germany has been victorious at sea. On the morrow of her marvellous victory Germany is by some sort of miracle to find shipyards, foundries, cotton mills, looms, factories, coal and iron mines, and all their equipment, suddenly spring up in Germany in order to take the trade that the most successful manufacturers and traders in the world have been generations in building up; Germany is to be able suddenly to produce three or four times what her population have hitherto been able to produce; for she must either do that or leave the markets which England has supplied heretofore still available to English effort. What has really fed these forty millions who are to starve on the morrow of Germany's naval victory is the fact that the coal and iron exploited by them have been sent in one form or another to populations which need those products. Is that need suddenly to cease, or are the forty millions to be suddenly struck with some sort of paralysis that all this vast industry suddenly comes to an end? What has the victory of Britain's ships at sea to do with the fact that the Canadian farmer wants to buy her ploughs and pay for them with his wheat? It may be true that Germany could stop the importation of that wheat. But why should she want to do so? How would it benefit her people to do so? By what sort of miracle is she suddenly to be able to supply products which have kept forty million people busy? By what sort of miracle is she suddenly to be able to double her industrial population? And by what sort of miracle is she to be able to consume the wheat, because if she cannot take that wheat the Cana-

dian cannot buy her plough? I am aware that
all this is elementary, that it is economics in
words of one syllable; but what are the economics
of Mr. Harrison and those who think like him
when he talks in the strain of the passage that
I have just quoted?

There is just one other possible meaning that
the patriot may have in his mind. He may plead
that great military and naval establishments
do not exist for the purpose of the conquest of
territory or of destroying a rival's trade, but for
"protecting" or indirectly aiding trade and
industry. We are allowed to infer that in some
not clearly-defined way a great Power can aid
the trade of its nationals by the use of the prestige which a great navy and a great army bring,
and by exercising bargaining powers in the matter
of tariffs with other nations. But again the fact
of the small nations in Europe gives the lie to
this assumption.

It is evident that the foreigner does not buy
England's products and refuse Germany's because
England has a larger navy. If one can imagine
the representatives of an English and of a German firm in Argentina, or Brazil, or Bulgaria, or
Finland meeting in the office of a merchant in
Argentina, or Brazil, or Bulgaria, or Finland,
both of them selling cutlery, the German is not
going to secure the order because he is able to
show the Argentinian, or the Brazilian, or the

Bulgarian, or the Finn that Germany has twelve "Dreadnoughts" and England only eight. The German will take the order if, on the whole, he can make a more advantageous offer to the prospective buyer, and for no other reason whatsoever, and the buyer will go to the merchant of whatever nation, whether he be German, or Swiss, or Belgian, or British, irrespective of the armies and navies which may lie behind the nationality of the seller. Nor does it appear that armies and navies weigh in the least when it comes to a question of a tariff bargain. Switzerland wages a tariff war with Germany, and wins. The whole history of the trade of the small nations shows that the political prestige of the great ones gives them practically no commercial advantage.

We continually talk as though the English carrying trade were in some special sense the result of the growth of England's great navy, but Norway has a carrying trade which, relatively to her population, is nearly three times as great as England's, and the same reasons which would make it impossible for a foreign nation to confiscate the gold reserve of the Bank of England would make it impossible for a foreign nation to confiscate British shipping on the morrow of a British naval defeat. In what way can the carrying trade or any other trade be said to depend upon military power?

As I write these lines there comes to my notice a series of articles in the *Daily Mail*, written by Mr. F. A. McKenzie, explaining how it is that England is losing the trade of Canada. In one article he quotes a number of Canadian merchants:

"We buy very little direct from England," said Mr. Harry McGee, one of the vice-presidents of the company, in answer to my questions. "We keep a staff in London of twenty, supervising our European purchases, but the orders go mostly to France, Germany, and Switzerland, and not to England."

And in a further article he notes that many orders are going to Belgium. Now the question arises: What more can England's navy do that it has not done in Canada? And yet the trade goes to Switzerland and Belgium. Are you going to protect the English merchant against the commercial "aggression" of Switzerland by building a dozen more "Dreadnoughts"? Suppose England could conquer Switzerland and Belgium with her "Dreadnoughts," would not the trade of Switzerland and Belgium go on all the same? Her arms have brought England Canada—but not the Canadian orders, which go to Switzerland.

If the traders of little nations can snap their fingers at the great war lords, why do British traders need "Dreadnoughts"? If Swiss commercial prosperity is secure from the aggression of a neighbour who outweighs Switzerland in military power a hundred to one, how comes it that the trade and industry, the very life-bread of her children, as Mr. Harrison would have us believe, of the greatest nation in history is in danger of imminent annihilation?

If the statesmen of Europe would tell us *how* the military power of a great nation is used to advance the commercial interest of its citizens, would explain to us the *modus operandi,* and not refer us to large and vague phrases about "exercising due weight in the councils of the nations," one might accept their philosophy. But until they do so we are surely justified in assuming that their political terminology is simply a survival —an inheritance from a state of things which has, in fact, long since passed away.

It is facts of the nature of those I have instanced which constitute the real protection of the small State, and which are bound as they gain in general recognition to constitute the real protection from outside aggression of all States, great or small.

One financial authority from whom I have quoted noted that this elaborate financial interdependence of the modern world has grown up in spite of ourselves, "without our noticing it until we put it to some rude test." Men are fundamentally just as disposed as they were at any time to take wealth that does not belong to them, which they have not earned. But their relative interest in the matter has changed. In very primitive conditions robbery is a moderately profitable enterprise. Where the rewards of labour, owing to the inefficiency of the means of production, are small and uncertain, and where all wealth is portable, raiding and theft offer the best reward for the enterprise of the courageous; in such conditions the size of man's wealth depends a good deal on the size of his club and the agility with which he wields it. But to the man whose wealth so largely depends upon his credit and on his paper being "good paper" in the City, dishonesty has become as precarious and profitless as honest toil was in more primitive times.

The instincts of the City man may at bottom be just as predatory as those of the cattle-lifter or the robber baron, but taking property by force has become one of the least profitable and the most speculative forms of enterprise in which he could engage. The force of commercial events has rendered the thing impossible. I know that the defender of arms will reply that it is the police who have rendered it impossible. This is not true. There were as many armed men in Europe in the days when the robber baron carried on his occupation as there are in our day. To say that the policeman makes him impossible is to put the cart before the horse. What created the police and made them possible, if it was not the general recognition of the fact that disorder and aggression make trade impossible?[1]

Just note what is taking place in South America. States in which repudiation was a commonplace of everyday politics have of recent years become as stable and as respectable as the City of London, and discharge their obligations as regularly. Does this mean that the people have become more moral, that the original wickedness of their nature, which made of their countries during hundreds of years a slough of disorder and a never-ending sanguinary scramble for the spoils, has in a matter of fifteen or twenty years completely changed? Probably not; and whether it has or not does not much matter. What matters is that the manifestations of their nature have changed a great deal.

These countries, like Brazil and the Argentine, have been drawn into the circle of international trade, exchange, and finance. Their economic relationships have become sufficiently extensive and complex to make repudiation the least profitable form of theft. The financier will tell you "they cannot afford to repudiate." If any attempt at repudiation were made, all sorts of property, either directly or indirectly connected with the orderly execution of governmental functions, would suffer, banks would become in-

[1] See Chap. v., Part II., for the completer explanation of the law underlying the fact.

volved, great businesses would stagger, and the whole financial community would protest. To attempt to escape the payment of a single loan would involve the business world in losses amounting to many times the value of the loan.[1]

It is only where a community has nothing to lose, no banks, no personal fortunes dependent upon public good faith, no great businesses, no industries, that the government can afford to repudiate its obligations or to disregard the general code of economic morality. This was the case with Argentina and Brazil a generation ago; and also to some extent with some Central American States to-day. *It is not because the armies in these States have grown* that the public credit has improved. Their armies were greater a generation ago than they are now. It is because they know that trade and finance are built upon credit—that is, confidence in the fulfilment of obligations, upon security of tenure in titles, upon the enforcement of contract according to law—and that if credit is profoundly touched, there is not a section of the elaborate fabric which is not affected.

The more our commercial system gains in complication, the more does the common prosperity of all of us come to depend upon the reliance which can be placed on the due performance of all contracts. This is the real basis

[1] Chap. IV., Part II.

of "prestige," national and individual; circumstances stronger than ourselves are pushing us, despite what the cynical critics of our commercial civilization may say, towards the unvarying observance of this simple ideal. Whenever we drop back from it, and such relapses occur as we should expect them to occur, especially in those societies which have just emerged from a more or less primitive State, punishment is generally swift and sure.

What was the real origin of the bank crisis in the United States, which had for American business men such disastrous consequences? It was the loss by American financiers and American bankers of the confidence of the American public. At bottom there was no other reason. One talks of cash reserves and currency errors; but London, which does the banking of the universe, works on the smallest cash reserve in the world, because, as an American authority has put it, "English bankers work with a 'psychological reserve.'"

I quote from Mr. Withers:

It is because they [English bankers] are so safe, so straight, so sensible, from an American point of view so unenterprising, that they are able to build up a bigger credit fabric on a smaller gold basis, and even carry this building to a height which they themselves have decided to be questionable. This "psychological reserve" is the priceless possession that has been handed down through generations of good bankers, and every individual of every generation who receives it can do something to maintain and improve it.

But it was not always thus, and it is merely the many ramifications of our commercial and financial world that have brought this about. In the end the Americans will imitate the London bankers, or they will suffer from a hopeless disadvantage in their financial competition. Commercial development is broadly illustrating one profound truth: that the real basis of social morality is self-interest. If English banks and insurance companies have become absolutely honest in their administration, it is because dishonesty of any one threatened the prosperity of all.

What bearing has the development of commercial morality on the matter in hand? A very direct one. If, as Mr. Chamberlain avers, the subject of rivalry between nations is business, the code which, despite the promptings of the natural man, has come to dominate business, must necessarily come, if their object really is business, to dominate the conduct of governments.

One cannot take up the speech of a statesman even of the first rank, or a leading article in even the foremost papers dealing with international relations, without finding it assumed as a matter of course, as Mr. Harrison assumes in the quotations that I have made, that European governments have the instincts of Congo savages, the foresight of cattle-lifters, and the business morals of South American adventurers. Are we to assume that the governments of the world, which, presumably, are directed by men as far-sighted as bankers, are permanently to fall below the banker in their conception of enlightened self-interest? Are we to assume that what is self-evident to the banker—namely, that the repudiation of our engagements, or any attempt at financial plunder, is sheer stupidity and commercial suicide—is for ever to remain unperceived by the ruler? But if the ruler sees that the seizure of an enemy's property is economically injurious to the nation seizing it, and is for that reason intangible, why do we go in such nightmare terror and spend our substance arming colossally against so problematic an attack?

The following correspondence, provoked by the first edition of this book, may throw light on some of the points dealt with in this chapter. A correspondent of *Public Opinion* criticized a part of the theses here dealt with as a " series of half-truths," questioning as follows:

What is "natural wealth," and how can trade be carried on with it unless there are markets for it when worked? Would the writer maintain that markets cannot be permanently or seriously affected by military conquest, especially if conquest be followed by

the imposition upon the vanquished of commercial
conditions framed in the interests of the victor? . . .
Germany has derived, and continues to derive, great
advantages from the most-favoured-nation clause
which she compelled France to insert in the Treaty of
Frankfurt. . . . Bismarck, it is true, underestimated
the financial resilience of France, and was sorely disappointed when the French paid off the indemnity with
such astonishing rapidity, and thus liberated themselves from the equally crushing burden of having
to maintain the German army of occupation.   He
regretted not having demanded an indemnity twice
as large.   Germany would not repeat the mistake,
and any country having the misfortune to be vanquished by her in future will be likely to find its
commercial prosperity compromised for decades.

To which I replied:

Will your correspondent forgive my saying that
while he talks of half-truths, the whole of this passage
indicates the domination of just that particular half-
truth which lies at the bottom of the illusion with
which my book deals?

What is a market?   Your correspondent evidently
conceives it as a place where things are sold.   That
is only half the truth.   It is a place where things are
bought and sold, and one operation is impossible
without the other, and the notion that one nation can
sell for ever and never buy is simply the theory of
perpetual motion applied to economics; and international trade can no more be based upon perpetual
motion than can engineering.   As between economi-

cally highly-organized nations a customer must also be a competitor, a fact which bayonets cannot alter. To the extent to which they destroy him as a competitor, they destroy him, speaking generally and largely, as a customer.

The late Mr. Seddon conceived England as making her purchases with "a stream of golden sovereigns" flowing from a stock all the time getting smaller. That "practical" man, however, who so despised "mere theories," was himself the victim of a pure theory, and the picture which he conjured up from his inner consciousness has no existence in fact. England has hardly enough gold to pay one year's taxes, and if she paid for her imports in gold she would exhaust her stock in six months; and the process by which she really pays has been going on for sixty years. She is a buyer just as long as she is a seller, and if she is to afford a market to Germany she must procure the money wherewith to pay for Germany's goods by selling goods to Germany or elsewhere, and if that process of sale stops Germany loses a market, not only the English market, but also those markets which depend in their turn upon England's capacity to buy—that is to say, to sell, for, again, the one operation is impossible without the other.

If your correspondent had had the whole process in his mind instead of half of it, I do not think that he would have written the passages I have quoted. In his endorsement of the Bismarckian conception of political economy he evidently deems that one nation's gain is the measure of another nation's loss, and that nations live by robbing their neighbours in a lesser or greater degree. This is economics à la Tamerlane and the Red Indian, and, happily, has no relation to the real facts of modern commercial intercourse.

The conception of one half of the case only dominates your correspondent's letter throughout. He says, "Germany has derived, and continues to derive, great advantage from the most-favoured-nation clause which she compelled France to insert in the Treaty of Frankfurt." Which is quite true, but leaves out the other half of the truth, which is somewhat important to our discussion—viz., that France has also greatly benefited, in that the scope of fruitless tariff war has been by so much restricted.

A further illustration: Why should Germany have been sorely disappointed at France's rapid recovery? The German people are not going to be the richer for having a poor neighbour—on the contrary, they are going to be the poorer, and there is not an economist with a reputation to lose, whatever his views of fiscal policy, who would challenge this for a moment.

How would Germany impose upon a vanquished England commercial arrangements which would impoverish the vanquished and enrich the victor? By enforcing another Frankfurt treaty, by which English ports should be kept open to German goods? But that is precisely what English ports have been for sixty years, and Germany has not been obliged to go to a costly war to effect it. Would Germany close her own markets to our goods? But, again, that is precisely what she has done— again without war, and by a right which we never dream of challenging. How is war going to affect the question one way or another? I have been asking

6

for a detailed answer to that question from European publicists and statesmen for the last ten years, and I have never yet been answered, save by much vagueness, much fine phrasing concerning commercial supremacy, a spirited foreign policy, national prestige, and much else, which no one seems able to define—but a real policy, a *modus operandi*, a balance-sheet which one can analyze, never. And until such is forthcoming I shall continue to believe that the whole thing is based upon an illusion.

The true test of fallacies of this kind is progression. Imagine Germany (as British Jingoes seem to dream of her) absolute master of Europe, and able to dictate any policy that she pleased. How would she treat such a European empire? By impoverishing its component parts? But that would be suicidal. Where would her big industrial population find their markets? If she set out to develop and enrich the component parts, these would become merely efficient competitors, and she need not have undertaken the costliest war of history to arrive at that result. This is the paradox, the futility of conquest— the great illusion which the history of our own Empire so well illustrates. England "owns" her Empire by allowing its component parts to develop themselves in their own way, and in view of their own ends, and all the empires which have pursued any other policy have only ended by impoverishing their own populations and falling to pieces.

Your correspondent asks: "Is Mr. Norman Angell prepared to maintain that Japan has derived no political or commercial advantages from her victories, and that Russia has suffered no loss from defeat?"

What I am prepared to maintain, and what the experts know to be the truth, is that the Japanese people are the poorer, not the richer, for their war, and that the Russian people will gain more from defeat than they could possibly have gained by victory, since defeat will constitute a check on the economically sterile policy of military and territorial aggrandisement and turn Russian energies to social and economic development; and it is because of this fact that Russia is at the present moment, despite her desperate internal troubles, showing a capacity for economic regeneration as great as, if not greater than, that of Japan.   This latter country has recently beaten all records for heavy taxation: on the average the people pay thirty per cent. of their net income in taxation in one form or another—a taxation which would create a revolution in Europe or America within twenty-four hours.   On the other side, for the first time in twenty years the Russian Budget shows a surplus.

This recovery of the defeated nation after wars is becoming one of the commonplaces of modern history. Ten years after the Franco-Prussian War France was in a better financial position than Germany, as she is in a better financial position to-day, and though her foreign trade does not show the expansion that that of Germany does—because her population remains absolutely stationary, while that of Germany increases by leaps and bounds—the French people as a whole are more prosperous, more comfortable, more economically secure, with a greater reserve of savings, and all the moral and social advantage that goes therewith, than are the Germans.   In the same way the social and industrial renaissance of modern Spain dates from the day that she was defeated and lost her colonies, and it is since her defeat that Spanish securities have just doubled in value. It is since England added the "gold-fields of the world" to her "possessions" that British Consols have dropped twenty points. Such is the outcome in terms of social well-being of military success and political prestige!

CHAPTER VI

THE INDEMNITY FUTILITY

What is the real profit of a nation from indemnity?—How a person differs from a State—An old illusion as to gold and wealth—What happened in 1870—Germany and France in the decade 1870–1880—Bismarck's testimony.

IN politics it is unfortunately true that ten sovereigns which can be seen bulk more largely in the public mind than a million which happen to be out of sight but are none the less real. Thus, however clearly the wastefulness of war and the impossibility of effecting by its means any permanent economic or social advantage for the conqueror may be shown, the fact that Germany was able to exact an indemnity of two hundred millions sterling from France at the close of the war of 1870–71 is taken as conclusive evidence that a nation can "make money by war."

A very prominent English public man, pushed recently in private conversation to show an adequate motive for Germany's aggression upon England, urged seriously that Germany would fight simply to make money; that she made money out of Austria, and again out of France, and that she would fight England for the sake of a thousand million indemnity.

In reply to such a plea, it would, of course, be easy to establish a balance-sheet, putting on the debit side some such list as the following: the cost of war preparation during the years that precede a conflict; the disorder and ruin which war itself causes; the killing and disablement of a large number of a nation's sturdiest citizens (sturdiest because selected, so that war constitutes the elimination, not of the unfit but of the fittest), the corresponding losses which limit the subsequent purchasing power of the defeated nation and which consequently react in the shape of lost markets on the conqueror; the subsequent burden which even victory entails—that is to say, the preventive measures to be taken against a *guerre de revanche;* the increase of force which it is necessary to offset against the enmity entailed in general politics by the efforts and intrigues of the vanquished; and, in addition to all this, the check in normal and social progress which the militarisation following upon war always involves, a setback which is shown in the case of Germany by the fact that she alone of the great States is forced by grave difficulties due to the survival of sheer feudalism, difficulties which are none the less great because they are in the eyes of Europe generally for the moment obscured by theatrical industrial success in foreign markets, and which are reflected by the growing power of the progressive party which, every educated German knows, cannot for ever be held at bay by sheer domination of Prussian autocracy. As against all this, an indemnity, even of a thousand million, would make the proposition very bad business indeed. On such a balance-sheet being roughly indicated, however, the public man in question immediately retorted by declaring that, so far as Germany is concerned, much of the cost has already been incurred and cannot be recovered, and must consequently be paid whether she fight or not. It is worth considering, therefore, whether in the circumstances of present-day politics an actual transfer of a thousand millions worth of real wealth from one nation to another is either possible, or, in the terms of predominant political economy, desirable from the point of view of those who are to receive it. Let it be said at once that there is nothing theoretically impossible in England's paying an indemnity of a thousand millions sterling (or more) provided that time were given, and provided that the German Government were prepared to see German trade and finance suffer to a greater extent probably than a thousand million, owing to the very grave embarrassment which would certainly affect a whole series of German trades by the withdrawal of English credit and English cheap money. It is impossible to give figures even approximately, but when it is remembered that 95 per cent. of the highly organized German industries exist on a basis of borrowed money, which, as we have seen, is in the last resort largely English money, and that greatly increased banking charges would simply and purely wipe out the very small margin of profit on which so much of German trade is done, it is easy to realize that a thousand millions paid to the Government would not seem a very brilliant compensation to the German manufacturer whose business had foundered in a welter of financial instability and high bank rate throughout Europe which the withdrawal of such a sum from London would infallibly cause.[1] For—and this is a capital factor in the whole matter—the situation would not be at all parallel to that which followed the Franco-Prussian war. German trade in 1870 was not in any way dependent upon French money—dependent, that is, upon being able to secure French credit; whereas, as we have seen, German trade in 1910 is in a very special sense dependent upon English money and the facilities of English credit. And all this is assuming—a very large assumption indeed—that the thousand millions, or any part

[1] The *Cologne Gazette* recently pointed out that so extensive, thanks to the industrial banks, has become the use of credit in German business that many of them may be considered in Stock Exchange jargon as "trading on a margin." Every operator knows what happens to a " marginal account " when the bank rate takes a jump and securities fall in value.

of it, would remain as booty after the payment of expenses of the war, repairing damage caused by the war, and providing against future hostility. If a war against a handful of farmers, without so much as a gunboat to their name, cost Great Britain a quarter of the sum in question, it is a little difficult to see how the actual cost of a war against the greatest Empire of history, with the greatest fleet of history, with the greatest naval traditions of history behind it, is going to leave much change out of a thousand millions—in any case not enough to make attack worth a government's while as a business proposition. Yet the public man who defended this thesis was described by a Liberal journal as the "most influential man in England, whether we like it or not." And if such a one talk in this strain, what sense of proportion in these matters can we expect from the mere man in the street?

Let us make in this matter, however, the largest assumption of all—that the entire sum becomes available for the German people as a whole.

Would it be possible for them really to profit by it?

I said just now that there is nothing inherently impossible or, indeed, any great difficulty in England's paying an indemnity of a thousand millions. But in the present state of national fiscal policies it is as certain as anything well could be that it would be impossible for the German people to receive anything more than a fraction of it, even though none of it were stopped en route for expenditure arising out of the war. *According to the economic doctrine now most in favour in Germany, and coming to be most in favour in England, German prosperity would suffer more by receiving this money than would English by paying it.* That this fact has never been brought into relief shows how little real attention the subject has received.

Notwithstanding that political economy is not a simple but a very complex subject, notwithstanding that the analogy as between an individual and a nation is always breaking down, it is accepted offhand that it is as simple a matter to enrich a nation by paying over a sum of money like a thousand millions in gold as it would be to enrich an individual. Yet the most summary examination shows that the two cases do not in any way go on all-fours: in this, as in so many matters in the domain of politics, the influence of mere words and metaphors—words which are generally inaccurate and metaphors which mislead—coupled with the sheer indolent inattention of the "average sensual man," have caused us to accept without doubt or question as absolutely identical in results an operation which the common facts of workaday politics render absolutely different.

What is this difference as between the transfer

of wealth from one individual to another, and from one nation to another?

If Jones, the individual, could by any means whatsoever induce his tradesmen to supply him with bread, meat, wine, clothes, and motor-cars for nothing, Jones would be completely satisfied, and there would never enter his mind for an instant that such was not an absolutely ideal arrangement.

But suppose that Jones is the Protectionist State of Jonesonia, is the matter in any way the same? Suppose that this Protectionist State were receiving its meat, bread, wine, clothes, and motor-cars from other countries for nothing, or even nearly nothing, what would the butchers, farmers, bakers, tailors, and motor-car makers of Jonesonia have to say? Do we not know that there would be such a howl about the ruin of home industry that no government could stand the clamour for a week, and do we not know that immediate steps would be taken as far as possible to shut out this flood of foreign goods poured in at prices so immensely below those at which the home producers could produce them? Do we not know that this influx of goods for nothing would be represented as a deep-laid plot on the part of foreign nations to ruin the trade of the State of Jonesonia, and that the citizens of Jonesonia would rise in their wrath to prevent the accomplishment of such a plot?

Do we not know that this very operation by which foreign nations tax themselves to send abroad goods, not for nothing (that would be a crime at present unthinkable), but at below cost, is an offence to which we have given the scientific name of "dumping," and that when it is carried very far, as in the case of sugar, even Free Trade nations like Great Britain join international conferences to prevent these gifts being made?

What, therefore, becomes of the analogy as between Jones and a State? And what shall be said of the political economy of those Protectionists who calmly talk as though the two operations were absolutely identical?

But, may object the militarist, when an indemnity is paid it is not paid in goods but in gold.

Really, ought not such an objector to buy a sixpenny text-book and get some elementary notion of the real process of international exchange? Is it necessary at this day to point out that, although the payment may be made in gold,[1] unless

---

[1] Such payment could not, of course, be made directly in gold; England could not make a payment of more than about fifty millions directly. Germany might conceivably convert the credit-equivalent she would receive from England into gold—although that would be extremely difficult and unprofitable, and only possible as long as England's credit remained unimpaired; but whether the final form of the indemnity were gold, or its equivalent in credit—paper money in some form, —the argument elaborated in this chapter remains unaffected.

that gold can be exchanged for meat, bread, fruit, clothes, and motor-cars the man receiving it gets nothing at all? Sooner or later the gold must be exchanged for commodities or it remains dead metal. In other words, if we can imagine a thousand millions of gold going into a country and never coming out, that country has not received any addition in real wealth. When Paris was besieged by the Germans and was starving for want of food and fuel, the hundreds of millions in the Bank of France might have been distributed among its starving population and none of them would have had so much as a mouthful the more of real wealth, unless the gold could have been taken outside the walls. And the same is as true of a community of twenty millions as of two.

What would have happened if the millions in the Bank of France had been distributed among the population of Paris? Food and fuel would have been as scarce as ever, and the population would have died as rapidly as ever and gone as hungry as ever. The only change would have been that everything would have gone up in price, roughly in direct ratio to the addition which had been made to their means of exchange; the population would have had more money corresponding to the rise of those prices, but general comfort would have been exactly what it was before. And this, indeed, is exactly what takes place when a Protectionist nation receives an in-

demnity of a large amount of gold. One of two
things happens: either the gold is exchanged for
real wealth with other nations, in which case the
greatly increased inports compete directly with
the home producers; or the money is kept within
the frontiers and is not exchanged for real wealth
from abroad, and prices inevitably rise, in which
case the situation, as just illustrated in the case of
Paris and the siege, is repeated. There is, however,
as compared with other nations, a further effect:
the rise in price of all commodities hampers
the receiving nation in selling those commodities
in the neutral markets of the world, especially
as the loss of so large a sum by the vanquished
nation has just the inverse effect of cheapening
prices, and therefore enabling that nation to
compete on better terms with the conqueror in
neutral markets. The dilemma, as stated above,
is clear and simple, and I challenge any economist
to show any real escape therefrom. Of two things
one happens: either the indemnity is paid in real
wealth (commodities) directly or indirectly, the
result which the Protectionist regards as unmiti-
gatedly mischievous; or the gold remains within the
frontiers, in which case there is no increase of real
wealth among the community, and prices rise, so
that the effect of the extra amount of gold in
circulation is nullified by its lower purchasing
power. There can be no question but that the
country paying the indemnity certainly does

lose that amount of wealth, because in order to obtain the gold she must get it from other countries, giving real wealth in exchange; but what is equally certain is that the country receiving such money receives it either in the form of real wealth, which constitutes a serious competition to their own manufacturers and traders, and constitutes in the terms of the Protectionist creed a grievous wrong, or it has the simple effect of raising prices, in which case the community do not receive any addition to their real wealth. The difficulty in the case of a large indemnity is not so much the payment by the vanquished as the receiving by the victor.

How far does the history of the period 1870–1880—the period, that is, during which the war indemnity was paid by France and spent by Germany[1]—bear out the apparent paradox just indicated? Preposterous as the thing may seem, it bears it out to the last detail, and the matter is worth a little careful examination.

The decade from 1870–1880 was for France a great recuperative period, and for Germany, after a boom in 1872, one of great depression. No less an authority than Bismarck himself testifies to the double fact. We know that Bismarck's life was clouded by watching what appeared to

[1] I am aware that part of the indemnity remained in the fortress of Spandau, but only a small part. The bulk was spent in the period indicated.

him an absurd miracle: the regeneration of France
after the war taking place more rapidly and more
completely than the regeneration in Germany,
to such an extent that in introducing his Protectionist Bill in 1879 he declared that Germany
was "slowly bleeding to death," and that if the
present process were continued she would find
herself ruined. Speaking in the Reichstag on
May 2, 1879, Bismarck said:

We see that France manages to support the present
difficult business situation of the civilized world better
than we do; that her Budget has increased since 1871
by a milliard and a half, and that thanks not only to
loans; we see that she has more resources than Germany, and that, in short, over there they complain
less of bad times.

And in a speech two years later (Nov. 29,
1881) he returns to the same idea:

It was towards 1877 that I was first struck with the
general and growing distress in Germany as compared
with France. I saw furnaces banked, the standard
of well-being reduced, and the general position of
workmen becoming worse, and business as a whole
terribly bad.

In the book from which these extracts are taken[1]
the author writes as an introduction to Bismarck's
speeches:

[1] *Die Wirtschafts Finanz und Sozialreform im Deutschen Reich.*
Leipzig, 1882.

Trade and industry were in a miserable condition. Thousands of workmen were without employment, and in the winter of 1876–7 unemployment took great proportions and soup-kitchens and State workshops had to be established.

Every author who deals with this period seems to tell the same tale. "If only we could get back to the general position of things before the war," says M. Block in 1879. "But salaries diminish and prices go up."[1]

In examining the effect which must follow the payment of a large sum of money by one country to another, we saw that either goods must be imported by the nation receiving the indemnity to compete with those produced at home; or the gold must be kept at home and prices rise and so hamper exportation; in the case of the country losing the gold, prices must fall and exports rise. That this, in varying degrees, is precisely what did take place after the payment of the indemnity we have ample confirmation. The German economist Max Wirth (*Geschichte der Handelskrisen*) expresses in 1874 his astonishment at France's financial and industrial recovery: "The most striking example of the economic force of the country is shown by the exports, which rose immediately after the signature of peace, despite a war which swallowed a hundred thousand lives

[1] "La Crise Économique," *Revue des Deux Mondes*, March 15, 1879.

7

and more than ten milliards (four hundred million sterling)." A similar conclusion is drawn by Professor Biermer (*Fürst Bismarck als Volnswort*), who indicates that the Protectionist movement in 1879 was in large part due to the result of the payment of the indemnity, a view which is confirmed by Maurice Block, who adds:

The five milliards provoked a rapid increase in imports, giving rise to extravagance, and as soon as the effect of the expenditure of the money had passed there was a slackening. Then followed a fall in prices, which has led to an increase in exports, which tendency has continued since.

But the temporary stimulus of imports—not the result of an increased capacity for consumption arrived at by better trade, but merely the sheer acquisition of bullion—did grave damage to German industry, as we have seen, and threw thousands of German workmen out of employment, and it was during that decade that Germany suffered the worst financial crisis experienced by any country in Europe. At the very time that the French millions were raining in upon Germany (1873), she was suffering from a grave financial crisis, and so little effect did the transfer of the money have upon trade and finance in general that twelve months after the payment of the last of the indemnity we find the bank rate higher in Berlin than in Paris, and, as was shown by the German economist Soetbeer, by the year 1878 far more money was in circulation in France than in Germany.[1]   Hans Blum, indeed, directly ascribed the series of crises between the years 1873 and 1880 to the indemnity: "A burst of prosperity and then ruin for thousands."[2]   Throughout the year 1875 the bank rate in Paris was uniformly three per cent.   In Berlin (Preussische Bank, which preceded the Reichs Bank) it varied from four to six per cent.   A like difference is reflected also by the fact that between the years 1872 and 1877 the deposits in the State savings banks in Germany actually *fell* by roughly twenty per cent., while in the same period the French deposits *increased* about twenty per cent.

It will be replied that after the first decade Germany's trade has shown an expansion which has not been shown by that of France.   Those who are hypnotized by this fact quietly ignore altogether one great fact which has marked both France and Germany, not since the war, but during the whole of the nineteenth century, and that fact is that the population of France, from causes in no way connected with the Franco-Prussian War, since the tendency was a pronounced one for fifty years before, is practically

[1] Maurice Block, "La Crise Économique," *Revue des Deux Mondes*, March 15, 1879.

[2] *Das Deutsche Reich zur Zeit Bismarcks.*

quite stationary; while the population of Germany, also for reasons in no way connected with the war, since the fact was also pronounced half a century previously, has shown an abounding expansion. Since 1875 the population of Germany has increased by twenty million souls. That of France has not increased at all. Is it astonishing that the labour of twenty million souls as against *nil* makes some stir in the industrial world, and is it not evident that the necessity of earning a livelihood for this increasing population gives to German industry an expansion outside the limits of her territory which cannot be looked for in the case of nations whose social energies are not met with any such problem? There is this moreover to be borne in mind: Germany has secured her foreign trade on what are in the terms of the relative comfort of her people hard conditions.   In other words, she has secured that trade by cutting profits in the way that a business fighting desperately for life will cut profits in order to secure orders and will make sacrifices that the comfortable business man will not do. Notwithstanding that France has made no sensational splash in foreign trade since the war, the standard of comfort among her people has been rising steadily and is without doubt generally higher to-day than is that of the German people. This higher standard of comfort is reflected in her financial situation. While

German Three Per Cents are quoted at 82, French Rentes are quoted at 98, and while the financial situation of Germany is at times notoriously bad, that of France is, generally speaking, the soundest in Europe. The French people have more invested wealth, more savings; and it is Germany, the victor, which is to-day in the position of a suppliant in regard to France, and it is revealing no diplomatic secrets to say that for many years now Germany has been employing all the wiles of her diplomacy to obtain the official recognition of German securities on the French Bourses. France financially has, in a very real sense, the whip hand.

Do not these facts and others like them confirm therefore the conclusion that in the conditions of the modern world it is economically impossible for a great nation, especially if that great nation be a Protectionist one, to realize any benefit from receiving a large indemnity? The nominal transfer of the money may indeed be made, but the social, commercial, financial benefit must necessarily, given the complications of our economy, be fictitious.

It may be argued that if the foregoing is true of an indemnity, it is equally true of a foreign loan received by a Protectionist State, and that therefore the millions that Russia receives from abroad in this way do not avail her anything. Russia has, however, large foreign commitments for the payment of interest on old loans, and much of the money raised abroad is returned abroad in that form. Then much of her war material is purchased abroad, so that she has generally sufficiently large payments to make abroad to avoid the financial stultification which the receipt of large sums would involve were it to be "spent in the country." That Russia does not altogether escape such stultification is shown by the facts, of which we are assured by Mr. Dillon, that the general rise in wages which has taken place in recent years in Russia has been more than nullified by the increased cost of living. It should be noted, moreover, that the steady increase of normal, honest revenue from abroad as the result of foreign investment or foreign trading is not in the same category economically as an indemnity secured by war. In the first case the increase of wealth is real, in the second fictitious, or evanescent, because in the first a market has been improved or created, and in the second injured or destroyed. If we were sending a hundred millions of goods a year to Germany in the ordinary course of ordinary business, it would mean that German industry had created a market for those goods by having previously found a market; if the amount were sent as part of a war indemnity, it would mean that Germany had not expanded its buying capacity that much by general commercial activity, and that it could only absorb those goods by depriving its own producers of the trade.

I have not complicated this exposition by the question of a gold reserve financially, as that does not, properly speaking, bear on the question. Some of the countries with the largest gold reserve have the worst finance—*e. g.*, Germany has a larger gold reserve than England, which has one of the smallest in Europe. This does not prevent Germany being a large borrower from England, and England being the banker of the universe. Some of the soundest banking and the largest trade in the world are done on the smallest gold reserve. Where banking is sound and conservative, gold in large part can be dispensed with. To add one final word as to anticipated criticism: I do *not* urge the absurdity that it is impossible for one government to make a payment of a large sum of money to another; or for the government receiving it to benefit thereby: but that the population as a whole of any nation receiving a large indemnity must suffer from any disturbance of the credit of the paying nation; that if the Protectionist doctrine is just they must suffer great disadvantage from the receipt of wealth which has not employed the home population; from the rise of prices which checks their exports; that these are factors which must be taken into consideration in estimating the *real* advantage to the *general population* of any country which may succeed in extorting bullion from another as war plunder.

The following, part of a reply to an article which appeared in the *Daily Mail*, professing to show that Germany had made a profit of two hundred millions out of the war, may give an idea of the *real* balance sheet:

"In arriving at this balance, my critic, like the company-promoting genius who promises you 150 per cent. for your money, leaves so much out of the account. Here are a few items not considered: For the purposes and period of the war Germany increased her peace army by five hundred and thirty thousand men, and kept them from civil occupations for over nine months; consequent losses, at least thirty million sterling. Some proportion of the families of forty thousand killed, and some, at least, of the eighty thousand wounded, were thrown upon the support of relatives, the pensions only covering a small fraction. Economists of repute, like De Molinari, have placed the cost under this head alone at eighty million sterling. The increase in the French army which took place immediately after the war, and as the direct result thereof, compelled Germany to increase her army by at least one hundred thousand men, and this increase has been maintained for forty years. The expenditure throughout amounts to at least two hundred million sterling. We are already as much on the debit side as my critic placed the result on the credit side, and I have not enumerated half the items yet—*e.g.*, loss of German trade during the war, loss of markets for Germany involved in the destruction of so many French lives and so much French wealth; loss from the general disturbance throughout Europe.

"But it is absurd to bring figures to bear on such a system of bookkeeping as that adopted by my critic. Germany had several years' preparation for the war, and has had, as the direct result thereof, and as an integral part of the general war system which her own policy supports, certain obligations during forty years. All this is ignored. Just note how the same principle would work if applied in ordinary commercial matters: because, for instance, on an estate the actual harvest only takes a fortnight, you disregard altogether the working expenses for the remaining fifty weeks of the year, charge only the actual cost of the harvest (and not all of that), deduct this from the gross proceeds of the crops, and call the result 'profit'! Such 'finance' is really luminous. Applied by the ordinary business man, it would in an incredibly short time put his business in the bankruptcy court and himself in gaol."

CHAPTER VII

HOW COLONIES ARE OWNED

The vagueness of our conceptions of statecraft—How England "owns" Colonies—Some little-recognized facts—Why foreigners could not fight England for her self-governing Colonies—She does not "own" them, since they are masters of their own destiny—The paradox of conquest: England in a worse position in regard to her own Colonies than in regard to foreign nations—Her experience as the oldest and most practised colonizer in history—Colonies not a source of fiscal profit—Could Germany hope to do better? —If not, inconceivable she should fight for sake of making hopeless experiment.

THE foregoing disposes of the first six of the seven propositions outlined in Chapter III. There remains the seventh, dealing with the notion that in some way Great Britain's security and prosperity would be threatened by a foreign nation "taking her Colonies from her,"—a thing which we are assured our rivals are burning to do, as it would involve the "breaking up of the British Empire" to their advantage.

Let us try to read some meaning into a phrase which, however childish it may appear on analysis, is very commonly in the mouths of those who are responsible for our political ideas.

I have stated the case thus:

No foreign nation could gain any advantage by the conquest of the British Colonies, and Great Britain could not suffer material damage by their loss, however much such loss would be regretted on sentimental grounds, and as rendering less easy certain useful social co-operation between kindred peoples. For the British Colonies are, in fact, independent nations in alliance with the Mother Country, to whom they are no source of tribute or economic profit, their economic relations being settled not by the Mother Country, but by the Colonies. Economically, England would gain by their formal separation, since she would be relieved of the cost of their defence. Their loss, involving, therefore, no change in economic fact (beyond saving the Mother Country the cost of their defence), could not involve the ruin of the Empire and the starvation of the Mother Country, as those who commonly treat of such a contingency are apt to aver. As England is not able to exact tribute or economic advantage, it is inconceivable that any other country, necessarily less experienced in colonial management, would be able to succeed where England had failed, especially in view of the past history of the Spanish, Portuguese, French, and British Colonial Empires. This history also demonstrates that the position of Crown Colonies in the respect which we are considering is not sensibly different from that of the self-governing ones. It is not to be presumed, therefore, that any European nation would attempt the desperately expensive business of the conquest of England for the purpose of making an experiment with her Colonies which all colonial history shows to be doomed to failure.

What are the facts? Great Britain is the most successful colonizing nation in the world, and the policy into which her experience has driven her is that outlined by Sir C. P. Lucas, one of the greatest authorities on colonial questions. He writes, speaking of the history of the British Colonies on the American continent, thus:

It was seen—but it might not have been seen had the United States not won their independence—that English colonists, like Greek colonies of old, go out on terms of being equal, not subordinate, to those who are left behind; that when they have effectively planted another and a distant land, they must, within the widest limits, be left to rule themselves; that, whether they are right, or whether they are wrong,— more, perhaps, when they are wrong than when they are right,—they cannot be made amenable by force; that mutual good feeling, community of interest, and abstention from pressing rightful claims to their logical conclusion can alone hold together a true Colonial Empire.

But what in the name of common-sense is the advantage of conquering them if the only policy is to let them do as they like, "whether they are right or wrong,—more, perhaps, when they are wrong than when they are right"? And what avails it to conquer them if they cannot be made amenable to force? Surely this makes the whole thing a *reductio ad absurdum*. Were a Power like Germany to use force to conquer colonies, she would find out that they were not amenable to force, and that the only working policy was to let them do exactly as they did before she conquered them, and to allow them, if they chose—and many of the British Colonies do so choose—to treat the Mother Country absolutely as a foreign country. There has recently been going on in Canada a discussion as to the position which that Dominion should hold with reference to the British in the event of war, and I take from a French-Canadian paper (*La Presse*, March 27, 1909) a passage which is quoted with approval by an English-Canadian publication. It is as follows:

If, after the organization of a Canadian Navy, England finds herself at war with a foreign Power, if that war is a just one, and Canada considers it to be so, England may always rely upon the eager support of Canadian soldiers and marines. But we must always be free to give or to refuse this support.

Could a foreign nation say more? In what sense does England "own" Canada when Canadians must always be free to give or refuse their military support to England; and in what way does Canada differ from a foreign nation when England may be at war while Canada can be at peace? Mr. Asquith formally endorses this conception. On August 26, 1909, in the House of Commons, after explaining the conclusions of the Imperial Conference, he said:

The result was a plan for so organising the forces of the Crown, wherever they are, that, *while preserving the complete autonomy* of each Dominion, *should these Dominions desire to assist* in the defence of the Empire in a real emergency, their forces could be rapidly combined into one homogeneous Imperial Army.[1]

This shows clearly that no Dominion is held to be bound by virtue of its allegiance to the Sovereign of the British Empire to place its forces at his disposition, no matter how real may

[1] The New York papers of November 16, 1909, report the following from Sir Wilfrid Laurier in the Dominion Parliament during the debate on the Canadian navy: "My honourable friend [Mr. Monk] has blamed the Government for proposing to begin the organization of a naval force. What is the object of that force—what is the occasion? We never had one before, he says. I remember the time when we had no railways, no public-school system. And if now we have to organize a naval force, it is because we are growing as a nation— it is the penalty of being a nation. I know of no nation having a seacoast of its own which has no navy, except Norway, but Norway will never tempt the invader. Canada has its coal mines, its gold-mines, its wheat-fields, and its vast wealth may offer a temptation to the invader."

be the emergency. If it should not desire so to do, it is free to refuse so to do. This is to convert the British Empire into a loose alliance of independent Sovereign States, which are not even bound to help each other in case of war. The alliance between Austria and Germany is far more stringent than the tie which unites for purposes of war the component parts of the British Empire.

One critic, commenting on this, says:

Whatever language is used to describe this new movement of Imperial defence, it is virtually one more step towards complete national independence on the part of the Colonies. For not only will the consciousness of the assumption of this task of self-defence feed with new vigour the spirit of nationality, it will entail the further power of full control over foreign relations. This has already been virtually admitted in the case of Canada, now entitled to a determinant voice in all treaties or other engagements in which her interests are especially involved. The extension of this right to the other colonial nations may be taken as a matter of course. Home rule in national defence thus established reduces the Imperial connection to its thinnest terms.[1]

[1] The recent tariff negotiations between Canada and the United States were carried on between Ottawa and Washington without the intervention of London. Sir Wilfrid Laurier, in a speech recently at Humbolt, said: "But while we acknowledge the sovereignty of the British King, we say

Is Germany really likely to fight England for the "ownership" of Colonies which are even now in reality independent, and might conceivably at the outbreak of war become so in name as well? Facts of very recent English history have established quite incontrovertibly this ridiculous paradox: England has more influence—that is to say, a freer opportunity of enforcing her point of view— with foreign nations than with her own Colonies. Indeed, does not Sir C. P. Lucas's statement that "whether they are right or wrong—still more, perhaps, when they are wrong," they must be left alone, necessarily mean that our position with the Colonies is weaker than our position with foreign nations? In the present state of international feeling Englishmen would never dream of advocating submission to foreign nations when they are wrong. Recent history is illuminating on this point.

What were the larger motives that pushed England into war with the Dutch Republics? It was to vindicate the supremacy of the British race in South Africa, to enforce British ideals as against Boer ideals, to secure the rights of British Indians and other British subjects, to protect the native against Boer oppression, to take the government of the country generally from a people whom such authorities as Doyle and

---

that the part Canada shall play is not the part of a dependency, but the part of a nation."

many of those who were loudest in their advocacy of the war described as "inherently incapable of civilization." What, however, is the outcome of spending two hundred and fifty millions upon the accomplishment of these objects? The present Government of the Transvaal is in the hands of the Boer party. England has achieved the union of South Africa in which the Boer element is predominant. Britain has enforced against the British Indian in the Transvaal and Natal the same Boer regulations which were one of our grievances before the war, and the Houses of Parliament have just ratified an Act of Union in which the Boer attitude with reference to the native is codified and made permanent. Sir Charles Dilke, in the debate in the House of Commons on the South African Bill, made this quite clear. He said:

The old British principle in South Africa, as distinct from the Boer principle, in regard to the treatment of natives was equal rights for all civilized men. At the beginning of the South African War the country was told that one of its main objects, and certainly that the one predominant factor in any treaty of peace, would be the assertion of the British principle as against the Boer principle. Now, the Boer principle dominates throughout the whole of South Africa.

Mr. Asquith, as representing the British Government, admitted that this was the case, and that "the opinion of this country is almost unanimous in objecting to the colour bar in the Union Parliament." He went on to say that "the opinion of the British Government and the opinion of the British people must not be allowed to lead to any interference with a self-governing Colony." So that, having expended in the conquest of the Transvaal a greater sum than Germany exacted from France at the close of the Franco-Prussian War, England has not even the right to enforce her views on those very subjects which constituted the motive of going to war. Again, it is to this paradox these conquests lead. As one critic declares:

The war has not made the Union, but it has made Dutch mastery within the Union. If Lord Milner had looked before he leaped ten years ago, he would have recognized that the surest way to render certain for the future that "dominion of Afrikanderdom" which he hated was to convert the two Republics by force into two self-governing British Colonies. Those who, ten years ago, insisted with so much assurance upon the inevitability of war in South Africa failed to recognize that the sequel of the war was equally inevitable. That the most redoubtable Boer generals, who eight years ago were in the field against our troops, should now be in London imposing on the British Government the terms of a national Constitution which will make them and their allies in the Cape the rulers of a virtually independent South

8

Africa is, indeed, one of the brightest humours of modern history.

The *National Review*, speaking of the South African Union Bill, remarks, not without justice:

Podsnap and Pecksniff were conspicuous throughout the debates. Government and Opposition vied with one another in hailing the millennium which must inevitably follow the adoption of a Constitution placing the British and the natives permanently under the heel of the Boers. Every tragedy has its comic aspect, and there is a certain grim humour in our sentimental, pro-native Radical Parliament passing a great measure of local self-government with a rigid colour bar virtually excluding the natives, who constitute at least four fifths of the population of South Africa, from all practical share in its government, either now or hereafter. We can imagine what would have been said by the Opposition had a Unionist Government proposed to hand over the population of South Africa to an "insignificant white oligarchy." The Radical Party would have seethed with indignation. But their delight at seeing Englishmen under the Boer harrow has completely reconciled them to the abandonment of their native *clientèle*.

Just recently there was in London a deputation from the British Indians in the Transvaal pointing out that the regulations there deprive them of the ordinary rights of British citizens. The British Government has informed them that the

Transvaal being a self-governing Colony, the Imperial Government can do nothing for them.[1] Now it will not be forgotten that, at a time when England was quarrelling with Paul Krüger, one of the liveliest of her grievances was the treatment of British Indians. Having conquered Krüger, now "owning" his country, does Great Britain act as she was trying to compel Paul Krüger as a foreign ruler to act? She does not. She (or rather the responsible Government of the

[1] A bill has been introduced into the Indian Legislative Council enabling the Government to prohibit emigration to any country where the treatment accorded to British Indian subjects was not such as met with the approval of the Governor-General. "As just treatment for free Indians has not been secured," says the *Times*, "prohibition will undoubtedly be applied against Natal unless the position of free Indians there is ameliorated. The position in Natal becomes more difficult as the number of free Indians increases; hence, it is desirable to stop emigration completely, though Natal may stave off prohibition by ameliorating the treatment of free Indians. A strong body of educated opinion desires the cessation of indentured emigration, because it injures free Indians. The immediate effect of prohibition on the districts from which the emigrants are mainly drawn may be severe."

Concerning some correspondence on the same subject appearing in the weekly paper *John Bull*, that journal comments (June 11, 1910: "This is the treatment meted out to a British subject in the Transvaal, an Indian gentleman, highly educated, and of unblemished character. Mr. L. W. Ritch, who directs our attention to this matter, and whose efforts on behalf of the Indians in the Transvaal have been so persistent and strenuous, tells us that he has appealed again and again to the Imperial Government to take some effective steps to correct the disgraceful state of things we have described; but either the power or the will, or both, would appear to be lacking."

Colony, with whom she dare not interfere, although she was ready enough to make representations to Krüger) simply and purely enforces his own regulations. Moreover, the Australian Colonies and British Columbia have since taken the view with reference to British Indians which President Krüger took, and which view England made almost a *casus belli*. Yet in the case of her Colonies she does absolutely nothing. So the process is this: The Government of a foreign territory does something which England asks it to cease doing. The refusal of the foreign Government constitutes a *casus belli*. England fights, and conquers, and the territory in question becomes one of her Colonies, and she allows the Government of that Colony to continue doing the very thing which constituted, in the case of a foreign nation, a *casus belli*. What did she undertake the war of conquest for? Do we not arrive, therefore, at the absurdity I have already indicated—*that a nation is in a worse position to enforce its views in its own territory—that is to say, in its colonies—than in foreign territory?* Would England submit tamely if a foreign Government should exercise permanently gross oppression on an important section of her citizens? Certainly she would not. But when the Government exercising that oppression happens to be the Government of her own Colonies she does nothing, and a great British authority lays it down that, even more when the

Colonial Government is wrong than when it is right, must she do nothing, and that, though wrong, the Colonial Government cannot be amenable to force. Nor can it be said that Crown Colonies differ essentially in this matter from self-governing Colonies. Not only is there an irresistible tendency for Crown Colonies to acquire the practical rights of self-governing Colonies, but it has become a practical impossibility to disregard their special interests. Experience is conclusive on this point.

I am not here playing with words or attempting to make paradoxes. This *reductio ad absurdum*—the fact that when Britain owns a territory she renounces the privilege of using force to ensure observance of her views—is becoming more and more a common-place of British Colonial Government.

As to the fiscal position of the Colonies, that is precisely what their political relation is in all but name; they are foreign nations. They erect tariffs against Great Britain; they exclude large sections of British subjects absolutely (practically speaking, no British Indian is allowed to set foot in Australia, and yet British India constitutes the greater part of the British Empire), and even against British subjects from Great Britain vexatious exclusion laws are enacted. Again the question arises: Could a foreign country do more? If fiscal preference is extended to Great

Britain, that preference is not the result of British "ownership" of the Colonies, but is the free act of the Colonial legislators, and could as well be made by any foreign nation desiring to court closer fiscal relations with Great Britain. [1]

Is it conceivable that Germany, if the real relations between Great Britain and her Colonies were understood, would undertake the costliest war of conquest in history in order to acquire an absurd and profitless position, in which she could not exact even the shadow of a material advantage?

It may be pleaded that Germany might on the morrow of conquest attempt to enforce a policy which gave her a material advantage in the Colonies, such as Spain and Portugal attempted to create for themselves. But in that case, is it conceivable that Germany, without colonial experience, would be able to enforce a policy which Great Britain was obliged to abandon a hundred years ago? Is it imaginable that, if Great Britain has been utterly unable to carry out a policy by which the Colonies shall pay

[1] Britain's total over-seas trade for 1908 was 1049 millions, of which 784 millions was with foreigners, and 265 millions with her own possessions. And while it is true that with some of her Colonies Britain has as much as 52 per cent. on their trade (e. g., Australia), it also happens that some absolutely foreign countries give greater percentage even of trade with Britain than do our Colonies. Britain possesses 38 per cent. of Argentina's foreign trade, but only 36 per cent. of Canada's, although Canada has recently given considerable preference.

anything resembling tribute to the Mother Country, Germany, without experience, and at an enormous disadvantage in the matter of language, tradition, racial tie, and the rest, would be able to make such a policy a success? Surely, if the elements of this question were in the least understood in Germany, such a preposterous notion could not be entertained for a moment.

There cannot be found a single authority, from Adam Smith to Seeley (or to Joseph Chamberlain, for that matter), prepared to risk his reputation by declaring that any fiscal arrangement constituting a monopoly benefit for the Mother Country can in our day be imposed upon colonies, or that any fiscal arrangement can be imposed upon any considerable colony of European people except by their consent and co-operation. And fiscal arrangements which are for the benefit of both parties, and are enforced by the consent of both, can be effected as between any communities, whether they stand in the relation of Mother Country and Colony or not.

Yet so little is the real relationship of modern colonies understood that I have heard it mentioned in private conversation by an English public man, whose position was such, moreover, as to enable him to give very great effect to his opinion, that one of the motives pushing Germany to war was the projected capture of South Africa, in order that she could seize the gold mines, and

by means of a tax of 50 per cent. on their output
secure for herself one of the chief sources of gold
in the world.

One heard a good deal at the outbreak of the
South African War of the part that the gold mines
played in precipitating that conflict. Alike in
England and on the Continent, it was generally
assumed that Great Britain was "after the gold
mines." A long correspondence took place in
the *Times* as to the real value of the mines, and
speculation as to the amount of money which it
was worth Great Britain's while to spend in their
"capture." Well, now that England has won the
war, how many gold mines has she captured? In
other words, how many shares in the gold mines
does the British Government hold? How many
mines have been transferred from their then owners
to the British Government as the result of British
victory? How much tribute does the Government
of Westminster exact as the result of investing
two hundred and fifty millions in the enterprise?

The fact is, of course, that England does not
hold a dollar's worth of the property. The mines
belong to the shareholders and to no one else,
and in the conditions of the modern world it is
not possible for a government to capture so
much as a single pound of such property as the
result of a war of conquest.

Supposing that Germany or any other conqueror were to put on the output of the mines a

duty of 50 per cent.[1] What would she get, and
what would be the result? The output of the
South African mines to-day is, roughly, thirty million sterling a year, so that she would get about
fifteen millions a year. The annual total income
of Germany is calculated at something like three
thousand million sterling, so that a tribute of fifteen million would hold about the same proportion to Germany's total income that, say, twenty
cents a day would to the income of a man in
receipt of $10,000 a year. It would represent
the expenditure that a middle-class householder
with an income of two or three thousand
dollars a year makes upon, say, matches.
Could one imagine such a householder in his
right mind committing burglary and murder
in order to economize thirty-five cents a week?
Yet that would be the position of the German
Empire engaging upon a great and costly war
for the purpose of exacting fifteen million sterling
a year from the South African mines; or, rather,
the situation for the German Empire would be
a great deal worse than that. For this householder having committed burglary and murder
for the sake of his thirty-five cents a week—the
German Empire, that is, having entered into one
of the most frightful wars of history to exact its

[1] A financier to whom I showed the proofs of this chapter
made a note at this point: "You can say that were such a tax
imposed the result would be nil."

tribute of fifteen millions sterling—would then find
that in order to get this thirty-five cents it had
to jeopardize many of the investments upon
which the bulk of its income depended. On the
morrow of imposing a tax of fifty per cent. on
the mines there would be such a slump in a class
of security now dealt in by every considerable
stock exchange in the world that there would
hardly be a considerable business firm in Europe
unaffected thereby. Englishmen know of the
difficulty that a relatively mild fiscal attack, delivered rather for social and moral than economic
reasons, upon a class of property like the brewing
trade, provokes. What sort of outcry, therefore,
would be raised throughout the world when
every South African mining share in the world
loses at one stroke half its value, and a great
many of them lose all their value? Who would
invest money in the Transvaal at all if property
were to be subject to that sort of shock? In-
vestors would argue that though it be mines
to-day, it might be other forms of property to-
morrow, and South Africa would find herself
in the position of being able hardly to borrow a
shilling for any purpose whatsoever, save at
usurious and extortionate rates of interest. The
whole of South African trade and industry would,
of course, feel the effect, and South Africa as
a market would immediately begin to dwindle
in importance. And those businesses bound up

with South African affairs would waver on the brink of ruin, and many of them topple over. Is that the way efficient Germany would 'set about the development of her newly acquired Empire? She would soon find that she had a ruined colony on her hands. And if in South Africa the sturdy Dutch and English stock did not produce a George Washington with a better material and moral case for independence than George Washington ever had, then history has no meaning. And if it cost England two hundred and fifty millions to conquer Dutch South Africa, what would it cost Germany to conquer Anglo-Dutch South Africa? Such a policy could not, of course, last six months, and Germany would end by doing what Great Britain has ended by doing—she would renounce all attempt to exact a tribute or commercial advantage other than those which are the result of free co-operation with the South African people. In other words, she would learn that the policy which Great Britain has adopted was not adopted by philanthropy, but in the hard school of bitter experience. Germany would see that the last word in colonial statesmanship is to exact nothing from your colonies, and where the greatest colonial power of history has been unable to follow any other policy, a poor intruder in the art of colonial administration would not be likely to prove more successful, and she, too, would find that the only way to treat colonies is to treat them as independent or foreign territories, and the only way to own them is to make no attempt at exercising any of the functions of ownership. And all the reasons which gave force to this principle in the seventeenth and eighteenth centuries—and the whole monopolistic system had broken down long before it was abolished by law—have been reinforced a hundredfold by all the modern contrivances of credit and capital, quick communication, popular government, popular press, the conditions and cost of warfare—the whole weight, indeed, of modern progress. It is not a question here of theorizing, of the erection of an elaborate thesis, nor is it a question of arguing what the relations of Colonies ought to be. The differences between the Imperialist and the Little Englander do not enter into the discussion at all. It is simply a question of what the unmistakable outstanding facts of experience have taught, and we all know, Imperialists and Little Englanders alike, that whatever the relations with the Colonies are to be, that relationship must be fixed by the free consent of the Colonies, by their choice, not ours. And Englishmen know, as informed Germans must know, that to attempt now what was impossible two hundred years ago, is sheer midsummer madness. And to suppose that Germany would seriously set about conquering first England and then South Africa, would attempt a policy which all history shows to be doomed to failure, is midsummer madness in still worse degree, yet it is the sort of madness that one may find blatant in the mouths of even respectable public men like Mr. Harrison, and in the columns of serious organs like the *Times*. Sir J. R. Seeley notes in his book, *The Expansion of England*, that because the early Spanish Colonies were in a true sense of the word " possessions," we acquired the habit of talking of " possessions " and " ownership," and our whole ideas of colonial policy were vitiated during three centuries, simply by the fatal hypnotism of an incorrect word. Is it not time that we shook off the influence of these fatal words? Canada, Australia, New Zealand, and South Africa are not "possessions." They are no more possessions than is Argentina or Brazil, and the nation which conquered England, which even captured London, would be hardly nearer to the conquest of Canada or Australia than if it happened to occupy Constantinople or St. Petersburg. Why, therefore, do we tolerate the loose talk which assumes that the master of London is also master of Montreal, Vancouver, Cape Town, Johannesburg, Melbourne, and Sydney? Have we not had about enough of this terrorist talk, which is persistently blind to the simplest and most elementary factors of the case?[1]

[1] As German opinion is presumably even less informed on this

side of the subject than is opinion in England or America, I have incorporated in the German edition of this book a good deal of additional matter, which will be found in the Appendix of this edition, and those who did not regard this as a closed question ought most emphatically to read the Appendix referred to. The position of the Philippines to the United States more nearly resembles that of a British Crown Colony to Great Britain than does that of the great self-governing colonies. But I have expressly excluded from the consideration of the benefits of conquest those cases in which a more civilized power employs its force for ensuring more stable conditions in less civilized territory. This whole matter is discussed in detail in Chapter V, part 2. Even where exclusive privileges are sought in such territory the real benefit to the people of the "owning" country is very questionable, as is shown by the history of Spain, Portugal, and France in the past as well as by the recent history of Spain and Portugal. Those points also are dealt with in the chapter which is referred to, as well as more specifically in the following chapter.

CHAPTER VIII

CONQUEROR OR POLICEMAN?

Alsace and Algeria—What is the difference?—How Germany
exploits without conquest—Or emigration—What is the
difference between an army and a police force?—The policing
of the world—Germany's share of it in the Near East.

THERE remain cases which apparently, however, do not come within the scope of the
facts outlined in the preceding chapter. Admitting that the conquest and exploitation for
the benefit of the conqueror of modern independent nations, such as are the self-governing
British Colonies, is a sheer physical impossibility,
that such a process belongs to the past and is
not possible in the modern world; admitting
that the transfer of a province like Alsace-Lorraine
from one Government to another is merely a
jugglery with administrative areas, benefiting
neither the "conqueror" nor the inhabitants of
such area; admitting that the advantages of the
pre-emption by force of empty territory suitable
for colonization by the white race, the process

that is which gave to Great Britain self-governing
Colonies, is also a thing of the past, and cannot
now be regarded as a contingency of practical
politics—there remain cases which do not at first
sight seem to be covered by the arguments of the
preceding chapter. It is urged that, though
Germany has received no tangible advantage
by the annexation of Alsace-Lorraine, the annexation of Algeria has been a tangible advantage
to France; that it is better for Americans that
California, which was acquired by conquest,
should be under American rather than under
Mexican rule; that both conquests have brought
territories suitable for colonization by the conqueror, and that they would not have been
suitable except for such conquest; that, to a
modified (a much modified!) degree, the same
would be true of the American conquest of the
Philippines; and that circumstances may arise in
which similar contingencies may present themselves (diplomacy does indeed attribute to Germany similar schemes of conquest in Asia Minor),
and that the scramble for semi-civilized territory
is likely to furnish as fruitful a source of conflict
between the great Powers as did the scramble for
the New World.

Here, as in every section of this subject,
we are dominated by the tyranny of an obsolete terminology, and are the victims of the confusion which results therefrom. It is important

to keep certain tangible facts of the case in mind.

In a subsequent section of this book[1] I have attempted to show how enormously the mechanical development of civilization is shifting the real conflict of humanity from the physical to the intellectual plane. It is as certain as anything can be that struggle will in the future go on as vigorously as ever. Force will rule the world in the future as in the past, but it will be the force of hard work and superior brain, not the force of cannon and *Dreadnoughts*.

When one nation, say England, occupies a territory, does it mean that that territory is "lost" to Germans? We know this to be an absurdity. Germany does an enormous and increasing trade with the territory that has been pre-empted by the Anglo-Saxon race. Millions of Germans in Germany gain their livelihood by virtue of German enterprise and German industry in Anglo-Saxon countries—indeed, it is the bitter and growing complaint of Englishmen that they are being driven out of these territories by the Germans; that where originally British shipping was universal in the East, German shipping is now coming to occupy the prominent place; that the trade of whole territories which Englishmen originally had to themselves is now being captured

[1] Chapter V., Part II., "The Diminishing Factor of Physical Force."

by Germans, and this not merely where the fiscal arrangements are more or less under the control of the British Government, as in the Crown Colonies, but in those territories originally British, like the United States, and nominally so no longer, as well as in those territories which are in reality independent, like Australia and Canada, though nominally still under British control.

Moreover, why need Germany occupy the extraordinary position of phantom "ownership" which England occupies, in order to enjoy all the real benefits which in our day result from a Colonial Empire? More Germans have found homes in the United States in the last half-century than Englishmen have in all their Colonies. It is calculated that between ten and twelve millions of the population of the United States are of direct German descent. It is true, of course, that these Germans do not live under their flag, but the truth is that they do not regret that fact, but rejoice in it! The majority of German emigrants do not desire that the land to which they go shall have the political character of the land which they leave behind. The fact that, in adopting the United States, they have shed something of the German tradition and create a new national type, partaking in part of the English and in part of the German, is, on the whole, very much to their advantage—and incidentally to ours. Writing recently of "Home-

Sickness among the Emigrants" (the *World*, July 19, 1910), Mr. Aflalo says:

The Germans are, of all nations, the least troubled with this weakness. Though far more warmly attached to the hearth than their neighbours across the Rhine, they feel exile less. Their one idea is to evade conscription, and this offers to all Continental nations a compensation for exile which to the Englishman means nothing. I remember a colony of German fishermen on Lake Tahoe, the loveliest water in California, where the pines of the Sierra Nevada must have vividly recalled their native Harz. Yet they rejoiced in the freedom of their adopted country and never knew a moment's regret for the Fatherland.

An English journalist, giving his experiences in Australia, writes[1]:

The history of the foundation of the Colony of South Australia is interesting. At one time Silesian Lutherans formed a tenth part of the population of the whole Colony, and there are now townships in which every name on the shop-front is German, and German is the common language of the home. One such township is Tanunda.

Almost every one of its inhabitants is German by descent, if not by birth. The churches are Lutheran, and one of them is old, with a flower-grown graveyard in front and a flagged path leading up to its door. I

[1] A. Marshall in the *Daily Mail*, London, April 11, 1910.

was there on Sunday, and saw the German farmers
from the surrounding district driving their families
home after service, and the German *hausfraus* walking
the streets with their service-books, dressed in their
best. The Germans make excellent colonists, and
have taken kindly to Australian life.

All this is very dreadful, of course, but, after
all, why should Anglo-Saxons of all people blame
Germans for preferring freedom to an irksome
regimentation? Carry the matter a little farther:
should we blame a Turk for preferring England
to Turkey? The blind dogma of patriotism
needs a little qualification, and if we give it
the qualification which interest and common-
sense justify, we shall realize that much of even
the sentimental motive for a nation like Germany
desiring colonies will vanish into thin air. Indeed, in our own case, are not certain foreign
countries much more of real colonies for our
children of the future, than certain territory
under our own flag? Will not England's children
find better and more congenial conditions, much
more of a colony, in Philadelphia, which is
"foreign," than in Bombay, which she "owns"?
And what is true of the Germans or English
in America or Australia is true of the French in
Canada. Are the French any the worse because
Canada is not "owned" by France? Is not the
whole question of the "ownership" of Colonies

becoming an academic one, since if the Colony succeeds it settles the question by "owning" itself; and if it does not succeed it is only a burden to the mother-country.

I know it will be urged that, despite all this, national sentiment of a nation will always desire for the overflow of its population territories in which that nation's language, law, and literature reign.

Again, to this objection we must point out that the day is past when it is possible for Germany to achieve such a result by conquest. The German conqueror of the future would have to say with Napoleon, "I come too late. The nations are too firmly set." Even when the English, the greatest colonizers of the world, conquer a territory like the Transvaal or the Orange Free State, they have no resort, having conquered it, but to allow its own law, its own literature, its own language to have free play, just as though the conquest had never taken place. This was even the case with Quebec more than one hundred years ago, and Germany will have to be guided by a like rule. On the morrow of conquest she would have to proceed to establish her real ascendancy by other than military means—a thing she is free to do to-day, if she can. It cannot throughout this discussion be too often repeated that the world has been modified, and that what was possible to the Canaanites or the Romans, or even to the Normans, is no longer possible to us. The edict can no longer go forth to "slay every male child" that is born into the conquered territory, in order that the race may be exterminated. Conquest in this sense is impossible. The most marvellous Colonial history in the world—British Colonial history—demonstrates that in this field physical force is no longer of avail.

Moreover, always as bearing upon the actual policy which concerns us, there is a further important fact to be considered: Germany's era of emigration has, for the time being at least, passed. Germans no longer emigrate, and the chief cause is that factor which modifies this whole problem at numberless points—the development of the means of communication. The manufacturer in Prussia, just as the manufacturer in Lancashire, is able to exploit a distant territory without going there, and will support himself and his factory out of such territory without ever moving from Prussia or Lancashire. England's greatest industry is carried on thanks to the product of States over which she has no sort of political control. Here again we see the distinction between modern and ancient conditions. Germany, by virtue of improved means of communication, is doing an enormous trade with South America; thousands, it may be millions, of Germans gain their livelihood in Germany by the exploitation of South American territory. In the pre-economic era such a thing would not have been possible except by virtue of the actual political conquest of such territory. To-day Germany knows such conquest to be impossible. Does she for that reason surrender any hope of having South America help support her population? Not the least in the world, and, as I have remarked in the next part of this book,[1] which deals more completely with this section of the subject, Germany, who never sent a soldier into South America, to-day draws more wealth therefrom, exacts infinitely more tribute therefrom, than does Spain, which has poured out oceans of blood in its "conquest." Here, as at every point, do we see the futility of mere military conquest.

This is the real struggle, therefore the real force of the future—the force of work, intelligence, efficiency, so fertile of useful results; not the force of arms, which is so barren.

At one point, however, one may look for armed intervention. There is a radical difference between cases like Alsace-Lorraine and cases like Algeria and California, which current political conception does not seem sufficiently to realize. The completer exposition of this difference, which reaches down into the fundamental principles of human progress, into the very biology of human development, belongs also to the next section of this book, dealing with the psychological aspect

[1] See Chapter V., Part II.

of the case. But it has also an economic side, which should briefly be touched on here. I will try to make this distinction clear by an apparent digression.

To a critic who maintained that the armies of the world were necessary and justifiable on the same grounds as the police forces of the world, adding, "Even in communities such as London, where, in our civic capacity, we have nearly realized all your ideals, we still maintain and are constantly improving our police force," I replied:

When we learn that the London County Council, instead of using its police for the running in of burglars and "drunks," is using them to lead an attack on Birmingham for the purpose of capturing that city as part of a policy of "municipal expansion," or "Civic Imperialism," or "Pan-Londonism," or what not; or is using its force to repel an attack from the Birmingham police acting as the result of a similar policy on the part of the Birmingham patriots—when that happens you can safely approximate a police force to a European army. But until it does, it is quite evident that the two—the army and the police force—have in reality diametrically opposed rôles. The police exist as an instrument of social co-operation; the armies as the natural outcome of the quaint illusion that though one city could never enrich itself by "capturing" or "subjugating" another, in some wonderful (and unexplained) way one country can enrich itself by capturing or subjugating another.

In the existing condition of things in Eng-land this illustration covers the whole case: the citizens of London would have no imaginable interest in "conquering" Birmingham, or *vice versa*. But suppose there arose in the cities of the North such a condition of disorder that London could not carry on its ordinary work and trade; then London, if it had the power, *would* have an interest in sending its police into Birmingham, presuming that that could be done. The citizens of London would have a tangible interest in the maintenance of order in the North—they would be the richer for it.

Order was just as well maintained in Alsace-Lorraine before the German conquest as after, and for that reason Germany has not benefited by the conquest. But order was not maintained in California, and would not have been as well maintained under Mexican as under American rule, and for that reason America has benefited by the conquest of California. France has bene-fited by the conquest of Algeria, England by that of India, because in each case the arms were employed not, properly speaking, for con-quest at all, but for police purposes, for the establishment and maintenance of order; and, so far as they filled that rôle, their rôle was a useful one.

How does this distinction affect the practical

problem under discussion? Most fundamentally. Germany has no need to maintain order in England, nor England in Germany, and the latent struggle therefore between these two countries is futile. It is not the result of any inherent necessity of either people; it is the result merely of that woful confusion which dominates statecraft to-day, and is bound, so soon as that confusion is cleared up, to come to an end.

Where the condition of a territory is such that the social and economic co-operation of other countries with it is impossible, we may expect the intervention of military force, not as the result of the "annexationist illusion," but as the outcome of real social forces pushing to the maintenance of order. That is the story of England in Egypt, or, for that matter, in India. And if America has any justification in the Philippines at all, it is not that she has "captured" those populations by force of conquest, as in the old days a raiding tribe might capture a band of cattle, but that she is doing there a work of police and administration which the natives cannot do for themselves. But foreign nations have no need to maintain order in the British Colonies, nor in the United States, the populations of those countries are quite capable of doing that for themselves; and though there might be such necessities in the case of countries like Venezuela, the last few years have taught us that by bringing these countries into the great economic currents of the world, and so setting up in them a whole body of interests in favour of order, more can be done than by forcible conquest. We occasionally hear rumours of German designs in Brazil and elsewhere, but even the modicum of education possessed by the average European statesman makes it plain to him that these nations are, like the others, "too firmly set" for military occupation and conquest by an alien people.

What, after all, is the practical question in this whole discussion? Even those who will not admit to the full the principles which I have attempted to elaborate in this book will certainly be obliged to admit, in the face of the facts outlined in the preceding chapter, that any talk of the German conquest of British Colonies is just so much moonshine. It will never be accomplished; it will never be attempted; and those who write and talk as though it would must be guilty either of very great ignorance or some insincerity. There will never be any duplication of that fight for empty territory which took place between European nations in the seventeenth and eighteenth centuries; the completely empty territory fit for white colonization is not there. Happily, as I have attempted briefly to indicate, the necessity for so finding territorial outlet for increasing populations is nothing like so great as it was. Germany is absorbing her increasing population, not by sending them abroad, but by so improving her

means of production that, thanks to them and
to the improved means of communication, she is
able to feed them at home. Indeed, it is doubtful,
judging solely by experience, whether even if she
had the empty territory she could create in it new
German nations of the German race, as England
has created new English nations of the English
race, since her very commercial success renders it
unnecessary for Germany's population to leave
home. It is not territory in the political sense
that she needs, but a safe field for investment and
rich markets for her products. To conquer England would not make such fields any safer or such
markets any richer. Germany's military activities, if used at all, will be used quite otherwise.

It is one of the humours of the whole Anglo-
German conflict that so much has the British
public been concerned with the myths and bogies
of the matter that it seems calmly to have ignored
the realities. While even the wildest Pan-German
has never cast his eyes in the direction of Canada,
he has cast them, and does cast them, in the direction of Asia Minor; and the political activities of
Germany may centre on that area for precisely
the reasons which result from the distinction
between policing and conquest which I have
drawn. German industry is coming to have a
dominating situation in the Near East, and as
those interests—her markets and investments—
increase, the necessity for better order in, and the

better organization of, such territories increases in corresponding degree. Germany may need to police Asia Minor.

What interest has England in attempting to prevent her? It may be urged that she would close the markets of those territories against England. But even if she attempted it, which she is never likely to do, a Protectionist Asia Minor organized with German efficiency would be better from the point of view of English trade than a Free Trade Asia Minor organized *à la Turque*. Protectionist Germany is one of the best markets that England has in Europe. If a second Germany were created in the Near East, if Turkey had a population with the German purchasing power and the German tariff, the markets would be worth some forty to fifty millions instead of some ten to fifteen. Why should England try to prevent Germany increasing her trade?

It is true that we touch here the whole problem of the fight for the open door in the undeveloped territories. But the real difficulty in this problem is not the open door at all, but the fact that Germany is beating England—or England fears she is beating her—in those territories where England has the same tariff to meet that she has, or even a smaller one; and that she is even beating the English in the territories that they already "own" —in their Colonies, in the East, in India. How, therefore, would England's final crushing of Germany in the military sense change anything? Suppose England crushed her so completely that she "owned" Asia Minor and Persia as completely as she owns India or Hong-Kong, would not the German merchant continue to beat the English merchant even then, as he is beating him now, in that part of the East over which England already holds political sway? Again, how would the disappearance of the German Navy affect the problem one way or the other?

Moreover, in this talk of the open door in the undeveloped territories we seem to lose all our sense of proportion. England's trade is in relative importance first with the great nations—the United States, France, Germany, Argentina, South America generally; after that with the white Colonies; after that with the organized East; and last of all, and to a very small extent, with the countries concerned in this squabble for the open door—territories in which the trade really is so small as hardly to pay for the making and upkeep of a dozen battleships.

When the man in the street, or, for that matter, the journalistic pundit, talks commercial diplomacy, his arithmetic seems to fall from him. Some years since the question of the relative position of the three Powers in Samoa exercised the minds of these wiseacres, who got quite fearfully warlike both in England and in the United States. Yet the trade of the whole island is not

worth that of an obscure Dorset village, and the
notion that naval budgets should be increased to
"maintain position," the notion that either of the
countries concerned should really think it worth
while to build so much as a single battleship the
more for such a purpose, is not throwing away a
sprat to catch a whale, but throwing away a whale
to catch a sprat—and then not catching it. For
even when one has the predominant political position, even when one has got extra *Dreadnoughts* or
extra twelve *Dreadnoughts*, it is the more efficiently
organized nation on the commercial side that will
take the trade. And while England is getting
excited over the trade of territories that matters
very little, rivals, including Germany, will be
quietly walking off with the trade that *does*
matter, will be increasing their hold upon such
markets as the United States, Argentina, South
America, and the lesser Continental States.

If we really examined these questions without
the old meaningless prepossessions, we should see
that it is more to the general interest to have an
orderly and organized Asia Minor under German
tutelage than to have an unorganized and disorderly one which should be independent. Perhaps it would be best of all that Great Britain
should do the organizing or share it with Germany,
though England has her hands full in that respect
—Egypt and India are problems enough. And
why should England forbid Germany to do in a

small degree what she has done in a large degree? Sir Harry Johnson, in the *Nineteenth Century* for December, 1910, comes a great deal nearer to touching the real kernel of the problem that is preoccupying Germany than any of the writers on the Anglo-German conflict of whom I know. As the result of careful investigation, he admits that Germany's real objective is not, properly speaking, England or England's Colonies at all, but the undeveloped lands of the Balkan Peninsula, Asia Minor, Mesopotamia, down even to the mouth of the Euphrates. He adds that the best informed Germans use this language to him:

In regard to England, we would recall a phrase dropped by ex-President Roosevelt at an important public speech in London, a phrase which for some reason was not reported by the London press. Roosevelt said that the best guarantee for Great Britain on the Nile is the presence of Germany on the Euphrates. Putting aside the usual hypocrisies of the Teutonic peoples, you know that this is so. You know that we ought to make common cause in our dealings with the backward races of the world. Let Britain and Germany once come to an agreement in regard to the question of the Near East, and the world can scarcely again be disturbed by any great war in any part of the globe, if such a war is contrary to the interests of the two Empires.

Such, declares Sir Harry, is German opinion. And in all human probability—so far as sixty-five

million people can be said to have the same opinion
—he is absolutely right.

It is because the work of policing backward or
disorderly populations is so often confused with
the annexationist illusion that the danger of squabbles in the matter is a real one.   Not the fact that
England is doing a real and useful work for the
world at large in policing India, creates jealousy
of her work there, but the notion that in some way
she "possesses" this territory, and draws tribute
and exclusive advantage therefrom.   When Europe is a little more educated on these matters, the
European populations will realize that they have
no primordial interest in furnishing the policemen.
German public opinion will see that, even if such
a thing were possible, the German people would
gain no advantage by replacing England in India,
especially as the final result of the administrative
work of Europe in the Near and Far East will be
to make populations like those of Asia Minor in
the last resort their own policemen.   Should some
Power, acting as policemen, ignoring the lessons
of history, try again the experiment tried by Spain
in South America and by England in North
America later, should she try to create for herself
exclusive privileges and monopolies, the other
nations have means of retaliation apart from
military conflict—in the numberless instruments
which the economic and financial relationships
of nations furnish.

PART II
The Human Nature of the Case

CHAPTER I

THE PSYCHOLOGICAL CASE FOR WAR

"You cannot leave human nature out of the account": vanity,
pride of place, pugnacity, the inherent hostility of nations
—Nations too good to fight; also too bad—Desire for mere
material comfort not the main motive in many human
activities—Military rivalry of nations needs long preparation—Such rivalry does not arise from "hot fit," therefore, but actual conflict may be precipitated thereby—
Scientific justification of international pugnacity—Struggle
between nations the law of survival—If a nation not
pugnacious in some degree, it will be eliminated in favour
of one that is—Pugnacity therefore a factor in the struggle
of nations, and must necessarily persist.

I OUGHT more properly, perhaps, to have entitled this section "The Case in its Biological
and Psychological Aspect." But it is as well
to avoid technical language when possible, and
the phrase used at the beginning of this part is
apposite for two reasons. Not only is it usually
urged that man's nature—the instinctive part of
him, his impulses—will always render war a
likely contingency between men, but also that
man's vital qualities, his virility and courage and
determination, hardihood, tenacity, and heroism,

149

are the legacy of war, and are preserved by war.

I have desired to get at the very best statement of this case, which, as we shall see presently, has not only the support of many authorities of the very greatest weight—of scientists, philosophers, soldiers, statesmen, poets, clergymen—but represents what is, perhaps, the very commonest objection urged to a purely economic statement of the case for peace: the objection that those who plead for rationalism in the international relationship "leave human nature out of account." With many the feeling that "all this logic does not amount to anything," even when they are unable to formulate any definite refutation of the arguments outlined in the first part of this book, is very profound and powerful. It is felt that, even admitting the general soundness of those arguments, there are a whole range of motives which remain unaccounted for. Nations do not fight merely about their material interests, but frequently on purely non-economic grounds: from vanity, from rivalry, from pride of place, the desire to be first, to occupy a great situation in the world, to have power or prestige, or from sheer hostility to people who differ from us; from quick resentment of insult or injury, the unreasoned desire, which comes of quarrel or disagreement, to dominate a rival at all costs; the "inherent hostility" that exists between rival nations; from the contagion of sheer passion—the blind strife of mutually hating men; and generally because men and nations always have fought and always will, and because, like the animals in Watt's doggerel, "It is their nature to."[1]

It should, however, be made clear that the term "ignoring human nature" is often used as implying, not that men are disposed to overlook their material interests, but that it is absurd to suppose they should ever do so. In other words, the phrase is often used indifferently to mean two diametrically opposed things. On the assumption—which, as pointed out in the first chapter of this book, certain phases of peace advocacy have done so much to foster—that those who oppose war are asking men, because the use of force is immoral and cruel, to forego an advantage which they might obtain by resort thereto, it is urged that in such a plea one is asking too much of "imperfect human nature." This view is reflected by Mr. St. Loe Strachey in his well-known pamphlet, *The New Way of Life*, when he writes (page 12):

We have got in future to face the world, not as we should like it to be, but as it is: the world of blood and

[1] A prominent international banker to whom I gave the first edition of this book said, "Though the economics of your book are unchallengeable, it is futile, for the simple reason that it deals with material interests, and people to-day do not go to war about business or material interest. I do not know what they go to war about, but I am quite sure it is not about business."

iron controlled by men who are not humanitarians and philanthropists, but persons intensely human on the other side of man's nature: persons who do not take what they would term a Sunday-school view of the world, but rather the view that man is still a wild beast; that the race is to the strong and not to the well-intentioned; that victory belongs to the big battalions, not to those who say that they envy no man anything, and who cannot understand that nations should hate or be jealous of each other. . . . We must not pretend that the world is better than it is, or different from what it is, but take its true measure and face the facts like men.[1]

The view plainly implied here is that men are too mercenary to take account of "sentiment" at all, or to be moved by anything but their interests. This point is sufficiently dealt with in the first part of this book. It is there shown that would men but approach the question from the simple view of their interests—from the purely selfish point of view, that is—it would be quickly realized that, owing to the change in the nature of wealth which the developments of the last generation have brought about, military force has been rendered futile for the achievement of any eco-

---

[1] Compare this with Major Stewart Murray's opinion: "Very plausible and very dangerous people are the peace idealists— too good and innocent for a hard, cruel world, where force is the chief law" (*Future Peace of the Anglo-Saxons*).

nomic aim. The idea that any sacrifice of self-
interest is needed on behalf of peace is there shown
to repose upon a series of political and economic
illusions, which are bound in the near future to
be recognized as illusions, however far from such
recognition Europe may at the moment appear
to be. The problem which is dealt with in this
section of this book is the precise reverse: It is
the fact that men, far from being too mercenary
to consider sentiment good or bad, are so sentimental both on the good and bad side as frequently to ignore their money interests.

The fact that there are very few opposed to
the peace ideal who, in speaking of "unchanging
human nature," do not swing at random between
the two contradictory contentions just indicated
shows how incoherent is the ordinary discussion
of this matter.

I do not think that any one who need be considered in this discussion challenges the fact that
around national conflicts do arise all those primitive, blind passions of the complex, elemental
impulses of our nature which have no relation to
material interest, and which are bound up with
so much of our conduct, and bound up with the
best as well as with the worst side.

After all, the normal motives in the case of
ordinary folk are not for the greater part of their
activities material at all. Herbert Spencer has
shown us that even the primitive savage is more

concerned to be decorated than to be dressed.[1]
If physical comfort and nothing else were our
aim, few of us would trouble to acquire more than
a hundred and fifty a year or thereabouts, as some
such sum will secure us three meals a day, and
few of us can eat more. Nevertheless, in our
cities we find thousands of men already enjoying
incomes more than sufficient to satisfy every
rational want, yet working feverishly and at
the sacrifice of comfort for the purpose of increasing such incomes to achieve simply social
consideration, not infrequently degenerating into
somewhat futile social display. Indeed, one may
say without much exaggeration that the greater
part of the English people socially above the
labouring classes are mainly concerned, not with
the increase of comfort, but with the keeping
up of appearances. The phenomenon is manifest as much in the spectacle of girls refusing
well-paid positions in domestic service to accept
ill-paid ones among the ranks of governesses or
shop-assistants as in that of the millionaire who
lives a life harder than that of his most obscure
clerk in order that he may outdo in financial

---

[1] Charles Darwin relates that, though many of the Patagonian
tribes possess fine furs, as soon as the rain and sleet come they
carefully take them off in order that they should not get spoiled.
Those familiar with the primitive men in South Africa have
noticed like behaviour when a Cape "boy" has a new set of
clothes.

influence some rival millionaire who is leading a
like life.

And vanity is evidently not the only non-
material motive behind much of our individual
conduct. To say nothing of the phenomenon of
religious fanatisism which has in the past drenched
the Western world in blood, and still does so much
of the Eastern world, the internal conflicts of
nations, the hostility which comes of mere difference of opinion and feeling and environment, is
very keen and real. Those who saw anything of
the state of feeling among Frenchmen during the
Dreyfus case had borne in upon them very strik-
ingly how deep and profound were the divisions
that could be created between people concerning
a matter in which their material interests were
not in the first instance directly involved.

A psychological factor exhibited thus early and
thus widely in social evolution is not likely to have
left international politics altogether unaffected.
Admiral Mahan, who has made the struggle
for domination among nations his especial study,
declares that some such consideration as that
which I have indicated does so animate the struggle of nations. He says:

Like individuals, nations and empires have souls as
well as bodies. Great and beneficent achievement
ministers to worthier contentment than the filling of
the pocket. Sentiment, imagination, aspiration, the
satisfaction of the rational and moral faculties in some

object better than bread alone, all must find a part in a worthy motive. That extension of national authority over alien communities which is the dominant note in the world politics of to-day dignifies and enlarges each citizen that enters its fold. . . .

It is useful, by the way, to compare Admiral Mahan's view with Mr. Strachey's view (quoted a few pages back) as to the sentiment of the matter. The two views well illustrate the flat contradiction involved in the common use of the phrase about ignoring human nature. Here we have two considerable authorities on the matter: one of them representing human nature as altogether too wedded to its material interest, too animal and brutal, to give up warfare; the other as so aspiring to better things as to take little account of its material interests, and so animated by a high ambition for "greater beneficent achievement," "ministering to worthier contentment than the filling of the pocket," as never likely to give up war.

The first contention we have dealt with; it is the second that now concerns us.

It may perhaps be some consciousness of the contradiction I have just touched on which gives rise to a somewhat widespread impression that the psychological motive of war is incapable of definite analysis, that war is purely "accidental," arising from sudden "hot fits" and war fevers too obscure in cause for examination. This surely is the extreme of unscientific fatalism. The view moreover is not one taken by the best of either side in this discussion; least of all is it taken by the great military writers who one and all declare that wars result from definite and determinable laws like all the great processes of human development. No one of the great masters of the art of war, from Grotius to Von der Goltz, accepts this view of the sudden and "accidental" nature of war. Indeed, there are certain very obvious objections to such an interpretation of the titanic conflicts that have shaken humanity. To say of human conduct in the mass that it is "motiveless" is, in any real sense, untrue, and such a view is only taken by those who do not trouble to disentangle causes that are often highly complex and obscure. Nor does the history of warfare justify any such conclusion. The causes of war in the past have at times been trivial enough, in all conscience, and generally divorced from any real interest of the people who suffered by and died in them. But the reasons which prompted those responsible for the wars— the diplomats and rulers—were definite enough. The causes may have been dynastic or religious or territorial, or simply for the purpose of diverting attention from things at home; or in more modern times merely that causes of quarrel readily capable of settlement between the governments concerned have grown into wars by reason of the agitation of unscrupulous politicians or a sensational press inflaming uninformed public opinion and setting up the irrational contagion known as war fever. But all these are causes and capable of analysis. Moreover, it is becoming almost impossible for a war to grow out of a mere "hot fit." Such can precipitate one in a day, it is true, but only if preparation for the particular war in question has been going on previously for a very long time—for years and even generations. The paraphernalia of war in the modern world cannot be improvised on the spur of the moment to meet each gust of ill-feeling and dropped when it is over. The building of battleships, the discussion of budgets, and the voting of them; the training of armies, the preparation of a campaign, is a long business, and more and more in our day does each distinctive campaign involve a special and distinctive preparation. The pundits declare that the German battleships have been especially built with a view to work in the North Sea. In any case, we know that the conflict with Germany has been going on for ten years. This is surely a rather prolonged "hot fit." The truth is that war in the modern world is the outcome of armed peace, and involves, with all its elaborate machinery of yearly budgets and slowly building warships and forts and slowly trained armies, a fixity of policy and purpose extending over years and sometimes generations. Men do not make these sacrifices month after month, year after year, pay taxes and upset governments and fight in Parliament for a mere passing whim; and as conflicts necessarily become more scientific, we shall in the nature of things be forced to prepare everything more thoroughly and have clearer and sounder ideas as to their essence, their cause, and their effects, and to watch more closely their relation to national motive and policy. Von der Goltz (*On the Conduct of War*) says:

One must never lose sight of the fact that war is the consequence and continuation of policy. One will act on the defensive strategically or rest on the defensive according as the policy has been offensive or defensive. An offensive and defensive policy is in its turn indicated by the line of conduct dictated historically. We see this very clearly in antiquity by the example furnished us by the Persians and the Romans. In their wars we see the strategical rôle following the bend of the historical rôle. The people which in its historical development has arrived at the stage of inertia, or even retrogression, will not carry on a policy of offence, but merely one of defence; a nation in that situation will wait to be attacked, and its strategy will consequently be defensive, and from a defensive strategy will follow necessarily a defensive tactic.

Lord Esher[1] expresses a like thought:

[1] *To-day and To-morrow*, p. 63.

A nation in case of war should have determined beforehand where to strike, and should be prepared to strike. In 1866, and again in 1870, Prussia reaped the advantage of forethought and scientific preparation. . . . Austria and France went to war *en amateur*. . . . It is well known that for years the Japanese fully foresaw the certainty of struggle with Russia. Schemes were elaborated and every detail of preparation attended to with precision and care, so that the long-expected blow fell where it had been planned to fall with extraordinary rapidity and success. . . . It is realized in Germany that the French have learned the lesson of 1870, and that some of the acutest minds in France have been for many years devoted to the consideration of problems of defence and offence.

It is true, of course, that the authorities just quoted write in the terms of the current political philosophy—that is to say, they assume that war is the outcome of man's struggle to advance his material interests. There are few authorities indeed who urge that the causes of war are purely or mainly psychological; that the struggles of nations are divorced from the questions of interest. Even Admiral Mahan does not get so far, since he only makes the "satisfaction of the worthier motive" one factor of several. Indeed, in the last analysis it is extremely difficult to separate the two. It may be said of the millionaire who works fourteen hours a day and lives like a clerk in order to dominate a financial rival, that he is spurred by a psychological motive—the desire for mastery and domination, pride, and vanity—all the motives, in short, which play so large a part in international rivalries. Nevertheless, the means —practically the only means—of his achieving his end is material success—by making money. So that whatever his motives may be, his energies are directed to filling his pockets just as much as though that were the end as well as the means; the millionaire's material success is the mark and token of his moral success. So must it be with nations. The nation that in the long run fails to achieve economic success cannot satisfy its national pride; it cannot in the modern world impose itself; it cannot even maintain great armies and great navies. It cannot in any way maintain its prestige.[1] For this reason it may be taken as an axiom that no nation of fair

---

[1] In a discussion of this matter one day the administrative head of one of the largest businesses in England scouted the idea that the making of money was the main motive of business competition. "Why am I really here in this office twelve hours a day, instead of fishing or playing golf? My income is large enough to enable me to amuse myself for the balance of my life. What I am really here for is to prevent X. across the street building up a bigger and more powerful business than ours." To which I replied, "And the condition of doing that is that you shall make more money than he does. You cannot make this a big business and beat him unless you make it an economic success. You have got to make money or have him beat you. It all comes to the same thing in the end." So far as the case is an analogy to national competition the question should be: "Would it satisfy your pride to have it out by fisticuffs, or to

political instruction will knowingly in the long run persist in a course of action which undermines its economic well-being. So again, in the last resort, the economic question lies purely at the bottom of the sentimental question.

The matter is admittedly more complicated in the field of politics by factors which do not exist in the field of business. There is the undeniable difference between men in their collective and individual capacities; the irrationalism of the "mob mind"; the fact that a man will in politics, in a matter where patriotism is involved, act with an irrationalism and an absence of any sense of responsibility which he would never display in the conduct of his private business. The political history of every nation reeks with examples. In politics old catch words and ideas which are the survival of conditions long since vanished still hold a sway which has no parallel in the ordinary conduct of commercial business.

It may well happen, therefore, that even though the economic futility of military force be fully demonstrated, a whole range of ideas which are the outcome of the old conditions will survive in various and elusive forms. I have tried by going to the most authoritative and most typical literature of the subject, not only to bring into relief what are commonly considered the outstand-

stick a knife into him? You have to beat him in business, not in boxing."

ing psychological motives for war, to give some
definite form to the feeling which exists as much
in the minds of the students of war as in the
minds of the mass of the people who create
public opinion in Christendom, that war can be
justified on other than economic grounds, and that
men will find plenty of cause for making war
even when the economic motive for it shall have
disappeared, but to give also the best scientific
defence or apologia of those motives. What is
that defence?

Man's tendency to fight, and especially his
tendency to fight for predominance and mastery
and to quarrel over matters affecting his pride
and prestige and vanity, is justified not only
as being rooted deep in "unchanging human
nature,"—a universal instinct so deep-seated that
no economic motive is necessary either to provoke
it or keep it alive,—but as furnishing the great
stimulus to our best efforts; and it is urged that
if we could shed it human nature would on the
whole be the poorer for it—that, in short, at the
bottom of man's tendency towards war lies some
quality which makes for his uplift and for his
material and moral advance. The plea has, of
course, received definite scientific expression in
the works of such philosophers as Ratzenhofer,
Nietzsche, and Ram, and even in the works of
economists like De Molinari, to mention only
one or two of the more notable. It is urged

that, whatever may be the case to-day, the condition of man's advance in the past has been the survival of the fit by struggle and warfare, and that in such struggle it is precisely those endowed with combativeness and readiness to fight that have survived. Thus the tendency to combat is not a mere human perversity, but is part of the self-protective instinct rooted in profound biological laws—the struggle of nations for survival. This point of view is well voiced by S. R. Steinmetz in his *Philosophie des Krieges*. War according to this author is an ordeal instituted by God who weighs the nations in its balance. It is the essential form of the State and the only function in which peoples can employ all their powers at once and convergently. No victory is possible save as the resultant of a totality of virtues; no defeat for which some vice or weakness is not responsible. Fidelity, cohesiveness, tenacity, heroism, conscience, education, inventiveness, economy, wealth, physical health, and vigour—there is hardly a moral or intellectual point of superiority that does not tell when "God holds his assizes" and hurls the peoples one upon another. "Die Weltgeschichte ist das Weltgericht," and Dr. Steinmetz does believe that, in the long run, chance and luck play some part in apportioning the issues. And international hostility is merely the psychological stimulus to that combativeness which is a necessary element of struggle; that though, like other ele-

mental instincts—our animal appetites, for instance—it may in some of its manifestations be
ugly enough, it makes for survival, and is to
that extent a part of the great plan.   It is urged
that too great a readiness to accept the friendly
assurances of another nation and an undue absence of distrust would, by the operation of a
sort of Gresham Law in international relationships, make steadily for the disappearance of
the human and friendly communities in favour
of the truculent and brutal.   If friendliness and
good feeling towards other nations lead us to
relax our self-defensive efforts, in the belief that,
since we are dealing with kindly and humane
fellow-men, we really need not take so much trouble
to defend ourselves against them, it is the quarrelsome communities which would see in this tendency an opportunity to commit aggression, and
there would be a tendency, therefore, for the least
civilized to wipe out the most.   Animosity and
hostility between nations, therefore, is a corrective
of this sentimental slackness, and to that extent
it plays a useful rôle, however ugly it may appear—"not pretty, but useful, like the dust-
man."   And though the material and economic
motives which prompt conflict may no longer
obtain, so profound is the psychological impetus
that other than economic motives will be found
for collision; that if rivalry can no longer formulate motives in material questions, it will convert

the moral conflicts of mankind into causes of war, and that just as in the past men made such moral differences as then existed (religious dogma, *e. g.*) causes of war, so in our day the moral differences of nations will be made to serve a like purpose; that an autocratic Germany or Russia will find sufficient ground in the defence of its special conception of national life for attacking a Liberal or Radical England whose influences threaten autocratic conceptions the world over; or that the fanaticism and vanity of Asiatic races will one day of itself furnish sufficient motive for attack upon a white race which in their view makes arrogant claims of domination and superiority.

Some such view has found lurid expression in the recent work of an American soldier, General Homer Lea.[1] The author urges not only that war is inevitable, but that any systematic attempt to prevent it is merely an unwise meddling with the universal law.

National entities, in their birth, activities, and death, are controlled by the same laws that govern all life—plant, animal, or national—the law of struggle, the law of survival. These laws, so universal as regards life and time, so unalterable in causation and consummation, are only valuable in the duration of national existence as the knowledge of and obedience to them is proportionately true or false. Plans to

[1] *The Valour of Ignorance.* I understand that General Homer Lea's title is based not upon the command of regular American but of irregular Chinese forces.

thwart them to shortcut them, to circumvent, to cozen, to deny, to scorn and violate them, is folly such as man's conceit alone makes possible. Never has this been tried—and man is ever at it—but what the end has been gangrenous and fatal.

In theory international arbitration denies the inexorability of natural laws, and would substitute for them the veriest Cagliostroic formulas, or would, with the vanity of Canute, sit down on the ocean-side of life and command the ebb and flow of its tides to cease.

The idea of international arbitration as a substitute for natural laws that govern the existence of political entities arises not only from a denial of their fiats and an ignorance of their application, but from a total misconception of war, its causes, and its meaning.

General Lea's thesis is emphasized in the introduction to his work written by another American soldier, General John J. P. Storey.

A few idealists may have visions that with advancing civilization war and its dread horrors will cease. Civilization has not changed human nature. The nature of man makes war inevitable. Armed strife will not disappear from the earth until human nature changes.

Many of the defenders of war, indeed, give a still further development to the thought revealed in these passages. They urge that human nature and human society have not yet reached a state of development in which they can dispense with the moral discipline of war; that without such, society would lose its virility and be in danger of rotting from sheer feeble effeminateness and lazy self-gratification. *Weltstadt und Friedensproblem*, the book of Professor Baron Karl von Stengel, a jurist, who was one of Germany's delegates at the first Hague Peace Conference, has a chapter entitled the "Significance of War for Development of Humanity," in which the author says:

War has more often facilitated than hindered progress. Athens and Rome, not only in spite of, but just because of their many wars, rose to the zenith of civilization. Great States like Germany and Italy are welded into nationalities only through blood and iron.

Storm purifies the air and destroys the frail trees, leaving the sturdy oaks standing. War is the test of a nation's political, physical, and intellectual worth. The State in which there is much that is rotten may vegetate for a while in peace, but in war its weakness is revealed.

Germany's preparations for war have not resulted in economic disaster, but in unexampled economic expansion, unquestionably because of our demonstrated superiority over France. It is better to spend money on armaments and battleships than luxury, motormania, and other sensual living.

We know that Moltke expressed a like view in his famous letter to Bluntschli. "A perpetual peace," declared the Field Marshal, "is a dream and not even a beautiful dream. War is one of the elements of order in the world established by God. The noblest virtues of man are developed therein. Without war the world would degenerate and disappear in a morass of materialism."[1]

At the very time that Moltke was voicing this sentiment, a precisely similar one was being voiced by no less a person than Ernest Renan. In his *La Réforme Intellectuelle et Morale* (1871, page 111) he writes:

If the foolishness, negligence, idleness, and short-sightedness of States did not involve their occasional collision, it is difficult to imagine the degree of degeneracy to which the human race would descend. War is one of the conditions of progress, the sting which prevents a country from going to sleep, and compels satisfied mediocrity itself to awaken from its apathy. Man is only sustained by effort and struggle. The day that humanity achieves a great pacific Roman Empire, having no external enemies, that day its morality and its intelligence will be placed in the very greatest peril.

In our own times a philosophy not very dissimilar has been voiced in the public declarations of ex-President Roosevelt. I choose a few phrases from his speeches and writings at random:

[1] For precisely similar views in more definite form see Ratzenhofer's *Die sociologische Erkentniss*, 1898, pages 233, 234.

We despise a nation just as we despise a man who submits to insult.   What is true of a man ought to be true of a nation.[1]

We must play a great part in the world and especially . . . perform those deeds of blood, of valour, which above everything else bring national renown.

We do not admire a man of timid peace.

By war alone can we acquire those virile qualities necessary to win in the stern strife of actual life.

In this world the nation that is trained to a career of unwarlike and isolated ease is bound to go down in the end before other nations which have not lost the manly and adventurous qualities.[2]

Exactly is this the point of view of an eminent English publicist, Mr. Sidney Low (*Nineteenth Century*, October, 1898):

The Cobdenite ideal of a State in which every citizen is ceaselessly engaged in the ennobling process of buying cheap and selling dear leaves something to be desired. The accumulation of riches and the steady pursuit of material comfort do not tend to the development of the highest type of character.

Professor William James covers the whole ground of these claims in the following passage:

[1] Speech at Stationers' Hall, June 6, 1910. Mr. Roosevelt seems to have overlooked the fact that among Anglo-Saxons the duel is dead. How does he propose that a man should resent an insult like a nation?

[2] *The Strenuous Life.*

The war party is assuredly right in affirming that the martial virtues although originally gained by the race through war are absolute and permanent human goods. Patriotic pride and ambition in their military form are, after all, only specifications of a more universal and enduring competitive passion. Pacifism makes no converts from the military party. The military party denies neither the bestiality, nor the horror, nor the expense; it only says that these things tell but half the story. It only says that war is worth these things; that taking human nature as a whole, war is its best protection against its weaker and more cowardly self, and that mankind cannot afford to adopt a peace-economy. . . . Militarism is the great preserver of our ideals of hardihood, and human life without hardihood would be contemptible. . . . This natural feeling forms, I think, the innermost soul of our army writings. Without any exception known to me, militarist authors take a highly mystical view of their subject and regard war as a biological and sociological necessity. . . . Our ancestors have bred pugnacity into our bone and marrow and thousands of years of peace won't breed it out of us. (*McClure's Magazine*, August, 1910.)

Even famous English clergymen have voiced the same view. Charles Kingsley, in his defence of the Crimean War as a "just war against tyrants and oppressors," wrote: "For the Lord Jesus Christ is not only the Prince of Peace, he is the Prince of War, too. He is the Lord of Hosts, the God of armies, and whoever fights in a just war against tyrants and oppressors, he is fighting on Christ's side, and Christ is fighting on his side. Christ is his captain and his leader, and he can be in no better service. Be sure of it, for the Bible tells you so."[1]

Canon Newbolt, Dean Farrar, the Archbishop of Armagh, have all written not dissimilarly.

The whole case may be résuméd thus:

Reasoning inductively: All the evidence bearing on the relations between nations shows that those relations always have been in part marked by a hostility in which merely material interest or cool reason may have no apparent or direct bearing; which may on the surface indeed appear illogical and reasonless. That there is no evidence that this characteristic of the relations between states ever has been or is being greatly modified; that it is more in complete accord with what we know of the everlasting unchangeability of human nature; that the warlike nations inherit the earth, and that the peaceful ones decline and degenerate.

Reasoning deductively: Since struggle is the law of life and a condition of survival as much with nations as with other organisms, pugnacity, which is merely intense energy in struggle, a readi-

---

[1] Thomas Hughes in his preface to the first English edition of the *Bigelow Papers* refers to the opponents of the Crimean War as a "vain and mischievous clique, who amongst us have raised the cry of peace." See also Mr. Hobson's *Psychology of Jingoism*, p. 52.

ness to accept struggle in its acutest form, must necessarily be a quality marking those individuals successful in the vital contests. A nation which, though in other respects superior to its neighbours, lacks that capacity and readiness for struggle which pugnacity and combativeness imply, is wiped out and replaced by it may be an inferior but more pugnacious rival, so that in the matter of pugnacity it is not necessarily the best which set the standard; it may well be the worst since the best have to be as pugnacious as any rival which threatens them. It is this deep-seated biological law which renders impossible the acceptance by mankind of the literal injunction to turn the other cheek to the smiter, or for human nature ever to conform to the ideal implied in that injunction, since, were it accepted, the best men and nations—in the sense of the kindliest and most humane—would be placed at the mercy of the most brutal, who, eliminating the least brutal, would stamp the survivors with the character of the worst, and the qualities of the militarist would remain in any case. And for this reason a readiness to fight, which means the qualities of rivalry and pride and combativeness, hardiness, tenacity, and heroism,—what we know as the manly qualities,—must in any case survive as the race survives, and since they stand in the way of the predominance of the purely brutal, are a necessary part of the highest morality.

Despite the apparent force of these two propositions, they are founded upon a profound illusion, and upon a gross misreading of all the facts of the case.

CHAPTER II

OUTLINE OF THE PSYCHOLOGICAL CASE FOR PEACE

The illusion on which conclusions of preceding chapter are based
—The real law of man's struggle: struggle with Nature, not
with other men—Mankind is the organism struggling to adapt
itself to its environment, the planet—Such struggle always
involves greater complexity of organism, closer co-ordination
of parts—Outline sketch of man's advance and main operating
factor therein—The progress towards elimination of physical
force—Co-operation across frontiers and its psychological
result—Impossible to fix limits of community—Such limits
irresistibly expanding—Break-up of State homogeneity—
State limits no longer coinciding with real conflicts between
men.

THE case outlined in the preceding chapter
reposes inductively, therefore, on an alleged
series of facts generalized respectively in these
two:

(1) The unchangeability of human nature in
the matter of pugnacity;

(2) The survival of the warlike nations of the
world; and

Deductively, on the general law drawn therefrom that, as struggle is the law of man's survival, pugnacity is explained by the condition

of that survival: the less pugnacious are eliminated in favour of the more; or, expressed otherwise, pugnacity is a form of energy in that struggle, a useful stimulus therein. This is at once the scientific explanation and the scientific justification of the plea for the virile qualities favouring warfare, and for rejecting any expectation that pugnacity between nations will seriously diminish, or that the process of man's development makes for its extinction.

In reply to the above case, I have written four chapters attempting to show:

(1) That the alleged unchangeability of human nature is not a fact, and all the evidence is against it (*e. g.*, the disappearance, or at least the attenuation, of the temper which leads us to enforce our religious belief on others; and of the temper which produced the duel);

(2) That the warlike nations do *not* inherit the earth;

(3) That physical force is a constantly diminishing factor in human affairs; that this involves profound psychological modifications; and

(4) That the increasing factor is co-operation, and that this factor tends to attenuate state divisions which in no way represent the limits of that co-operation.

The first two chapters present the facts of the case; the second two the factors, displaying the general law underlying and defining the real character of man's struggle and advance, and the psychological development involved therein.

The illusion underlying the case detailed in the preceding chapter and outlined above arises from the indiscriminate application of scientific formula. Struggle is the law of survival with man, as elsewhere, but it is the struggle of man with the universe, not man with man. "Dog does not eat dog." Even tigers do not live on one another; they live on their prey. The planet is man's prey. Man's struggle is the struggle of the organism, which is human society, in its adaptation to its environment, the world—not the struggle between different parts of the same organism.[1]

The error here indicated arises, indeed, from mistaking the imperfect working of different parts of the same organism for the conflict of individual organisms. Britain to-day supports forty millions in greater comfort than it supported twenty a little over half a century ago. This has

[1] Since the publication of the first edition of this book there has appeared in France an admirable work by Mr. J. Novikow, *Le Darwinisme Social*, in which this application of the Darwinian theory to sociology is discussed with great ability and at great length and in full detail. Mr. Novikow has established in biological terms what, previous to the publication of his book, I attempted to establish in economic terms. The real application of the biological law to human society had, moreover, already been partly anticipated, in correcting some of the conclusions drawn by Spencer and Huxley, by Professor Karl Pearson (*The Grammar of Science*, pp. 433–438).

been accomplished, not by the various groups—
Scots, English, Welsh, Irish—preying upon one
another, but by exactly the reverse process:
closer co-operation between themselves and with
populations outside.

That mankind as a whole represents the
organism and the planet the environment, to
which he is more and more adapting himself,
is the only conclusion that consorts with the
facts. If struggle between men is the true
reading, those facts are absolutely inexplicable,
for he is drifting away from conflict, from the
use of physical force and towards co-operation.
This much is unchallengeable, as the facts which
follow will show.

But in that case, if struggle for extermination
of rivals between men is the law of life, mankind
is setting at naught the natural law, and must be
on its way to extinction.

Happily the natural law in this matter has been
misread. Man in his sociological aspect is not
the complete organism. The man who attempts
to live without association with his fellows, dies.
Nor is the nation the complete organism. If
Britain attempted to live without co-operation
with other nations, half the population would
starve. The completer the co-operation, the
greater the vitality; the more imperfect the co-
operation, the less the vitality. Now a body, the
various parts of which are so interdependent that

without co-ordination vitality is reduced or death ensues, must be regarded, in so far as those functions are concerned, not as a collection of rival organisms, but as one. This is in accord with what we know of the character of living organisms in their conflict with environment. The higher the organism, the greater the elaboration and interdependence of its parts, the greater the need for co-ordination.[1]

If we take this as the reading of the biological law, the whole thing becomes plain: man's irresistible drift away from conflict and towards co-operation is but the completer adaptation of the organism (man) to its environment (the planet, wild nature), resulting in a more intense vitality.

The foregoing is the law stated biologically.

The psychological development involved in man's struggle along these lines may best be stated by an outline sketch of the character of his advance.

When I kill my prisoner (cannibalism was a very common characteristic of early man), it is in "human nature" to keep him for my own

---

[1] Co-operation does not exclude competition. If a rival beats me in business, it is because he furnishes more efficient co-operation than I do; if a thief steals from me, he is not co-operating at all, and if he steals much will prevent my co-operation. The organism (society) has every interest in encouraging the competitor and suppressing the parasite.

larder.   It is the extreme form of the use of force, the extreme form of human individualism. But putrefaction sets in before I can consume him (it is as well to recall these real difficulties of the early man, because, of course, "human nature does not change"), and I am left without food.

But my two neighbours, each with his butchered prisoner, are in like case, and though I could quite easily defend my larder, we deem it better on the next occasion to join forces and kill one prisoner at a time.   I share mine with the other two; they share theirs with me.   There is no waste through putrefaction.   It is the earliest form of the surrender of the use of force in favour of co-operation—the first attenuation of the tendency to act on impulse.   But when the three prisoners are consumed, and no more happen to be available, it strikes us that on the whole we should have done better to make them catch game and dig roots for us.   The next prisoners that are caught are not killed, a further diminution of impulse and the factor of physical force, they are only enslaved, and the pugnacity which in the first case went to kill them is now diverted to keeping them at work.   But the pugnacity is so little controlled by rationalism that the slaves starve, and in an access of hunger become unmanageable.   They are better treated; there is a diminution of pugnacity.   They become sufficiently manageable for the masters themselves, while the slaves are digging roots, to do a little hunting. The pugnacity recently expended on the slaves is redirected to keeping hostile tribes from capturing them—a difficult matter, because the slaves themselves show a disposition to try a change of mastership. They are bribed into good behaviour by better treatment: a further diminution of force, a further drift towards co-operation; they give labour, we give food and protection. As the tribes enlarge, it is found that those have most cohesion where the position of slaves is recognized by definite rights and privileges. Slavery becomes serfdom or villeiny. The lord gives land and protection, the serf labour and military service: a further drift from force, a further drift towards co-operation, exchange. With the introduction of money even the form of force disappears: the labourer pays rent and the lord pays his soldiers. It is free exchange on both sides, and economic force has replaced physical force. And the further the drift from force towards simple economic interest the better the result for the effort expended. The Tartar khan who seizes by force the wealth in his State, giving no adequate return, soon has none to seize. Men will not work to create what they cannot enjoy, so that, finally, the khan has to kill a man by torture to obtain a sum which is the thousandth part of what a London tradesman will spend to secure a title carrying no right to the exercise of force from a sovereign who has lost all right to the use or exercise of physical force, the head of the wealthiest country in the world, the sources of whose wealth are the most removed from any process involving the exercise of physical force.

But while this process is going on inside the tribe, or group, or nation, force and hostility as between differing tribes or nations remain; but not undiminished. At first it suffices for the fuzzy head of a rival tribesman to appear above the bushes for primitive man to want to kill it. He is a foreigner: kill him. Later he only wants to kill him if he is at war with his tribe. There are periods of peace: diminution of hostility. In the first conflicts all of the other tribe are killed—men, women, and children. Force and pugnacity are absolute. But the use of slaves both as labourers and as concubines attenuates this: there is a diminution of force. The women of the hostile tribe bear children by the conqueror: there is a diminution of pugnacity. At the next raid into the hostile territory it is found that there is nothing to take, because everything has been killed or carried off. So on later raids the conqueror kills the chiefs only (a further diminution of pugnacity, a further drift from mere impulse), or merely dispossesses them of their lands and divides them among the conquerors (Norman Conquest type). We have already passed the stage of extermination.[1] The conqueror simply absorbs the conquered—or the conquered absorbs the conqueror, whichever you like. It is no longer the case of one gobbling up another. Neither is gobbled. In the next stage we do not even dispossess the chiefs—a further sacrifice of physical force—we merely impose tribute. But the conquering nation soon finds itself in

[1] Without going to the somewhat obscure analogies of biological science, it is evident from the simple facts of the world that if at any stage of human development warfare ever did make for the survival of the fit, we have long since passed out of that stage. When we conquer a nation in these days, we do not exterminate it. We leave it where it was. When we "overcome" the servile races, far from eliminating them, we give them added chances of life by introducing order, etc., so that the lower human quality tends to be perpetuated by conquest by the higher. If it ever happens that the Asiatic races challenge the white in the industrial or military field, it will be in large part thanks to the work of race conservation which has been the result of England's conquest in India, Egypt, and Asia generally, and her action in China when she imposed commercial contact with the Chinese by virtue of military power. War between people of roughly equal development makes also for the survival of the unfit, since we no longer exterminate and massacre a conquered race, but only their best elements (those carrying on the war), and because the conqueror uses up *his* best elements in the process, so that the less fit of both sides are left to perpetuate the species. Nor do the facts of the modern world lend any support to the theory that preparation for war under modern conditions tends to preserve virility, since those conditions involve an artificial barrack life, a highly mechanical training tending to the destruction of initiative, and a mechanical uniformity and centralization tending to crush individuality, and accentuating the drift towards a centralized bureaucracy already too great.

the position of the khan in his own State—the more he squeezes the less he gets, until finally the cost of getting the money by military means exceeds what is obtained. It is the case of Spain in Spanish America—the more territory she "owned" the poorer she became. The wise conqueror, then, finds that better than the exaction of tribute is an exclusive market—old English colonial type. But in the process of ensuring exclusivity more is lost than is gained: the colonies are allowed to choose their own system—further drift from the use of force, further drift from hostility and pugnacity. Final result: complete abandonment of physical force, co-operation on basis of mutual profit the only relationship, with reference not merely to colonies which have become in fact foreign States, but also to States foreign in name as well as in fact. We have arrived not at the intensification of the struggle between men, but at a condition of vital dependence upon the prosperity of foreigners. Could England by some magic kill all foreigners, half the British population would starve. This is not a condition making indefinitely for hostility to foreigners; still less is it a condition in which such hostility finds its justification in any real instinct of self-preservation or in any deep-seated biological law. With each new intensification of dependence between the parts of the organism must go that psychological development which has marked every stage of progress in the past, from the day that we killed our prisoner in order to eat him, and refused to share him with our fellow, to the day that the telegraph and the bank have rendered military force economically futile.

But the foregoing does not include all the facts, or all the factors. If Russia does England an injury—sinks a fishing fleet in time of peace for instance—it is no satisfaction to Englishmen to go out and kill a lot of Frenchmen or Irishmen. The English want to kill Russians. But if they knew a little less geography, if for instance they were Chinese Boxers, it would not matter the least in the world which they killed, because to the Chinaman all alike would be "foreign devils": his knowledge of the case does not enable him to differentiate between the various nationalities of Europeans. In the case of a wronged negro in the Congo the collective responsibility is still wider; for a wrong inflicted by one white man he will avenge himself on any other—German, English, French, Dutch, Belgian, or Chinese. As our knowledge increases, our sense of the collective responsibility of outside groups narrows. But immediately we start on this differentiation there is no stopping. The yokel is satisfied if he can "get a whack at them foreigners"—Germans will do if Russians are not available. The more educated man wants Russians; but if he stops a moment longer he will see that in killing Russian peasants he might as well be killing so many Hindoos, for all they had to do with the matter. He then wants to get at the Russian Government. But so do a great many Russians—Liberals, Reformers, etc. He then sees that the real conflict is not English against Russians at all, but the interest of all law-abiding folk—Russian and English alike— against oppression, corruption, and incompetence. And to give the Russian Government an opportunity of going to war would only strengthen its hands against those with whom the English were in sympathy—the Reformers. As war would increase the influence of the reactionary party in Russia, it would do nothing to prevent the recurrence of such incidents, and so quite the wrong party would suffer. Were the real facts and the real responsibilities understood, a Liberal people would reply to such an aggression by taking every means which the social and economic relationship of the two States affords to enable Russian Liberals to hang a few Russian admirals and establish a Russian Liberal Government. In any case the realization of the facts attenuates English hostility. In the same way, as the real facts of the case become more familiar will hostility to Germans be attenuated. Englishmen will realize that many Germans are just as much opposed as they are to German naval aggression. Englishmen will not want to kill *those*

Germans at least. Englishmen will want to help them realize their anti-naval plans. The capacity for differentiation in this sense is fatal to any sustained hostility between large nations. International hostilities repose for the most part upon our conception of the foreign State with which we are quarrelling as a homogeneous personality having the same characteristic of responsibility as an individual, whereas the variety of community interests, both material and moral, regardless of State boundaries, renders the analogy between nations and individuals an utterly false one.

Indeed, where the co-operation between the parts of the social organism is as complete as our mechanical development has recently made it, it is impossible to fix the limits of the community, and to say what is one community and what is another. Certainly the State limits no longer define the limits of the community; and yet it is only the State limits which international antagonism predicates. If the Louisiana cotton crop fails, a part of Lancashire starves. There is closer community of interest in a vital matter between Lancashire and Louisiana than between Lancashire and, say, the Orkneys, part of the same State. There is much closer intercommunication between Britain and the United States in all that touches social and moral development than between Britain and, say, Bengal, part of the same State. An English nobleman has more community of thought and feeling with a European Continental aristocrat (will marry his daughter, for instance) than he would think of claiming with such "fellow" British countrymen as a Bengal babu, a Jamaica negro, or even a Dorset yokel. A professor at Oxford will have closer community of feeling with a member of the French Academy than with, say, a Whitechapel publican. One may go further and say that a British subject of Quebec has closer contact with Paris than with London; the British subject of Dutch-speaking Africa with Holland than with England; the British subject of Hong Kong with Pekin than with London; of Egypt with Constantinople than with London, and so on. In a thousand respects association cuts across State boundaries, which are purely conventional, and renders the biological division of mankind into independent and warring States a scientific ineptitude.

Allied factors, introduced by the character of modern intercourse, have already gone far to render territorial conquest futile for the satisfaction of natural human pride and vanity. Just as in the economic sphere factors peculiar to our generation have rendered the old analogy as between State and persons a false one, so do these factors render the analogy in the sentimental sphere a false one. While the individual of great possessions does in fact obtain, by reason of his wealth, a deference which satisfies his pride and vanity, the individual of the great nation has no such sentimental advantage as against the citizen of the small. No one thinks of respecting a Russian mujik because he belongs to a great nation, or despising a Scandinavian or Belgian gentleman because he belongs to a small one; and any society will accord prestige to the nobleman of Norway, Holland, Belgium, Spain, or even Portugal, where it refuses it to an English "bounder." The nobleman of any country will marry the noblewoman of another more readily than a woman from a lower class of his own country. The prestige of the foreign country rarely counts for anything in the matter when it comes to the real facts of everyday life, so shallow is the real sentiment which now divides States. Just as in material things community of interest and relationship cut clear across State boundaries, so inevitably will the psychic community of interest come so to do.

Just as in the material domain the real biological law, which is association and co-operation between individuals of the same species in the struggle with their environment, has pushed men in their material struggle to conform with that law, so will it do so in the sentimental sphere. We shall come to realize that the real psychic and moral divisions are not as between nations but as between opposing conceptions of life. Though it is unlikely that man's nature will ever lose the

combativeness, hostility, and animosity which are
so large a part of it (although the manifestations of
such feeling have so greatly changed within the
historical period as almost to have changed in
character), what we shall see is the diversion of
those psychological qualities to the real instead
of the artificial conflict of mankind.   We shall see
that at the bottom of any conflict between the
armies or governments of Germany and England
lies not the opposition of "German" interests to
"English" interests, but the conflict in both
States between democracy and autocracy, or
between Socialism and Individualism, or reaction
and progress, however one's sociological sympathies may classify it.   That is the real division in
both countries, and for Germans to conquer English or English, Germans, would not advance
the solution of such a conflict one iota; and
as such conflict becomes acuter, the German in-
dividualist will see that it is more important to
protect his freedom and property against the
Socialist and trade unionist, who can and are attacking them, than against the British army, which
cannot.   In the same way the British Tory will
be more concerned with what Mr. Lloyd George's
Budgets can do than with what the Germans
can do.   And from the realization of that fact
to the realization on the part of the British
democrat that what stands in the way of his
securing for social expenditure enormous sums

that now go to armaments is mainly a lack of co-operation between himself and the democrats of a hostile nation who are in a like case, is but a step, and a step that, if history has any meaning, is bound shortly to be taken, and when it is taken, property, capital, Individualism will have to give to its international organization, already far-reaching, a still more definite form, in which international differences will play no part. And when that condition is reached, both States will find inconceivable the idea that artificial State divisions (which are coming more and more to approximate to mere administrative divisions, leaving free scope within them or across them for the development of genuine nationality) could ever in any way define the real conflicts of mankind.

There remains, of course, the question of time: that these developments will take "thousands" or "hundreds" of years. Yet the interdependence of modern nations is the growth of little more than fifty years. A century ago, England could have been self-supporting and little the worse for it. One must not overlook the Law of Acceleration. Man probably dates from the Tertiary Period[1] —three hundred thousand years. He has developed more in the last three thousand than in the preceding two hundred and ninety-seven thousand,

[1] I am indebted to Mr. Novikow's admirable *Darwinisme Social* for this illustration.

and more in the last three hundred than in the preceding three thousand, and in some respects more in the last fifty than in the preceding two hundred ninety-nine thousand nine hundred and fifty. We see more change now in ten years than originally in ten thousand. Who shall foretell the developments of a generation?

CHAPTER III

UNCHANGING HUMAN NATURE

The progress from cannibalism to Herbert Spencer — The disappearance of religious oppression by government— Disappearance of the duel — The Crusaders and the Holy Sepulchre — The wail of militarist writers at man's drift away from militancy.

WE have seen (Chapter I., Part II.) that the psychological case against peace reposes *a priori* upon the alleged unchangeability of human nature—the alleged persistence, notably, of those forms of pugnacity which lead to fight and quarrel. All of us, who have had occasion to discuss this subject, are familiar with the catch phrases with which the whole matter is so often dismissed: "You cannot change human nature," "What man always has been during thousands of years, he always will be," are the sort of dicta delivered generally as self-evident propositions that do not need discussion. Or if, in deference to the fact that very profound changes in which human nature is involved *have* taken place in the habits of mankind, the statement of the proposition is somewhat less dogmatic, we are given to understand that any serious modification of the tendency to go to war can only be looked for in "thousands of years."

What are the facts? They are these:

That the alleged unchangeability of human nature in this matter is not true; that man's pugnacity, though not disappearing, is very visibly, under the forces of mechanical and social development, being transformed and diverted from ends that are wasteful and destructive to ends that are less wasteful, which render easier that co-operation between men in the struggle with their environment which is the condition of their survival and advance; that changes which, in the historical period, have been extraordinarily rapid are necessarily quickened—quickened in geometrical rather than arithmetical ratio by virtue of the law of motion which we know as the Law of Acceleration.

With very great courtesy, one is impelled to ask those who argue that human nature in all its manifestations must remain unchanged, how they interpret history. We have seen man progress from the mere animal fighting with other animals, seizing his food by force, seizing also by force his females, eating his own kind, the sons of the family struggling with the father for the possession of the father's wives; we have seen this incoherent welter of animal struggle at least partly abandoned for settled industry, and partly surviving as a more organized tribal warfare or a more ordered pillaging, like that of the Vikings and the Huns; we have seen even these pillagers abandon in part their pillaging for ordered industry, and in part for the more ceremonial conflict of feudal struggle; we have seen even the feudal conflict abandoned in favour of dynastic and religious and territorial conflict, and then dynastic and religious conflict abandoned, and there remains now only the conflict of States, and that, too, at a time when the character and conception of the State is being radically and profoundly modified.

Pari passu with this collective progress, from the preying of one animal upon another, has gone on a like progress in individual conduct. For æons man's life and property depended upon his club or a well-aimed stone, then upon a flint hatchet, then upon a sword, then upon individual fight hedged round with the form of law, and finally upon none of these things, but upon law alone. And to our ancestor the notion that he could ever depend upon anything but his strong right arm for the defence of his property would have appeared as absurd as does the notion of international dependence upon law to our patriots to-day. And even to-day, outside the Anglo-Saxon world, while the individual does not defend his property by arms, he does so defend his honour.

Human nature may not change, whatever that vague phrase may mean; but human nature is a complex factor. It is made up of numberless motives, many of which are modified in relation to the rest as circumstances change; so that the manifestations of human nature change out of all recognition. Do we mean by the phrase that "human nature does not change" that the feelings of the paleolithic man who ate the bodies of his enemies and of his own children are the same as those of a Herbert Spencer, or even of the modern Londoner who catches his train to town in the morning? And if human nature does not change, may we therefore expect the city clerk to brain his mother and serve her up for dinner, or suppose that Lord Roberts or Lord Kitchener is in the habit, while on campaign, of catching the babies of his enemies on spear-heads, or driving his motor car over the bodies of young girls, in the fashion that the leaders of the old Northmen drove their ox wagons over the bodies of their enemies' womenkind?

What *do* these phrases mean? These and many like them are repeated in a knowing way with an air of great wisdom and profundity by journalists and writers of repute, and one may find them blatant any day in our own newspapers and reviews; yet the most cursory examination proves them to be neither wise nor profound, but simply a parrot-like repetition of catch-phrases which lack common-sense and fly in the face of facts of everyday experience.

The truth is that the facts of the world as they stare us in the face show that in our common attitude we not only overlook the modifications in human nature which have occurred historically since yesterday—occurred even in our generation —but that we ignore the modification of "human nature" which mere difference of social habit and custom and outlook effect. Take the case of the duel. Even educated people in Germany, France, Italy, will tell you that it is "not in human nature" to expect a man of gentle birth to abandon the habit of the duel; the notion that honourable people should ever so place their honour at the mercy of whoever may care to insult them is, they assure you, both childish and sordid. With them the matter will not bear discussion.

Yet the great societies which exist in England, North America, Australia—the whole Anglo-Saxon world, in fact—have abandoned the duel, and we cannot lump the whole Anglo-Saxon race as either sordid or childish.

That such a change as this which must have collided with human pugnacity in its most insidious form, pride and personal vanity, the traditions of an aristocratic status—every one of the psychological factors now involved in international conflict—has been effected in our own generation should surely give pause to those who dismiss as chimerical any hope that rationalism will ever dominate the conduct of nations. Yet, profound as is this change, a still more universal change, affecting still more nearly our psychological impulses, has been effected within a relatively recent historical period. I refer to the abandonment by the governments of Europe of their right to enforce the religious belief of their citizens. For hundreds of years, generation after generation, it was regarded as an evident part of a ruler's right and duty to dictate what his subjects should believe. And this originated not merely from a thirst for oppression on the part of the governments, but also from the fact that the governments realized that if parties in the State having religious opinions hostile to their own became powerful, they would utilize that influence to replace rulers hostile in religious opinion to themselves by rulers of their own belief. The more purely instructive motive of fanaticism was therefore reinforced by the more rational motives of statecraft—the motives, indeed, of political self-defence. "It is not that I want to prevent Protestants worshipping God as they please," argued the Liberal Catholic, "but if the Protestant gets the upper hand he will cut my throat, or at least turn all Catholics from power. It is in human nature that he should do so. It is asking too much to assume that if our religious rivals get the power to dominate us, they will not use it. Of course they will. You cannot ask us to commit political and religious suicide, and as we have the force, we must use it. It is the law of life." And from this reasoning arose hecatomb on hecatomb—all the long series of religious wars which swept over Europe. Any one who should have argued that the differences between Catholics and Protestants were not such as force could settle, and that the time would come when man would realize this truth, and regard a religious war between European States as a wild and unimaginable anachronism, would have been put down as a futile doctrinaire, completely ignoring the most elementary facts of "Unchanging Human Nature."

There is one striking incident of the religious struggle of States which illustrates vividly the change which has come over the spirit of man. For nearly two hundred years Christians fought the Infidel for the conquest of the Holy Sepulchre. All the nations of Europe joined in this great endeavour. It seemed to be the one thing which could unite them, and for generations, so profound was the impulse which affected the movement, the struggle went on. There is nothing in history, perhaps, quite comparable to it. Suppose that during this struggle one had told a European statesman of that age, that the time would come when, assembled in a room, the representatives

of a Europe which had made itself the absolute
master of the Infidel could by a single stroke of
the pen have secured the Holy Sepulchre for all
time to Christendom, but that, having discussed
the matter cursorily twenty minutes or so would
decide that on the whole it was not worth
while!   Had such a thing been told to such mediæval statesman, he would certainly have regarded
the prophecy as that of a madman.   Yet this,
of course, is precisely what took place.

But perhaps the very strongest evidence that
the whole drift of human tendencies is away from
such conflict as is represented by war between
States is to be found in the writings of those who
declare war to be inevitable.   Among the writers
quoted in the first chapter of this section, there
is not one who, if his arguments are examined
carefully, does not show that he realizes, con-
sciously or subconsciously, that man's disposition
to fight, far from being unchanged, is becoming
rapidly enfeebled.   Take, for instance, the latest
work voicing the philosophy that war is inevitable; that, indeed, it is both wicked and childish to
try and prevent it.[1]   Notwithstanding that the
inevitability of war is his thesis, he entitles the
first section of his book "The Decline of Militancy," and shows clearly, in fact, that the com-

[1] See quotations p. 150 from General Lea's book, *The Valour
of Ignorance.*

mercial activities of the world lead directly away from war:

"Trade, ducats, and mortgages are regarded as far greater assets and sources of power than armies or navies. They produce national effeminacy and effeteness."

Now, as this tendency is common to all nations of Christendom, indeed, of the world, since commercial and industrial development is world-wide, it necessarily means, if it is true of any one nation, that the world as a whole is drifting away from the tendency to warfare.

A large part of General Lea's book is a sort of Carlylean girding at what he terms "protoplasmic gourmandizing and retching" (otherwise the busy American industrial and social life of his countrymen). He declares that, when a country makes wealth production and industries its sole aim, it becomes "a glutton among nations, vulgar, swinish, arrogant"; "commercialism, having seized hold of the American people, overshadows it, and tends to destroy not only the aspirations and world-wide career open to the nation, but the Republic itself." "Patriotism in the true sense" (*i. e.*, the desire to go and kill other people) General Lea declares almost dead in the United States. The national ideals, even of the native-born American, are deplorably low:

There exists not only individual prejudice against

military ideals, but public antipathy; antagonism of politicians, newspapers, churches, colleges, labour unions, theorists, and organized societies. They combat the military spirit as if it were a public evil and a national crime.

But in that case, what in the name of all that is muddle-headed comes of the "unchanging tendency towards warfare"? What is all this curious rhetoric of General Lea's (and I have dealt with him at some length, because his principles if not his language are those animating much similar literature in England, France, Germany, and the Continent of Europe generally) but an admission that the whole tendency is not, as he would have us believe, towards war, but away from it? Here is an author who tells us that war is to be for ever inevitable, and in the same breath that men are rapidly conceiving not only a "slothful indifference" to fighting, but a profound antipathy to the military ideal.

Of course General Lea implies that this tendency is peculiar to the American Republic and is for that reason dangerous to his country; but, as a matter of fact General Lea's book might be a free translation of much nationalist literature of either France or Germany. I cannot recall a single author of either of the four great countries who, treating of the inevitability of war, does not bewail the falling away of his own country from the military ideal, or, at least, the tendency so to fall away. Thus the English journalist reviewing in the *Daily Mail* General Lea's book cannot refrain from saying:

Is it necessary to point out that there is a moral in all this for us as well as for the American? Surely almost all that Mr. Lea says applies to Great Britain as forcibly as to the United States. We too have lain dreaming. We have let our ideals tarnish. We have grown gluttonous, also. . . . Shame and folly are upon us as well as upon our brethren. Let us hasten with all our energy to cleanse ourselves of them, that we can look the future in the face without fear.

Exactly the same note dominates the literature of a protagonist like Mr. Blatchford. He talks of the "fatal apathy" of the British people; "the people," he says, breaking out in anger at the small disposition they show to kill other people "are conceited, self-indulgent, decadent, and greedy. They will shout for the Empire, but they will not fight for it."[1] A glance at such publications as *Blackwood's*, the *National Review*, the *Spectator*, the *World*, will reveal precisely similar outbursts.

Of course, Mr. Blatchford declares that the Germans are very different, and that what General Lea (in talking of *his* country) calls the "gourmandizing and retching" is not at all true of

[1] *Germany and England*, p. 19.

Germany. As a matter of fact, however, the phrase I have quoted might have been "lifted" from the work of any average pan-German, or even from more responsible quarters. Have Mr. Blatchford and General Lea forgotten that no less a person than Prince von Bülow, in a speech made in the Prussian Diet, did, as a matter of fact, use almost the words I have quoted from Mr. Blatchford, and dwelt at length on the self-indulgence and degeneracy, the rage for luxury, etc., which possess modern Germany, and told how the old qualities which had marked the founders of the Empire were disappearing?[1]

Indeed, do not a great part of the governing classes of Germany almost daily bewail the infiltration of anti-militarist doctrines among the German people, and does not the extraordinary increase in the Socialist vote justify the complaint?

A precisely analogous plea is made by the Nationalist writer in France when he rails at the pacifist tendencies of *his* country, and points to the contrasting warlike activities of neighbouring nations. A glance at a copy of practically any Nationalist or Conservative paper in France will furnish ample evidence. Hardly a day passes but that the *Écho de Paris*, *Gaulois*, *Figaro*, *Journal des Débats*, *Patrie*, or *Presse* does not sound this

---

[1] See the first chapter of Mr. Harbutt Dawson's admirable work, *The Evolution of Modern Germany*.

note, while one may find it rampant in the works of such serious writers as Paul Bourget, Barrès, Faguet, Brunetière, Paul Adam, to say nothing of more popular publicists like Déroulède, Millevoye, Drumont, etc.

All these advocates of war, therefore,—American, English, German, French,—are at one in declaring that foreign countries are very warlike, but their own country "sunk in sloth," drifting away from war. But as, presumably, they know more of their own country than of others, their own testimony therefore involves mutual destruction of their own theories. They are thus unwilling witnesses to the truth, which is that we are all alike—English, Americans, Germans, French—losing the psychological impulse to war, just as we have lost the psychological impulse to kill our neighbours on account of religious differences, or (at least, in the case of the Anglo-Saxon) to kill our neighbours in duel for some cause of wounded vanity.

How, indeed, could it be otherwise? How can modern life, with its overpowering proportion of industrial activities and its infinitesimal proportion of military, keep alive the instincts associated with war as against those developed by peace?

Not alone evolution but common-sense and common observation teach us that we develop most those qualities which we exercise most, which serve us best in the occupation on which we are most engaged. A race of seamen is not developed by agricultural pursuit carried on hundreds of miles from the sea.

Take the case of what is reputed (quite wrongly, incidentally) to be the most military nation in Europe—Germany. The immense majority of adult Germans—speaking practically, all who make up what we know as Germany—have never seen a battle, and in all human probability never will. In forty years eight thousand Germans have been in the field about twelve months—against naked blacks.[1] So that the proportion of war-like activities as compared with peaceful activities works out at one as against hundreds of thousands. I wish it were possible to illustrate this diagrammatically; but it could not be done in this book, because if a single dot, the size of a full-stop, were to be used to illustrate the expenditure of time in actual war, I should have to fill most of the book with dots to illustrate the time spent by the balance of the population in peace activities.[2]

[1] I have excluded the " operations " with the allies in China. But they only lasted a few weeks. And are they war ? This illustration appears in Mr. Novikow's *Darwinisme Social*.

[2] The most recent opinion on evolution would go to show that environment plays an even larger rôle in the formation of character than selection. (See Prince Kropotkin's article, *Nineteenth Century*, July, 1910, in which he shows that experiment reveals the direct action of surroundings as the main factor of evolution.)

In that case, how can we possibly expect to keep alive warlike qualities, when all our interests and activities—all our environments, in short—are peace-like ?

In other words, the occupations which develop the qualities of industry and peace are so much in excess of those which would develop the qualities we associate with war that such excess has almost now passed beyond any ordinary means of visual illustration, and has entirely passed beyond any ordinary human capacity fully to appreciate. How can we expect the survival of qualities which, according to the military pundits, are closely associated with an occupation the immense majority, even in the case of nations reputed warlike, never undertake, as against qualities associated with the occupations which are those of practically all, practically every day? Peace is with us now nearly always; war is with us rarely, yet we are told that it is the qualities of war which will survive, and the qualities of peace which will be subsidiary.

I am not forgetting, of course, the military training, the barrack life, which is to keep alive the military tradition. I have dealt with the question in the next chapter. It suffices for the moment to note that such training is justified on the ground (notably among those

---

How immensely, therefore, must our industrial environment modify the pugnacious impulse of our nature !

who would introduce it into England)—(1) That it ensures peace; (2) renders a population more efficient in the art of peace—that is to say, perpetuates the condition of "slothful ease" which we are told is so dangerous to our characters, in which we are bound to lose the "warlike qualities," and which renders society still more "gourmandizing" in General Lea's contemptuous phrase, still more "Cobdenite" in Mr. Sidney Low's. One cannot have it both ways. If long-continued peace is enervating, it is mere self-stultification to plead for conscription, on the ground that it will still further prolong that enervating condition. If Mr. Sidney Low sneers at industrial society and the peace ideal—"the Cobdenite ideal of buying cheap and selling dear"—he must not defend German conscription (though he does) on the ground that it renders German commerce more efficient—that, in other words, it advances that "Cobdenite ideal." In that case, the drift away from war will be stronger than ever. Perhaps some of all this inconsistency was in Mr. Roosevelt's mind when he declared that by "war alone" can man develop those many qualities, etc. If conscription really does prolong peace and increase our aptitude for the arts of peace, then conscription itself is but a factor in man's temperamental drift away from war, in the change of his nature towards peace.

It is not because man is degenerate or swinish or

gluttonous (such language, indeed, applied as it is by General Lea to the larger and better part of the human race, suggests a not very high-minded ill-temper at the stubbornness of facts which rhetoric does not affect) that he is showing less and less disposition to fight, but because he is condemned by the real "primordial law" to earn his bread in the sweat of his brow, and his nature in consequence develops those qualities which the bulk of his interests and capacities demand and favour.

These are the facts of the world as we know it to-day. Of course, it is always open to the dogmatic to declare, as he does declare, that the emotional habits of a lifetime will go for nothing when national pride is affronted, or when national honour needs vindication. Again, the dogmatist of this sort is so apt to overlook what actually has taken place.

Discussing this subject in London recently, Mr. Roosevelt remarked: "We despise a nation just as we despise a man who fails to resent an insult"[1]—this as justification for large national armaments. Mr. Roosevelt seems to forget that the duel with us is extinct. Do *we*, the English-speaking people of the world, to whom presumably Mr. Roosevelt must have been referring, despise a man who fails to resent an insult by arms? Would we not, on the contrary, despise the man

[1] Speech at Stationers' Hall, June 6, 1910.

who should do so? Yet, as I have pointed out earlier in this chapter, so recent is this change that it has not yet reached the majority of Continental people. But if this reform has been effected in the case of the individual, why on earth should it be a manifest impossibility to bring about an analogous habit of mind among governments and peoples, most especially when we remember that when individuals fight a duel at least the individuals who have quarrelled fight, whereas in the case of a nation, thousands of Englishmen may be slaughtered in a quarrel with Germany, in which a great many Germans take the English view. In fact, this overlapping of views, in which division of opinion follows more and more the divisions of political philosophy rather than of political frontiers, is the characteristic of most modern wars. It is no longer possible to hold an entire nation collectively responsible for the action of its Government, and educated people are coming more and more the world over to realize this fact.

Even when harmless fishermen are sunk by incompetent or drunken Russian naval officers, opinion in England differentiates between the Government and the people; there is certainly no ill-feeling again the Russian Reformers, engaged at the time in a struggle with their own Government to put an end to that very condition of things which made the Hull outrage possible; and the English people realized thoroughly that the Russian people as a whole could not be held responsible for the outrage. The same realization of the facts will go more and more to modify that senseless notion of the collective responsibility of an entire nation for the acts of its Government which we seem to have borrowed from the Chinese, who, if the real author of a murder cannot be found, hang his brother or his son.

This phase of the subject—the false representation of a whole nation of, it may be, one hundred million people as a homogeneous personality—belongs to another section of the case.[1] But I refer to it here as bearing on the relation between the old code of the duel, which, in so far as Anglo-Saxons are concerned, has passed away, and the still existent but happily modifying code of national honour. The vague talk of national honour as a quality under the especial protection of the soldier shows, perhaps more clearly than aught else, how much our notions concerning international politics have fallen behind the notions that dominate us in everyday life. When an individual begins to rave about his honour, we may be pretty sure he is about to do some irrational, most likely disreputable, deed. The word is like an oath, serving with its vague yet large meaning to intoxicate the fancy. Its vagueness

[1] See Chapter VI of this section.

and elasticity make it possible to regard a given incident at will as either harmless or a *casus belli*. Our sense of proportion in these matters approximates to that of the schoolboy. The passing jeer of a foreign journalist, a foolish cartoon, is sufficient to start the dogs of war baying up and down the land.[1] We call it "maintaining the national prestige," "enforcing respect," and I know not what other high-sounding name. But it amounts to the same thing in the end.

The one distinctive advance in civil society achieved by the Anglo-Saxon world is fairly betokened by the passing away of this old notion of a peculiar possession in the way of honour which has to be guarded by arms. It stands out as the one clear moral gain of the nineteenth century; and, when we observe the notion resurging in the minds of men, we may reasonably expect to find that it marks one of those reversions in the ongoing of moral development which so often occur in the realm of mind as well as in that of organic forms.

But two or three generations since this progress, even among Anglo-Saxons, towards a rational

[1] I have in mind here the ridiculous furore that was made by the Jingo Press over some French cartoons that appeared at the outbreak of the Boer War. It will be remembered that at that time France was the "enemy," and Germany was, on the strength of a speech by Mr. Chamberlain, a quasi-ally. We were at that times as warlike towards France as we are now towards Germany. And this is barely ten years ago!

standard of conduct in this matter, as between individuals, would have seemed as unreasonable as do the hopes of international peace in our day. Even to-day the Continental officer is as firmly convinced as ever that the maintenance of personal dignity is impossible save by the help of the duel. Such will ask in triumph, "What will you do if one of your own order openly insult you? Shall you preserve your self-resepct by summoning him to the police-court?" And the question is taken as settling the matter off-hand.

The survival, where national prestige is concerned, of the standards of the *code duello* is daily brought before us by the rhetoric of the patriots. Our army and our navy, not the good faith of our statesmen, are the "guardians of our national honour." Like the duellist, the patriot would have us believe that a dishonourable act is made honourable if the party suffering by the dishonour be killed. The patriot is careful to withdraw from the operation of possible arbitration all questions which could affect the "national honour." An "insult to the flag" must be "wiped out in blood." Small nations, which in the nature of the case cannot so resent the insults of great empires, have apparently no right to such a possession as "honour." It is the peculiar prerogative of worldwide empires. The patriots who would thus resent "insults to the flag" may well be asked whether they would condemn the conduct of the

German lieutenant who kills the unarmed civilian in cold blood "for the honour of the uniform."

It does not seem to have struck the patriot that, as personal dignity and conduct have not suffered but been improved by the abandonment of the principle of the duel, there is litttle reason to suppose that international conduct or national dignity would suffer by a similar change of standards.

The whole philosophy underlying the duel where personal relations are concerned excites in our day the infinite derision of all Anglo-Saxons. Yet these same Anglo-Saxons maintain it as vigorously as ever in the relations of States.

In view of changes as psychologically profound as these, what justification have we for the common dogmatism that "thousands of years" or "hundreds of years" must separate us from international Rationalism? "Thousands of years" takes us back to primitive savagery in Great Britain; a hundred and fifty years to the approval of slavery and belief in witchcraft.[1] In 1775 slavery was regarded as indispensable to the prosperity of England. Fifty years later it was regarded as the very worst of evils, and this change of opinion was effected in fifty years mainly through the intellectual work of two or three

---

[1] Thomasius calculated that during the seventeenth century a hundred thousand persons were burned as witches in Germany alone. The English Act of Parliament punishing witchcraft was only repealed in 1745.

men. Less than half a century ago Russia still
preserved one of the worst forms of feudalism.
To-day she has a Parliamentary Constitution.
In 1830 a ship going from Marseilles to Constantinople still ran the risk of pillage by pirates.

Those who talk thus seem to take no account
of the Law of Acceleration, as true in the domain
of sociology as of physics, which I have touched
on at the close of the preceding chapter. The
most recent evidence would seem to show that
man as a fire-using animal dates back to the
Tertiary epoch—say, three hundred thousand
years. Now, in all that touches this discussion,
man in Northern Europe (in Great Britain, say)
remained unchanged for two hundred and ninety-
eight thousand of those years. In the last two
thousand years he changed more than in the two
hundred and ninety-eight thousand preceding,
and in one hundred he has changed more perhaps
than in the preceding two thousand. The comparison becomes more understandable if we
resolve it into hours. For, say, fifty years the
man was a cannibal savage or a wild animal,
hunting other wild animals, and then in the space
of three months he became John Smith of Surbi-
ton, attending church, passing laws, using the
telephone, and so on. That is the history of
European mankind. And in the face of it the
wiseacres talk sapiently, and lay it down as a
self-evident and demonstrable fact that the

abandonment of inter-state war, which, by reason of the mechanics of our civilization, accomplishes nothing and can accomplish nothing, will for ever be rendered impossible because, once man has got the habit of doing a thing, he will go on doing it, although the reason which in the first instance prompted it has long since disappeared— because, in short, of the "unchangeability of human nature."

I have not in the foregoing chapter touched on the underlying principle which explains this change in man's nature: it suffices for the present to draw attention to the facts. The second series of facts—the relative advance made by the military and the less military nations—remains to be presented, which is done in the next chapter; and then the general law which underlies and explains both series of facts will be elucidated.

CHAPTER IV

DO THE WARLIKE NATIONS INHERIT THE EARTH?

The confident dogmatism of militarist writers on this subject—
The facts—The lessons of Spanish-America—How conquest
makes for the survival of the unfit—Spanish method and
English method in the New World—The virtues of military
training—The Dreyfus case—The threatened Germanization
of England.

THE militarist authorities I have quoted in the
preceding chapter admit, therefore, and
admit very largely, man's drift, in a sentimental
sense, away from war. But that drift, they declare, is degeneration; without those qualities
which "war alone," in Mr. Roosevelt's phrase,
can develop, man will "rot and decay."

This plea is, of course, directly germane to our
subject. To say that the qualities which we
associate with war, and nothing else but war, are
necessary to assure a nation success in its struggles
with other nations is equivalent to saying that
those who drift away from war will go down
before those whose warlike activity can conserve
those qualities essential to survival; which is but
another way of saying that men must always

remain warlike if they are to survive; that the warlike nations inherit the earth; that men's pugnacity, therefore, is the outcome of the great natural law of survival, and that a decline of pugnacity marks in any nation a recession and not an advance in its struggle for survival. I have already indicated (Chapter II, Part 2) the outlines of the proposition, which leaves no escape from this conclusion. This is the scientific basis of the proposition voiced by the authorities I have quoted—Mr. Roosevelt, Von Moltke, Renan, Nietzsche, and various of the warlike clergy[1]— and it lies at the very bottom of the plea that man's nature, in so far as it touches the tendency of men as a whole to go to war, does not change; that the warlike qualities are a necessary part of human vitality in the struggle for existence; that, in short, all that we know of the law of evolution forbids the conclusion that man will ever lose this warlike pugnacity, or that nations will survive other than by the struggle of physical force.

[1] See citations, p. 152, notably Mr. Roosevelt's dictum: "In this world the nation that is trained to a career of unwarlike and isolated ease is bound to go down in the end before other nations which have not lost the manly and adventurous qualities." This view is even emphasized in the speech which Mr. Roosevelt recently delivered at the University of Berlin (see *Times*, May 13, 1910). "The Roman civilization," declared Mr. Roosevelt— perhaps, as the *Times* remarks, to the surprise of those who have been taught to believe that *latifundia perditere Roma*—" went down primarily because the Roman citizen would not fight, because Rome had lost the fighting edge." See footnote, p. 156.

The view is best voiced, perhaps, by General Homer Lea, whom I have already quoted. He says:

As physical vigour represents the strength of man in his struggle for existence, in the same sense military vigour constitutes the strength of nations; ideals, laws, constitutions are but temporary effulgences (p. 11). The deterioration of the military force and the consequent destruction of the militant spirit have been concurrent with national decay (p. 24). International disagreements are . . . the result of the primordial conditions that sooner or later cause war, . . . the law of struggle, the law of survival, universal, unalterable . . . to thwart them, to short-cut them, to circumvent them, to cozen, to deny, to scorn, to violate them, is folly such as man's conceit alone makes possible. . . . Arbitration denies the inexorability of natural laws . . . that govern the existence of political entities (pp. 76, 77). Laws that govern the militancy of a people are not of man's framing, but follow the primitive ordinances of nature that govern all forms of life from a simple protozoa, awash in the sea, to the empires of man (*The Valour of Ignorance*).

I have already indicated the grave misconception which lies at the bottom of the interpretation of the evolutionary law here indicated. What we are concerned with now is to deal with the facts on which this alleged general principle is inductively based. We have seen from the foregoing chapter that man's nature certainly does change; we are concerned to show here from the facts of the present-day world that the warlike qualities do not make for survival, that the warlike nations do not inherit the earth.

Which are the military nations? We generally think of them in Europe as Germany and France, or perhaps also Russia, Austria, and Italy. Admittedly (*vide* all the English and American military pundits and economists) England is the least militarized nation in Europe, the United States perhaps in the world. It is, above all, Germany that appeals to us as the type of the military nation, one in which the stern school of war makes for the preservation of the "manly and adventurous qualities."

The facts want a little closer examination. What is a career of unwarlike ease, in Mr. Roosevelt's phrase? In the last chapter we saw that during the last forty years, eight thousand out of sixty million Germans have been engaged in warfare during a trifle over a year, and that against Hottentots or Hereros. This gives a proportion of war days per German as against peace-days per German which is as one to some hundreds of thousands. So that if we are to take Germany as the type of the military nation, and if we are to accept Mr. Roosevelt's dictum that by war alone can we acquire "those virile qualities necessary to win in the stern strife of actual life," we shall nevertheless be doomed to lose them, for under conditions like those of Germany how many of us can ever see war, or can pretend to fall under its influence? As already pointed out, the men who really give the stamp to the German nation, to German life and conduct—that is to say, the majority of adult Germans—have never seen a battle and never will. France has done much better. Not only has she seen infinitely more of actual fighting, but her population is much more militarized than that of Germany, 50 per cent. more, in fact, since, in order to maintain from a population of forty millions the same military effective as Germany does with sixty millions, $1\frac{1}{2}$ per cent. of the French population is under arms as against 1 per cent. of the German.[1]

Still more military in both senses is Russia, as we know, and more military than Russia is Turkey, and more military than Turkey as a whole are the semi-independent sections of Turkey, Arabia, and Albania, and then, perhaps, comes Morocco.

On the Western Hemisphere we can draw a like table as to the "warlike, adventurous, manly and progressive peoples" as compared with the "peaceful, craven, slothful, and decadent." The least warlike of all, the nation which has had the least training in war, the least experience of it, which

[1] See M. Messimy's Report on the War Budget for 1908 (annexe 3, p. 474). France's military activities since 1870 have, of course, been much greater than those of Germany,—Tonkin, Madagascar, Algiers, Morocco. As against these, Germany has only had the Hereros Campaign.

has been the least purified by it, is Canada.
After that comes the United States, and after that
the best (excuse me, I mean, of course, the worst)
—*i. e.*, the least warlike of the Spanish American
Republics—like Mexico and Argentina; while the
most warlike of all, and consequently the most
"manly and progressive," are the "Sambo" republics, like San Domingo, Nicaragua, Colombia,
and Venezuela.   They are always fighting.   If
they cannot manage to get up a fight between one
another, the various parties in each republic will
fight between themselves.   Here we get the real
thing.   The soldiers do not pass their lives in
practising the "goose-step," cleaning harness,
pipeclaying belts, but in giving and taking hard
pounding.   Several of these progressive republics
have never known a year since they declared their
independence from Spain in which they have not
had a war.   And quite a considerable proportion
of the populations spend their whole lives in
fighting.   During the first twenty years of Venezuela's independent existence she fought no less
than one hundred and twenty important battles,
either with her neighbours or with herself, and
she has maintained the average pretty well ever
since.   Every election is a fight—none of your
"mouth fighting," none of your craven talking-
shops for them.   Good, honest, hard, manly
knocks, with anything from one to five thousand
dead and wounded left on the field.   The presi-

dents of these strenuous republics are not pol-
troons of politicians, but soldiers—men of blood
and iron with a vengeance—men after Mr.
Roosevelt's own heart, all following "the good
old rule, the simple plan." These are the people
who have taken Carlyle's advice to "shut up
the talking-shops." *They* fight it out like men;
they talk with Gatling-guns and Mausers. Oh,
they are a very fine, manly, military lot! If
fighting makes for survival, they should completely oust from the field Canada and the United
States, one of which has never had a real battle
for the best part of its hundred years of craven,
sordid, peaceful life, and the other of which
General Homer Lea assures us is surely dying,
because of its tendency to avoid fighting.

General Lea makes no secret of the fact (and
if he did, some of his rhetoric would display it)
that he is out of sympathy with predominant
American ideals. He might emigrate to Venezuela, or Colombia, or Nicaragua. He would
be able to prove to each military dictator in turn
that, in converting the country into a shambles,
far from committing a foul crime for which such
dictators should be, and are, held in execration by
civilized men the world over, they are, on the contrary, but obeying one of God's commands in
tune with all the immutable laws of the universe.
I desire to write in all seriousness, but to one who
happens to have seen at first hand something of

the conditions which arise from a real military conception of civilization it is very difficult. How does Mr. Roosevelt, who declares that "by war alone can we acquire those virile qualities necessary to win in the stern strife of actual life"; how does von Stengel, who declares that "war is a test of a nation's health political, physical, and moral"; Mr. Sidney Low, who infers that the military state is so much finer than the Cobdenite one of commercial pursuits; M. Ernest Renan, who declares that war is the condition of progress, and that under peace we should sink to a degree of degeneracy difficult to realize; and how do the various English clergymen who voice a like philosophy reconcile their creed with military Spanish-America? How can they urge that non-military industrialism, which, with all its short-comings, has on the Western Continent given us Canada and the United States, makes for decadence and degeneration, while militarism and the qualities and instincts that go with it have given us Venezuela and San Domingo? Do we not all recognize that industrialism—Mr. Lea's "gourmandizing and retching" notwithstanding—is the one thing which will save these military republics; that the one condition of their advance is that they shall give up the stupid and sordid gold-braid militarism and turn to honest work?

If ever there was a justification for Herbert Spencer's sweeping generalization that "advance to the highest forms of man and society depends on the decline of militancy and the growth of industrialism," it is to be found in the history of the South and Central American republics. Indeed, Spanish-America at the present moment affords more lessons than we seem to be drawing, and, if militancy makes for advance and survival, it is a most extraordinary thing that all who are in any way concerned with those countries, all who live in them and whose future is wrapped up in them, can never sufficiently express their thankfulness that at last there seems to be a tendency with some of them to get away from the blood and valour nonsense which has been their curse for three centuries, and to exchange the military ideal for the Cobdenite one of buying cheap and selling dear which so excites the scorn of Mr. Sidney Low.

Some years ago an Italian lawyer, a certain Tomasso Caivano, wrote a letter detailing his experiences and memories of twenty years' life in Venezuela and the neighbouring republics, and his general conclusions have for this discussion a direct relevancy. As a sort of farewell exhortation to the Venezuelans, he wrote:

The curse of your civilization is the soldier and the soldier's temper. It is impossible for two of you, still less for two parties, to carry on a discussion without one wanting to fight the other about the matter in hand. You regard it as a derogation of dignity to consider the point of view of the other side, and to attempt to meet it, if it is possible to fight about it. You deem that personal valour atones for all defects. The soldier of evil character is more considered amongst you than the civilian of good character, and military adventure is deemed more honourable than honest labour. You overlook the worst corruption, the worst repression, in your leaders if only they gild it with military fanfaronade and declamation about bravery and destiny and patriotism. Not until there is a change in this spirit will you cease to be the victims of evil oppression. Not until your general populace—your peasantry and your workers—refuse thus to be led to slaughter in quarrels of which they know and care nothing, but into which they are led because they also prefer fighting to work—not until all this happens will those beautiful lands which are among the most fertile on God's earth support a happy and prosperous people living in contentment and secure possession of the fruits of their labour.[1]

Spanish-America seems at last in a fair way of throwing off the domination of the soldier and awakening from these nightmares of successive military despotisms tempered by assassination, though, in abandoning, in Signor Caivano's words, "military adventure for honest labour," she will necessarily have less to do with those deeds of blood and valour of which her history has been so full. But those in South America who matter are not mourning. Really they are not.[2]

[1] *Vox de la Naçion*, Caracas, April 22, 1897.

[2] Even Mr. Roosevelt calls South American history mean and

The thing can be duplicated absolutely on this side of the hemisphere. Change a few names, and you get Arabia or Morocco. Listen to this from a recent *Times* article[1]:

The fact is that for many years past Turkey has almost invariably been at war in some part or other of Arabia. . . . At the present moment Turkey is actually conducting three separate small campaigns within Arabia or upon its borders, and a fourth series of minor operations in Mesopotamia. The last-named movement is against the Kurdish tribes of the Mosul district. . . . Another, and more important advance is against the truculent Muntefik Arabs of the Euphrates delta. . . . The fourth, and by far the largest, campaign is the unending warfare in the province of Yemen, north of Aden, where the Turks have been fighting intermittently for more than a decade. The peoples of Arabia are also indulging in conflict on their own account. The interminable feud between the rival potentates of Nedjd, Ibn Saud

bloody. It is noteworthy that, in his article published in the *Bachelor of Arts* for March, 1896, Mr. Roosevelt, who lectured Englishmen so vigorously on their duty at all cost, not to be guided by sentimentalism in the government of Egypt, should write thus at the time of Mr. Cleveland's Venezuelan message to England: "Mean and bloody though the history of the South American republics has been, it is distinctly in the interest of civilization that . . . they should be left to develop along their own lines. . . . Under the best of circumstances, a colony is in a false position; but if a colony is a region where the colonizing race has to do its work by means of other and inferior races, the condition is much worse. There is no chance for any tropical colony owned by a Northern race."

[1] June 2, 1910.

of Riadh and Ibn Rashid of Hail, has broken out
afresh, and the tribes of the coastal province of El
Katar are supposed to have plunged into the fray.
The Muntefik Arabs, not content with worrying the
Turks, are harrying the territories of Sheikh Mur-
barak of Koweit. In the far south the Sultan of
Shehr and Mokalla, a feudatory of the British
Government, is conducting a tiny war against a hostile
tribe in the mysterious Hadramaut. In the west the
Beduin are spasmodically menacing certain sections
of the Hedjaz Railway, which they very much dislike.
. . . Ten years ago the Ibn Rashids were nominally
masters of a great deal of Arabia, and grew so aggres-
sive that they tried to seize Koweit. The fiery old
Sheikh of Koweit marched against them, and alter-
nately won and lost. He had his revenge. He sent
an audacious scion of the Ibn Sauds to the old
Wahabi capital of Riadh, and by a remarkable
stratagem the youth captured the stronghold with
only fifty men at his back. When the new Ibn Saud
raised afresh the white and red banner of the Wahabis,
thousands flocked to his aid. The rival parties have
been fighting at intervals ever since.

And so on and so on to the extent of a column. So
that what Venezuela and Nicaragua are to the
American Continent, Arabia, Albania, Armenia,
Montenegro and Morocco are to the Eastern Hemisphere. We find exactly the same rule—that
just as one gets away from militancy one gets
towards advance and civilization; as men lose
the tendency to fight they gain the tendency to

work, and it is by working with one another, and not by fighting against each other, that men advance.

Take the progression away from militancy, and it gives us a table something like this:

Arabia and Morocco.

Turkish territory as a whole.

The more unruly Balkan States. Montenegro.

Russia.

France.

Germany.

Scandinavia. Holland. Belgium.

England.

Do Mr. Roosevelt, Admiral Mahan, Baron von Stengel, Marshal von Moltke, General Lea, and the English clergymen seriously argue that this list should be reversed, and that Arabia and Turkey should be taken as the types of progressive nations, and England and Germany and Scandinavia as the decadent?

It may be urged that my list is not absolutely accurate, in that England, having fought more little wars (though the conflict with the Boers, waged with a small, pastoral people, shows how little wars may drain a great country), is more militarized than Germany, which has not been fighting at all. But I have tried in a very rough fashion to arrive at the degree of militancy in each State, and the absence of actual fighting in the case of Germany (as in that of the smaller States) is balanced by the fact of the military training of her people. As I have already indicated, France is more military than Germany, both in the extent to which her people are put through the mill of universal military training and by virtue of the fact that she has done so much more small fighting than Germany (Madagascar, Tonkin, Africa, etc.); while, of course, Russia and the Balkan States are still more military in both senses—more actual fighting, more military training.

Perhaps the militarist will argue that, while useless and unjust wars make for degeneration, just wars are a moral regeneration. But did a nation, group, tribe, family or individual ever yet enter into a war which he did not think just? The British, or most of them, believed the war against the Boers just, but most of the authorities in favour of war in general outside of Great Britain believed it unjust. Nowhere do you find such deathless, absolute, unwavering belief in the justice of war as in those conflicts which all Christendom knows to be at once unjust and unnecessary. I refer to the religious wars of Mohammedan fanaticism.

Do you suppose that when Nicaragua goes to war with San Salvador or Costa Rica, or Colombia with Peru, or Peru with Chili, or Chili with the Argentine, they do not each and every one of them believe that they are fighting for immutable and deathless principles? The civilization of most

of them is, of course, as like as two peas, and there
is no more reason, except their dislike of rational
thought and hard work, why they should fight
with one another, despite General Lea's fine words
as to the primordial character of national differences, than that Dorset should fight with Devon;
to one another they are as alike, and whether San
Salvador beats Costa Rica or Costa Rica San
Salvador does not, so far as essentials are concerned, matter twopence. But their rhetoric of
patriotism—the sacrifice, and the deathless glory,
and the rest of it—is often just as sincere as
ours. That is the tragedy of it, and it is that
which gives to the solution of the problem in
Spanish-America its real difficulty.

But even if we admit that warfare *à l'espagnole*
may be degrading, and that just wars are ennobling
and necessary to our moral welfare, we should
nevertheless be condemned to degeneracy and
decline. A just war implies that someone must
act unjustly towards us, but as the general condition improves—as it is improving in Europe as
compared with Central and South America, or
Morocco, or Arabia—we shall get less and less
"moral purification"; as men become less and less
disposed to make unjustifiable attacks, they will
become more and more degenerate. In such
incoherence are we landed by the pessimistic and
impossible philosophy that men will decay and die
unless they go on killing each other.

What is the fundamental error at the base of the theory that war makes for the survival of the fit—that warfare is any necessary expression of the law of survival? It is the illusion induced by the hypnotism of a terminology which is obsolete. The same factor which leads us so astray in the economic domain leads us also astray in this.

Conquest does not make for the elimination of the conquered; the weakest do not go to the wall, though that is the process which those who adopt the formula of evolution in this matter have in their minds.

Great Britain has conquered India. Does that mean that the inferior race is replaced by the superior? Not the least in the world; the inferior race not only survives, but is given an extra lease of life by virtue of the conquest. If ever the Asiatic threatens the white race, it will be thanks in no small part to the work of race conservation which England's conquests in the East have involved. War, therefore, does not make for the elimination of the unfit and the survival of the fit. It would be truer to say that it makes for the survival of the unfit.

What is the real process of war? You carefully select from the general population on both sides the healthiest, sturdiest, the physically and mentally soundest, those possessing precisely the virile and manly qualities which you desire to preserve, and, having thus selected the *élite* of the two populations, you exterminate them by battle and disease, and leave the worst of both sides to amalgamate in the process of conquest or defeat—because, in so far as the final amalgamation is concerned, both processes have the same result—and from this amalgam of the worst of both sides you create the new nation or the new society which is to carry on the race. Even supposing the better nation wins, the fact of conquest results only in the absorption of the inferior qualities of the beaten nation—inferior presumably because beaten, and inferior because we have killed off their selected best and absorbed the rest, since we no longer exterminate the women, the children, the old men, and those too weak or too feeble to go into the army.[1]

You have only to carry on this process long enough and persistently enough to weed out completely from both sides the type of man to

---

[1] Dr. Otto Seeck (*Der Untergang der Antiken Welt*) finds the downfall of Rome due solely to the rooting out of the best—die Ausrottung der Besten. Seeley says: "The Roman Empire perished for want of men."

Three million men—the élite of Europe—perished in the Napoleonic wars. It is said that after those wars the height standard of the French adult population fell abruptly one inch. However that may be, it is quite certain that the physical fitness of the French people was immensely lowered by the drain of the Napoleonic wars, since, as the result of a century of militarism, France is compelled every few years to reduce the standard of physical fitness in order to keep up her effective military strength, so that now even three-foot dwarfs are impressed. There is no height limit at all.

whom alone we can look for the conservation of virility, physical vigour, and hardihood. That such a process did play no small rôle in the degeneration of Rome and the populations on which the crux of the Empire reposed there can hardly be any reasonable doubt. And the process of degeneration on the part of the conqueror is aided by this added factor: If the conqueror profits much by his conquest, as the Romans did in one sense, it is the conqueror who is threatened by the enervating effect of the soft and luxurious life; while it is the conquered who are forced to labour for the conqueror, and who learn in consequence those qualities of steady industry which are certainly a better moral training than living upon the fruits of others, upon labour extorted at the sword's point. It is the conqueror who becomes effete, and it is the conquered who learn discipline and the qualities making for a well-ordered state.

To say of war, therefore, as does Baron von Stengel, that it destroys the frail trees, leaving the sturdy oaks standing, is merely to state with absolute confidence the exact reverse of the truth: to take advantage of loose catch-phrases, which by inattention not only distort common thought in these matters, but often turn the truth upside down. Our everyday ideas are full of illustrations of the same thing. For hundreds of years we talked of the "riper wisdom of the ancients," implying that this generation is the youth in experience, and that the early ages had the accumulated experience—the exact reverse, of course, of the truth. Yet "the learning of the ancients" and "the wisdom of our forefathers" was a common catch-phrase, even in the British Parliament, until an English country parson killed this nonsense by ridicule.[1]

I do not urge that the somewhat simple, elementary, selective process which I have described accounts in itself for the decadence of military Powers. That is only a part of the process: the whole of it is somewhat more complicated, in that the process of elimination of the good in favour of the bad is quite as much sociological as biological; that is to say, if during long periods a nation gives itself up to war, trade languishes, the population loses the habit of steady industry, government and administration become corrupt, abuses escape punishment, and the real sources of a people's strength and expansion dwindle. What has caused the relative failure and decline of Spanish, Portuguese, and French expansion in Asia and the New World, and the relative success of English expansion therein? Was it the mere hazards of war which gave to Great Britain the domination of India and half of the New World? That is surely a superficial reading of history. It

[1] I think one may say fairly that it *was* Sidney Smith's ridicule which killed this curious illusion.

was, rather, that the methods and processes of Spain, Portugal, and France were military, while those of the Anglo-Saxon world were commercial and peaceful. Is it not a commonplace that in India, quite as much as in the New World, the trader and the settler drove out the soldier and the conqueror? The difference between the two methods was that one was a process of conquest, and the other of colonizing, or non-military administration for commercial purposes. The one embodied the sordid Cobdenite idea, which so excites the scorn of the militarists, and the other the lofty military ideal. The one was parasitism; the other co-operation.[1]

Those who confound the power of a nation with the size of its army and navy are mistaking the cheque-book for the money. A child, seeing its father paying bills in cheques, assumes that you only need plenty of cheque-books in order to have plenty of money; it does not see that for the cheque-book to have power there must be unseen resources on which to draw. Of what use is domination unless there be individual capacity, social training, industrial resources, to profit thereby? How can you have these things if energy is wasted as in military adventure? Is not the failure of Spain explicable by the fact that she failed to realize this truth? For three

[1] See the distinction established at the beginning of the next chapter.

centuries she attempted to live upon conquest, upon the force of her arms, and year after year got poorer in the process, and her modern social renaissance dates from the time when she lost the last of her American colonies. It is since the loss of Cuba and the Philippines that Spanish national securities have doubled in value. (At the outbreak of the Hispano-American War Spanish Fours were at 45; they have since touched par.) And if Spain has shown in the last decade a social renaissance not shown perhaps for a hundred and fifty years, it is because a nation still less military than Germany, and still more purely industrial, has compelled Spain once and for all to surrender all dream of empire and conquest. The circumstances of the last surrender are eloquent in this connection as showing how even in warfare itself the industrial training and the industrial tradition—the Cobdenite ideal of Mr. Sydney Low's scorn—are more than a match for the training of a society in which military activities are predominant. If it be true that it was the German schoolmaster who conquered at Sedan, it was the Chicago merchant who conquered at Manila. The writer happens to have been in touch both with Spaniards and Americans at the time of the war, and well remembers the scorn with which Spaniards referred to the notion that the Yankee pork-butchers could possibly conquer a nation of their military tradition, and to the idea that trades-

men would ever be a match for the soldiery and
pride of old Spain.   And French opinion was not
so very different.[1]   Shortly after the war I wrote
in an American journal as follows:

Spain represents the outcome of some centuries
devoted mainly to military activity.   No one can say
that she has been unmilitary or at all deficient in
those qualities which we associate with soldiers and
soldiering.   Yet, if such qualities in any way make
for national efficiency, for the conservation of national
force, the history of Spain is absolutely inexplicable.
In their late contest with America, Spaniards showed
no lack of the distinctive military virtues.   Spain's
inferiority—apart from deficiency of men and money
—was precisely in those qualities which industrialism
has bred in the unmilitary American.   Authentic
stories of wretched equipment, inadequate supplies,
and bad leadership show to what depths of inefficiency
the Spanish service, military and naval, had fallen.
We are justified in believing that a much smaller
nation than Spain, but one possessing a more industrial and less military training, would have done
much better, both as regards resistance to America
and the defence of her own Colonies.   The present
position of Holland in Asia seems to prove this.

[1] M. Pierre Loti, who happened to be at Madrid when the
troops were leaving to fight the Americans, wrote: "They are,
indeed, still the solid and splendid Spanish troops, heroic in every
epoch; one only needs to look at them to divine the woe that awaits
the American shopkeepers when brought face to face with such
soldiers."   He prophesied *des surprises sanglantes.*   M. Loti is a
member of the French Academy.

The Dutch, whose traditions are industrial and non-military for the most part, have shown greater power and efficiency as a nation than the Spanish, who are more numerous.

Here, as always, it is shown that, in considering national efficiency, even as expressed in military power, the economic problem cannot be divorced from the military, and that it is a fatal mistake to suppose that the power of a nation depends solely upon the power of its public bodies, or that it can be judged simply from the size of its army. A large army may, indeed, be a sign of national—that is, military—weakness. Warfare in these days is a business like most else, and no courage, no heroism, no "glorious past," no "immortal traditions," will atone for deficient rations and fraudulent administration. Good civilian qualities are the ones that will in the end win a nation's battles. The Spaniard is the last one in the world to see this. He talks and dreams of Castilian bravery and Spanish honour, and is above shopkeeping details. . . . A writer on contemporary Spain remarks that any intelligent middle-class Spaniard will admit every charge of incompetence which can be brought against the conduct of public affairs. "Yes, we have a wretched Government. In any other country somebody would be shot." This is the hopeless military creed: killing somebody is the only remedy.

Here we see a trace of that intellectual legacy which Spain has left to the New World, and which has stamped itself so indelibly on the history of

Spanish-America. On a later occasion in this connection I wrote as follows:

To appreciate the outcome of much soldiering, the condition in which persistent military training may leave a race, one should study Spanish-America. Here we have a collection of some score of States, all very much alike in social and political make-up. Most of the South-American States so resemble one another in language, laws, institutions, that to an outsider it would seem not to matter a straw under which particular six-months-old republic one should live; whether one be under the government of the pronunciamento-created President of Colombia, or the pronunciamento-created President of Venezuela, one's condition would appear to be much the same. Apparently no particular country has anything which differentiates it from another, and, consequently, nothing to protect against the other. Absolutely the Governments might all change places and the people be none the wiser. Yet, so hypnotized are these little States by the "necessity for self-protection," by the glamour of armaments, that there is not one which has not a relatively elaborate and expensive military establishment to protect it from the rest.

No conditions seem so propitious for a practical confederation than those of Spanish-America; with a few exceptions, the virtual unity of language, laws, general race-ideals would seem to render protection of frontiers supererogatory. Yet the citizens give untold wealth, service, life, and suffering to be protected against a Government exactly like their own. All this waste of life and energy has gone on without it ever occurring to one of these States that it were preferable to be annexed a thousand times over, so trifling would be the resulting change in their condition, than continue the everlasting and futile tribute of blood and treasure. Over some absolutely unimportant matter—like that of the Patagonian roads, which nearly brought Argentina and Chili to grips the other day—as much patriotic devotion will be expended as ever the Old Guard lavished in protecting the honour of the Tricolour. Battles will be fought which will make all the struggles in South Africa appear mean in comparison. Actions in which the dead are counted in thousands will excite no more comment in the world than that produced by a skirmish in Natal, in which a score of yeomen are captured and released.

In the decade since the foregoing was written things have enormously improved in South America. Why? For the simple reason, as pointed out in Chapter V. of the first part of this book, that Spanish-America is being brought more and more into the economic movement of the world; and with the establishment of factories, in which large capital has been sunk, banks, businesses, etc., the whole attitude of mind of those interested in these ventures is changed. The Jingo, the military adventurer, the fomenter of trouble, are seen for what they are—not as patriots, but as representing exceedingly mischievous and maleficient forces.

This general truth has two facets: if long warfare diverts a people from the capacity for industry, so in the long run economic pressure—the influences, that is, which turn the energies of people to pre-occupation with social well-being—is fatal to the military tradition.   Neither tendency is constant: warfare produces poverty; poverty pushes to thrift and work, which result in wealth; wealth creates leisure and pride and pushes to warfare.

Where Nature does not respond readily to industrial effort, where it is at least apparently more profitable to plunder than to work, the military tradition survives.   The Bedouin has been a bandit since the time of Abraham, for the simple reason that the desert does not support industrial life nor respond to industrial effort.   The only career offering a fair apparent return for effort is plunder.   In Morocco, in Arabia, in all very poor pastoral countries, the same phenomenon is exhibited; in mountainous countries which are arid and are removed from the economic centres, *idem*.   It may have been to some extent the case in Prussia before the era of coal and iron; but the fact that to-day 99 per cent. of the population is normally engaged in trade and industry, and 1 per cent. only in military preparation, and some fraction too small to be properly estimated engaged in actual war, shows how far she has outgrown such a state—shows, incidentally, what little chance the ideal and tradition represented by 1

per cent. or some fractional percentage has against
interests and activities represented by 99 per cent.
The recent history of South and Central America,
because it is recent, and because the factors are
less complicated, illustrates best the tendency with
which we are dealing.   Spanish-America inherited
the military tradition in all its vigour.   As I have
already pointed out, the Spanish occupation of the
American Continent was a process of conquest
rather than of colonizing; and while the Mother-
country got poorer and poorer by the process of
conquest, the new countries also impoverished
themselves in adherence to the same fatal illusion.
The glamour of conquest was, of course, Spain's
ruin.   So long as it was possible for her to live
on extorted bullion, neither social nor industrial
development seemed possible.   Despite the common idea to the contrary, Germany has known
how to keep this fatal hypnotism at bay, and, far
from allowing her military activities to absorb her
industrial, it is precisely the military activities
which are in a fair way now of being absorbed by
the industrial and commercial, and her world
commerce has its foundation, not in tribute or
bullion exacted at the sword's point, but in sound
and honest exchange.   So that to-day the legiti-
mate commercial tribute which Germany, who
never sent a soldier there, exacts from Spanish-
America, is immensely greater than that which
goes to Spain, who poured out blood and treasure

during three centuries on these territories. In this way, again, do the warlike nations inherit the earth!

If Germany is never to duplicate Spain's decadence, it is precisely because (1) she has never had historically Spain's temptation to live by conquest, and (2) because, having to live by honest industry, her commercial hold, even upon the territories conquered by Spain, is more firmly set than that of Spain herself.

How may we sum up the whole case, keeping in mind every empire that ever existed—the Assyrian, the Babylonian, the Mede and Persian, the Macedonian, the Roman, the Frank, the Saxon, the Spanish, the Portuguese, the Bourbon, the Napoleonic? In all and every one of them we may see the same process, which is this: If it remains military it decays; if it prospers and takes its share of the work of the world it ceases to be military. There is no other reading of history.

It may, of course, be argued that the whole thing is a question of degree; that while it may be quite true that Spain and Portugal have worn themselves out with military conquest—mistaking the means for the end—that, while the Anglo-Saxon world has triumphed by the non-military labour of her settlers, traders, and manufacturers, yet the fact remains that had the Anglo-Saxon world not done *some* fighting she would have been driven from the New World or would never have gained a foothold there.

I am not concerned to deny the truth of this. The principle by which we may determine the difference between advantageous and disadvantageous employment of military force—a principle which most clearly establishes the difference which has distinguished the expansion of Spain and England—is explained at the beginning of the next chapter. What we are now more concerned with is not so much processes and principles as the physical and psychological facts of the case. As explained in the first section of this book, I am arguing the main thesis on the facts of the world as they stand to-day; and just what proportion of fighting may have been useful in the past and what proportion useless is an interesting but academic question I am not concerned to solve. If I have appealed to the historical facts, it is because we are at present dealing with the human nature of the case—the biological origins of the sentimental and moral motives pushing nations into war—and because I wish to show from a brief historical review of national development that the broad features of such do not justify the plea that pugnacity and antagonism between nations is bound up in any way with the real process of national survival. Those facts show clearly enough that nations nurtured normally in peace are more than a match for nations nurtured normally in war; that communities of non-military tradition and instincts, like the Anglo-Saxon communities of the New World, show elements of survival stronger than those possessed by communities animated by the military tradition, like the Spanish and Portuguese nations of the New World; that the position of the industrial nations in Europe as compared with the military give no justification for the plea that the warlike qualities make for survival. It is clearly evident that there is no biological justification in the terms of man's political evolution for the perpetuation of antagonism between nations, or any justification for the plea that the diminution of such antagonism runs counter to the teachings of the "natural law." There is no such natural law; natural laws are thrusting men irresistibly towards co-operation between communities and not towards conflict.

There remains the argument that, though the conflict itself may make for degeneration, the preparation for that conflict makes for survival, for the improvement of human nature. I have already touched upon the hopeless confusion which comes of the plea that, while long-continued peace is bad, military preparations find their justification in the plea that they insure peace.

Mr. Low, in the passage which I have quoted, sneers at the idea of peace because it involves the Cobdenite state of buying cheap and selling dear.

But he goes on to argue for great armaments, not as a means of promoting war, that valuable school, etc., but as the best means of securing peace; in other words, that condition of "buying cheap and selling dear" which but a moment before he had condemned as so defective. As though to make the stultification complete, he pleads for the peace value of military training, on the ground that German commerce has benefited from it—that, in other words, it has promoted the "Cobdenite ideal." The analysis of the reasoning gives a result something like this: (1) War is a great school of morals, therefore we must have great armaments to insure peace; (2) secure peace engenders the Cobdenite ideal, which is bad, therefore we should adopt conscription, (a) because it is the best safeguard of secure peace, (b) because it is an excellent training for commerce—the Cobdenite ideal.

Is it true that barrack training—the sort of school which the competition of armaments during the last generation has imposed on the people of Continental Europe—makes for moral health? Is it likely that a "perpetual rehearsal for something never likely to come off, and when it comes off is not like the rehearsal," should be a training for life's realities? Is it likely that such a process would have the stamp and touch of closeness to real things? Is it likely that the mechanical routine of artificial occupations, artificial crimes, artificial virtues, artificial punishments should form any real training for the battle of real life?[1] What of the Dreyfus case? What of the abominable scandals that have marked German military life of late years? If peace military training is such a fine school, how could the *Times* write thus of France after she had submitted to a generation of a very severe form of it:

A thrill of horror and shame ran through the whole civilized world outside France when the result of the Rennes Court Martial became known. . . . By their [the officers'] own admission, whether flung defiantly at the judges, their inferiors, or wrung from them under cross-examination, Dreyfus's chief accusers were convicted of gross and fraudulent illegalities which, anywhere, would have sufficed, not only to discredit their testimony—had they any serious testimony to offer—but to transfer them speedily from the witness-box to the prisoner's dock. . . . Their vaunted honour " rooted in dishonour stood." . . . Five judges out of the seven have once more demonstrated the truth of the astounding axiom first propounded during the Zola trial, that " military justice is not as

[1] "For permanent work the soldier is worse than useless; his whole training tends to make him a weakling. He has the easiest of lives; he has no freedom and no responsibility. He is, politically and socially, a child, with rations instead of rights—treated like a child, punished like a child, dressed prettily and washed and combed like a child, excused for outbreaks of naughtiness like a child, forbidden to marry like a child, and called 'Tommy' like a child. He has no real work to keep him from going mad except housemaid's work " (*John Bull's Other Island*).

other justice." . . . We have no hesitation in saying
that the Rennes Court Martial constitutes in itself
the grossest, and, viewed in the light of the surrounding circumstances, the most appalling prostitution
of justice which the world has witnessed in modern times . . . Flagrantly, deliberately, mercilessly,
trampled justice underfoot. . . . The verdict, which
is a slap in the face to the public opinion of the civilized
world, to the conscience of humanity. . . . France
is henceforth on her trial before history. Arraigned
at the bar of a tribunal far higher than that before
which Dreyfus stood, it rests with her to show
whether she will undo this great wrong and rehabilitate
her fair name, or whether she will stand irrevocably
condemned and disgraced by allowing it to be con-
summated. We can less than ever afford to underrate
the forces against truth and justice. . . . Hypnotized
by the wild tales perpetually dinned into all credulous
ears of an international " syndicate of treason," con-
spiring against the honour of the army and the safety
of France, the conscience of the French nation has
been numbed, and its intelligence atrophied. . . .
Amongst those statesmen who are in touch with the
outside world in the Senate and Chamber there must
be some that will remind her that nations, no more
than individuals, can bear the burden of universal
scorn and live. . . . France cannot close her ears to
the voice of the civilized world, for that voice is the
voice of history [September 11, 1899].

And what the *Times* said then all England was
saying, and not only all England, but all America.

And has Germany escaped a like condemnation? We commonly assume that the Dreyfus case could not be duplicated in Germany. But this is not the opinion of very many Germans themselves. Indeed, just before the Dreyfus case reached its crisis, the Kotze scandal—in its way just as grave as the Dreyfus affair, and revealing a military condition just as serious—prompted the *Times* to declare that "certain features of German civilization are such as to make it difficult for Englishmen to understand how the whole State does not collapse from sheer rottenness." And if that could be said of the Kotze scandal, what shall be said of the state of things which, among others, has been revealed by Maximilian Harden?

Need it be said that the writer of these lines does not desire to represent Germans as a whole as more corrupt than their neighbours? But impartial observers are not of opinion, and very many Germans are not of opinion, that there has been either economic, social, or moral advantage to the German people from the victories of 1870 and the state of regimentation which the sequel has imposed. This is surely evidenced by the actual position of affairs in the German Empire, the complex difficulty with which the German people are now struggling, the growing discontent, the growing influence of those elements which are nurtured in discontent, the growth on one side of radical *intransigeance* and on the other of almost feudal autocracy, the failure to effect normally and easily those democratic developments which have been effected in almost every other European State, the danger for the future which such a situation represents, the precariousness of German finance, the relatively small benefit which her population as a whole has received from the greatly increased foreign trade—all this, and much more, confirms that view. England seems to be affected with the German superstition just now. With the curious perversity that marks "patriotic" judgments, the whole tendency at present is to make comparisons with Germany to the disadvantage of ourselves and of other European countries. Yet if Germans themselves are to be believed, much of that superiority which we see in Germany is as purely non-existent as the phantom German war-balloon to which our Press devoted serious columns, to the phantom army corps in Epping Forest, to the phantom stores of arms in London cellars, and to the German spy which our patriots see in every Italian waiter.[1]

Despite the hypnotism which German "progress" seems to exercise on the minds of British

[1] Things must have reached a pretty pass in England when the owner of the *Daily Mail* and the patron of Mr. Blatchford can devote a column and a half over his own signature to reproaching in vigorous terms the hysteria and sensationalism of his own readers.

Jingoes, the German people themselves, as distinct from the small group of Prussian Junkers, are not in the least enamoured of it, as is proved by the unparalleled growth of the social democratic element, which is the negation of military imperialism, and which, as the figures in Prussia prove, receives support not from one class of the population merely, but from the mercantile, industrial, and professional classes as well. The agitation for electoral reform in Prussia shows how acute the conflict has become: on the one side the increasing democratic element showing more and more of a revolutionary tendency, and on the other side the Prussian autocracy showing less and less disposition to yield. Does any one really believe that the situation will remain there, that the Democratic parties will continue to grow in numbers and be content for ever to be ridden down by the "booted Prussian," and that German democracy will indefinitely accept a situation in which it will be always possible—in the words of the Junker von Oldenburg, member of the Reichstag—for the German Emperor to say to a lieutenant, "Take ten men and close the Reichstag"?[1]

[1] I take the following from the *Anti-Socialistische Korresponddenz:* "The social democratic problem, and the social problem in general, are becoming more difficult and more acute. The social democracy at the present moment is more than ever a party of class; it is at bottom losing nothing of its revolutionary

Has not the last ten years, indeed, revealed very striking symptoms in this respect? Was not the outburst of German public opinion which followed the publication of the Kaiser's interview in the *Daily Telegraph*, and the still more unprecedented attitude of abject apology adopted by the Chancellor on that occasion, a revelation of the change in German spirit which has taken place within the last decade? It may be urged, indeed, that the whole outcry rapidly died down; but does it not show a tremendous gulf separating us from the time when *lèse-majesté* prosecutions were counted by thousands, when the punishments therefor ran in the sum to some thousands of years of

---

character." We know what the social democracy party is—controls twenty-five per cent. of the votes in the Reichstag, owns seventy-four daily papers, and has a revenue of considerably over a million marks a year. Professor Delbruck, the editor of the *Preussische Jahrbücher*, prophesies that the Socialists will have one hundred and twenty seats in the next Reichstag (at present they hold forty-nine).

The following from the Berlin correspondent of the *Daily Mail* (August 1, 1910) is suggestive: "The tide of German Socialism still rises. The victory in the Reichstag by-election in Wurtemburg again points to a problem which must dwarf all others in the minds of German statesmen. The Socialists have achieved the extraordinary feat of winning seven Reichstag by-elections in succession. The approach of the 1911 elections makes the phenomenon all the more alarming from the Government's point of view. Pre-eminent among the causes of the 'red flood' is Prince Bülow's failure with his Finance Reform Bill in face of the opposition of the Extreme Conservatives, and Herr von Bethmann-Hollweg's unfortunate attempt at franchise reform in Prussia."

imprisonment, and when such convictions included lads in their teens and the venerable rectors of Universities.

But what must be the German's appreciation of the value of military victory and militarization when, mainly because of such, he finds himself engaged in a struggle which elsewhere less militarized nations settled a generation since? And what has the English defender of the militarist regimen, who holds the German system up for imitation, to say of it as a school of national discipline, when the Imperial Chancellor himself defends the refusal of democratic suffrage like that obtaining in England on the ground that the Prussian people have not yet acquired those qualities of public discipline which make it workable in England?

Yet what Prussia in the opinion of the Chancellor is not yet fit for, Scandinavian nations, Switzerland, Holland, Belgium have fitted themselves for without the aid of military victory and subsequent regimentation. Did not some one once say that the war had made Germany great and Germans small?[1]

---

[1] Mr. Dawson (*The Evolution of Modern Germany*, page 16) says: "It is questionable whether Germany counts as much to-day as an intellectual and moral agent in the world as when she was little better than a geographical expression. . . . When it comes to working with human material the German system [of education] breaks down. . . . German systems of education are very far from being successful in the making of

When we ascribe so large a measure of Germany's social progress (which no one as far as I know is concerned to deny) to the victories and regimentation, why do we conveniently overlook the social progress of the small States which I have just mentioned, where such progress on the material side has certainly been as great as, and on the moral side greater than, in Germany? Why do we overlook the fact that, if Germany has done well in certain social organizations, Scandinavia and Switzerland have done better? And why do we overlook the fact that, if regimentation is of such social value, it has been so completely inoperative in States which are more highly militarized even than Germany—in Turkey, in Russia?

But even assuming—a very large assumption—that regimentation has played the rôle in German progress which our Germano-maniacs would have us believe, is there any justification for supposing that a like process would be in any way adaptable to English conditions, social, moral, material, and historical?

Some of the acutest foreign students of English progress—men like Edmond Demolins—ascribe such to the very range of qualities which the German system is bound to crush: our aptitude

---

character and individuality. Educated Germans know this: hence the discontent of the enlightened classes with the political laws under which they live."

for initiative, our reliance upon our own efforts, our sturdy resistance to State interference (already weakening), our impatience with bureaucracy and red tape (also weakening), all of which is wrapped up with our general rebelliousness toward regimentation.

Though we base part of the defence of armaments on the plea that, economic interest apart, we desire to live our own life in our own way, to develop in our own fashion, is there no danger that with this mania for the imitation of German method Englishmen may Germanize England, though never a German soldier land on English soil?

Of course Englishmen argue thus: that, though we may adopt the French and German system of conscription, we could never fall a victim to the defects of those systems, and that the scandals which break out from time to time in France and Germany could never be duplicated by *our* barrack system, and that the military atmosphere of our own barracks, the training in our own army, would always be wholesome. But what do even its defenders say?

Mr. Blatchford himself says[1]:

Barrack life is bad. Barrack life will always be bad. It is never good for a lot of men to live together apart from home influences and feminine. It is not good

---

[1] See also the confirmatory verdict of Captain March Phillips quoted in the next chapter.

for women to live or work in communities of women. The sexes react upon each other; each provides for the other a natural restraint, a wholesome incentive. . . . The barracks and the garrison town are not good for young men. The young soldier, fenced and hemmed in by a discipline unnecessarily severe, and often stupid, has at the same time an amount of licence which is dangerous to all but those of strong good-sense and strong will. I have seen clean, good, nice boys come into the Army and go to the devil in less than a year. I am no Puritan. I am a man of the world; but any sensible and honest man who has been in the Army will know at once that what I am saying is entirely true, and is the truth expressed with much restraint and moderation. A few hours in a barrack-room would teach a civilian more than all the soldier stories ever written. When I joined the Army I was unusually unsophisticated for a boy of twenty. I had been brought up by a mother. I had attended Sunday-school and chapel. I had lived a quiet, sheltered life, and I had an astonishing amount to learn. The language of the barrack-room shocked me, appalled me. I could not understand half I heard; I could not credit much that I saw. When I began to realize the truth, I took my courage in both hands and went about the world I had come into with open eyes. So I learnt the facts, but I must not tell them.[1]

[1] *My Life in the Army*, p. 119.

CHAPTER V

THE DIMINISHING FACTOR OF PHYSICAL FORCE: PSYCHOLOGICAL RESULTS

Diminishing factor of physical force—Though diminishing, physical force has always been important in human affairs—What is underlying principle, determining advantageous and disadvantageous use of physical force?—Force that aids co-operation in accord with law of man's advance; force that is exercised for parasitism in conflict with such law and disadvantageous for both parties—Historical process of the abandonment of physical force—The Kahn and the London tradesman—Ancient Rome and modern Britain—The sentimental defence of war as the purifier of human life—The facts—The redirection of human pugnacity.

DESPITE the general tendency indicated by the facts touched on in the preceding chapter, it will be urged (with perfect justice) that, though the methods of Anglo-Saxondom as compared with those of the Spanish, Portuguese, and French Empires, may have been mainly commercial and industrial rather than military, war was a necessary part of expansion; that but for some fighting the Anglo-Saxons would have been ousted from North America or Asia, or would never have gained a footing there.

Does this, however, prevent us establishing on the basis of the facts exposed in the preceding chapter a general principle sufficiently definite to serve as a practical guide in policy, and to indicate reliably a general tendency in human affairs? Assuredly not. The principle which explains the uselessness of much of the force exerted by the military type of empire, and justifies in large part that employed by Britain, is neither obscure nor uncertain, although empiricism, rule of thumb (which is the curse of political thinking in our days, and more than anything else stands in the way of real progress), gets over the difficulty by declaring that no principle in human affairs can be pushed to its logical or theoretical conclusion; that what may be " right in theory " is wrong in practice.

Thus Mr. Roosevelt, who expresses with such admirable force and vigour the average thoughts of his hearers or readers, generally takes this line: We must be peaceful, but not too peaceful; warlike, but not too warlike; moral, but not too moral.[1]

With such verbal mystification are we encouraged to shirk the rough and stony places along the hard road of thinking. If we cannot carry a principle to its logical conclusion, at what point are we to stop? One will fix one and one another

[1] I do not think this last generalization does any injustice to the essay "Latitude and Longitude among Reformers" (*Strenuous Life*, pp. 41–61.

with equal justice. What is it to be "moderately" peaceful, or "moderately" warlike? Temperament and predilection can stretch such limitations indefinitely. This sort of thing only darkens counsel.

If a theory is right, it can be pushed to its logical conclusion; indeed, the only real test of its value is that it *can* be pushed to its logical conclusion. If it is wrong in practice, it is wrong in theory, for the right theory will take cognizance of all the facts, not only of one set.

In Chapter II. of this part (p. 161–6), I have very broadly indicated the process by which the employment of physical force in the affairs of the world has been a constantly diminishing factor since the day that primitive man killed his fellow man in order to eat him. Yet throughout the whole process the employment of force has been an integral part of progress, until even to-day in the most advanced nations force—the police-force—is an integral part of their civilization.

What, then, is the principle determining the advantageous and the disadvantageous employment of force?

Preceding the outline sketch just referred to, is another sketch indicating the real biological law of man's survival and advance; the key to that law is found in co-operation between men and struggle with nature. Mankind as a whole is the organism which needs to co-ordinate its parts in order to insure greater vitality by better adaptation to its environment.

Here, then, we get the key: force employed to secure completer co-operation between the parts makes for advance; force which runs counter to such co-operation, which is in any way a form of parasitism, makes for retrogression.

Why is the employment of force by the police justified? Because the bandit refuses to co-operate. He does not want to do his work, and live by what it is worth; he wants to live as a parasite, to take wealth, and give nothing in exchange. If he increased in numbers, co-operation between the various parts of the organism would be impossible; he makes for disintegration. He must be restrained, and so long as the police use their force in such restraint they are merely insuring co-operation. The police are not struggling against man; they are struggling with nature—crime.

Now, suppose that this police-force becomes the army of a political Power and the diplomats of that Power say to a smaller one: "We outnumber you; we are going to annex your territory, and you are going to pay us tribute." And the smaller Power says: "What are you going to give us for that tribute?" And the larger replies: "Nothing. You are weak; we are strong; we gobble you up. It is the law of life; always has been—always will be to the end."

Now, that police-force, become an army, is no longer making for co-operation; it has simply and purely taken the place of the bandits; and to approximate such an army to a police-force, and to say that because both operations involve the employment of force they both stand equally justified, is to ignore half the facts, and to be guilty of those lazy generalizations which we associate with savagery.

But the difference is more than a moral one. If the reader will again return to the little sketch referred to on a preceding page, he will probably agree that the diplomats of the larger power are acting in an extraordinarily stupid fashion. I say nothing of their sham philosophy (which happens, however, to be that of European state-craft to-day), by which this aggression is made to appear in keeping with the law of man's struggle for life, when, as a matter of fact, it is the very negation of that law; but we know *now* that they are taking a course which gives the least result, even from *their* point of view, for the effort expended.

Here we get the key also to the difference be-tween the respective histories of the military empires, like Spain, France, and Portugal, and the more industrial type, like England, which has been touched upon in the preceding chapter. Not the mere hazard of war, not a question of mere efficiency in the employment of force, has given to Great Britain influence in half a world, and taken it from Spain, but a radical, fundamental difference in underlying principles, however imperfectly realized. England's exercise of force has approximated on the whole to the rôle of police; Spain's to that of the diplomats of the suppositious Power just referred to. England's has made for co-operation; Spain's for the embarrassment of co-operation. England's has been in keeping with the real law of man's struggle; Spain's in keeping with the sham law, which the "blood and iron" empiricists are for ever throwing at our heads. For what has happened to all attempts to live on extorted tribute? They have all failed—failed miserably and utterly[1]—to such an extent that to-day the exaction of tribute has become an economic impossibility.

If, however, our suppositious diplomats, instead of asking for tribute, had said: "Your country is in disorder; your police is insufficient; our merchants are robbed and killed; we will lend you police and help you to maintain order. You will pay the police their just wage, and that is all," and had honestly kept to this office, their exercise of force would have aided human co-operation, not checked it. Again, it would have been a struggle, not against man, but against crime; the "predominant Power" would have been

---

[1] See Chapter VII., Part I.

living, not on other men, but by more efficient organization of man's fight with nature.

That is why in the first section of this book I have laid emphasis on the truth that the justification of past wars has no bearing on the problem which confronts us: the precise degree of fighting which was necessary a hundred and fifty years ago is a somewhat academic problem. The degree of fighting which is necessary to-day is the problem which confronts us, and a great many factors have been introduced into the problem since England won India and North America. The face of the world has changed, and the factors of conflict have changed radically: to ignore that is to ignore facts and to be guided by the worst form of theorizing and sentimentalism— the theorizing that will not recognize the facts. England does not need to maintain order in Germany, nor Germany in France; and the struggle between those nations is no part of man's struggle with nature—has no justification in the real law of human struggle; it is an anachronism; it finds its justification in a sham philosophy that will not bear the test of facts, and, responding to no real need, and achieving no real purpose, is bound with increasing enlightenment to come to an end.

I wish it were not everlastingly necessary to reiterate the fact that the world has moved. Yet for the purposes of this discussion it is. If to-day an Italian warship were suddenly to bombard Liverpool without warning, the Bourse in Rome would present a condition, and the bank-rate in Rome would take a jump that would ruin tens of thousands of Italians—do far more injury, probably, to Italy than to England. Yet if five hundred years ago Italian pirates had landed from the Thames and sacked London itself, not an Italian in Italy would have been a penny the worse for it.

Is it seriously urged that in the matter of the exercise of physical force therefore there is no difference in these two conditions: and is it seriously urged that the psychological phenomena which go with the exercise of physical force are to remain unaffected?

The preceding chapter is, indeed, the historical justification of the economic truths established in the first section of this book in the terms of the facts of the present-day world, which show that the predominating factor in survival is shifting from the physical to the intellectual plane. This evolutionary process has now reached a point in international affairs which involves the complete economic futility of military force. In the last chapter but one I dealt with the psychological consequence of this profound change in the nature of man's normal activities, showing that his nature is coming more and more to adapt itself to what he normally and for the greater part of his life—in most cases all his life—is engaged in, and is losing the impulses concerned with an abnormal and unusual occupation.

Why have I presented the facts in this order, dealt with the psychological result involved in this change before the change itself? I have adopted this order of treatment because the believer in war justifies his dogmatism for the most part by an appeal to what he alleges is the one dominating fact of the situation—i. e., that human nature is unchanging. Well, as will be seen from the penultimate chapter, such alleged fact does not bear investigation. Human nature is changing out of all recognition. Not only is man fighting less, but he is using all forms of physical compulsion less, and as a very natural result is losing those psychological attributes that go with the employment of physical force. And he is coming to employ physical force less because accumulated evidence is pushing him more and more to the conclusion that he can accomplish more easily that which he strives for by other means.

Few of us realize to what extent economic pressure—and I use that term in its just sense, as meaning, not only the struggle for money, but everything implied therein, well-being, social consideration, and the rest—has replaced physical force in human affairs. The primitive mind could not conceive a world in which everything was not regulated by force: even the great minds of antiquity could not believe the world would be an industrious one unless the great mass were made industrious by the use of physical force—*i. e.*, by slavery. Three fourths of those who peopled what is now Italy in Rome's palmiest days were slaves, chained in the fields when at work, chained at night in their dormitories, and those who were porters chained to the doorways. It was a society of slavery—fighting slaves, working slaves, cultivating slaves, official slaves, and Gibbon adds that the Emperor himself was a slave, "the first slave to the ceremonies he imposed." Great and penetrating as were many of the minds of antiquity, none of them show much conception of any condition of society in which the economic impulse could replace physical compulsion. And had they been told that the time would come when the world would work very much harder under the impulse of an abstract thing known as economic interest, they would have regarded such a statement as that of a mere sentimental theorist. Indeed, one need not go so far: if one had told an American slave-holder of sixty years since that the time would come when the South would produce more cotton under the free pressure of economic forces than under slavery, he would have made a like reply. He would probably have declared that "a good cowhide whip beats all economic pressure"—pretty much the sort of thing that one may hear from the mouth of the

average militarist to-day. Very "practical" and
virile, of course, but it has the disadvantage of
not being true.

And the presumed necessity for physical compulsion did not stop at slavery. As we have
already seen, it was accepted as an axiom in
statecraft that men's religious beliefs had to be
forcibly restrained, and not merely their religious
belief, but their very clothing; and we have hundreds of years of complicated sumptuary laws,
hundreds of years, also, of forcible control, or,
rather, the attempted forcible control, of prices and
trade, the elaborate system of monopolies, absolute prohibition of the entrance into the country
of certain foreign goods, the violation of which
prohibition was treated as a penal offence. We
had even the use of forced money, the refusal to
accept which was treated as a penal offence. In
many countries for years it was a crime to send
gold abroad—all indicating the domination of the
mind of man by the same curious obsession that
man's life must be ruled by physical force, and
it is only very slowly and very painfully that we
have arrived at the truth that men will work best
when left to unseen and invisible forces. And a
world in which physical force was withdrawn
from the regulation of men's labour, faith, clothes,
trade, language, travel, would have been absolutely
inconceivable to even the best minds during the
three or four thousand years of history which

mainly concern us. What is the central explanation of the profound change involved here—the shifting of the pivot in all human affairs in so far as they touch both the individual and the community, from physical ponderable forces to economic imponderable forces? It is surely that, strange as it may seem, the latter forces accomplish the desired result more efficiently and more readily than do the former, which even when they are not completely futile are in comparison wasteful and stultifying. It is the law of the economy of effort. Indeed, the use of physical force usually involves on those employing it the same limitation of freedom (even if in lesser degree) as that which it is desired to impose. Herbert Spencer illustrates the process in the following suggestive passage:

The exercise of mastery inevitably entails on the master himself some sort of slavery more or less pronounced. The uncultured masses and even the greater part of the cultured will regard this statement as absurd, and though many who have read history with an eye to essentials rather than to trivialities know that this is a paradox in the right sense—that is, true in fact though not seeming true—even they are not fully conscious of the mass of evidence establishing it and will be all the better for having illustrations recalled. Let me begin with the earliest and simplest which serves to symbolize the whole.

Here is a prisoner, with his hands tied and a cord

round his neck (as suggested by figures in Assyrian bas-reliefs), being led home by his savage conqueror, who intends to make him a slave. The one you say is captive and the other free. Are you quite sure the other is free? He holds one end of the cord and, unless he means his captive to escape, he must continue to be fastened by keeping hold of the cord in such way that it cannot easily be detached. He must be himself tied to the captive while the captive is tied to him. In other ways his activities are impeded and certain burdens are imposed on him. A wild animal crosses the track and he cannot pursue. If he wishes to drink of the adjacent stream he must tie up his captive lest advantage be taken of his defenceless position. Moreover, he has to provide food for both. In various ways he is no longer, then, completely at liberty; and these worries adumbrate in a simple manner the universal truth that the instrumentalities by which the subordination of others is effected themselves subordinate the victor, the master, or the ruler.[1]

Thus it comes that all nations attempting to live by conquest end by being themselves the victims of a military tyranny precisely similar to that which they hope to inflict; or, in other terms, that the attempt to impose by force of arms a disadvantageous commercial situation to the advantage of the conqueror ends in the conqueror's falling a victim to the very disadvantages from which he hoped by a process of spoliation to profit.

[1] *Facts and Comments*, p. 112.

But the truth that economic force always in the long run outweighs physical or military force is illustrated by the simple fact of the universal use of money—the fact that the use of money is not a thing which we choose or can shake off, but a thing imposed by the operation of forces stronger than our volition, stronger than the tyranny of the cruellest tyrant who ever reigned by blood and iron. I think it is one of the most astounding things, to the man who takes a fairly fresh mind to the study of history, that the most absolute despots—men who can command the lives of their subjects with a completeness and a nonchalance of which the modern western world furnishes no parallel—cannot command money. One asks oneself, indeed, why such an absolute ruler, able as he is by the sheer might of his position and by the sheer force of his power to take everything that exists in his kingdom, and able as he is to exact every sort and character of service, needs money, which is the means of obtaining goods or services by a freely consented exchange. Yet, as we know, it is precisely in ancient as in modern times the most absolute despot who is often the most financially embarrassed.[1] Is not this a demonstration that in

---

[1] Buckle (*History of Civilization*) points out that Philip II., who ruled half the world and drew tribute from the whole of South America, was so poor that he could not pay his personal servants or meet the daily expenses of the Court!

reality physical force is operative in only very narrow limits? It is no mere rhetoric but the cold truth to say that under absolutism it is a simple thing to get men's lives, but often impossible to get money. And the more, apparently, that physical force was exercised, the more difficult did the command of money become. And for a very simple reason—a reason which reveals in rudimentary form that principle of the economic futility of military power with which we are dealing. The phenomenon is best illustrated by a concrete case. If one go to-day into one of the independent despotisms of Central Asia one will find generally a picture of the most abject poverty. Why? Because the ruler has absolute power to take wealth whenever he sees it, to take it by any means whatever—torture, death, up to the completest limit of uncontrolled physical force. What is the result? The wealth is not created and torture itself cannot produce a thing which is non-existent. Step across the frontier into a State under British or Russian protection, and where the Khan has some sort of limits imposed on his powers. The difference is immediately perceptible: evidence of wealth and comfort in relative profusion, and other things being equal, the ruler whose physical force over his subjects is limited, is a great deal richer than the ruler whose physical force over his subjects is unlimited. In other words, the farther one gets away from physical force in the acquisition of wealth, the greater is the result for the effort expended. At the one end of the scale you get the despot in rags, exercising sway over what is probably a potentially rich territory, reduced to having to kill a man by torture in order to obtain a sum which, at the other end of the scale, a London tradesman will spend on a restaurant dinner for the purpose of sitting at table with a duke—or the thousandth part of the sum which the same tradesman will spend in philanthrophy or otherwise, for the sake of acquiring an empty title from a monarch who has lost all power of exercising any physical force whatsoever.

Which process, judged by all things that men desire, gives the better result, the physical force of blood and iron which we see, or the intellectual or psychic force which we cannot see? But the principle which operates in the limited fashion which I have indicated, operates with no less force in the larger domain of modern international politics. The wealth of the world is not represented by a fixed amount of gold or money now in the possession of one power, and now in the possession of another, but depends on all the unchecked multiple activities of a community for the time being. Check that activity, whether by imposing tribute, or disadvantageous commercial conditions, or an unwelcome administration which sets up sterile political agitation, and you get less wealth—less wealth for the conqueror, quite as much as for the conquered. The broadest statement of the case is that all experience— especially the experience indicated in the last chapter—shows that in trade by free consent carrying mutual benefit, we get larger results for effort expended than in the exercise of physical force which attempts to exact advantage for one party at the expense of the other. I am not arguing over again the thesis of the first part of this book; but, as we shall see presently, the general principle of the diminishing factor of physical force in the affairs of the world carries with it a psychological change in human nature which modifies radically our impulses to sheer physical conflict. What it is important just now to keep in mind is the incalculable intensification of this diminution of physical force by our mechanical development. The principle was obviously less true for Rome than it is for Great Britain: Rome, however imperfectly, lived largely by tribute. The sheer mechanical development of the modern world has rendered tribute in the Roman sense impossible. Rome did not have to create markets and find a field for the employment of her capital. We do. What result does this carry? Rome could afford to be relatively indifferent to the prosperity of her subject territory. We cannot. If the territory is not prosperous we have no market, and we have no field for our investments, and that is why we are checked at every point from doing what Rome was able to do.   You can to some extent exact tribute by force; you cannot compel a man to buy your goods by force if he does not want them, and has not got the money to pay for them.   Now, the difference which we see here has been brought about by the interaction of a whole series of mechanical changes—printing, gunpowder, steam, electricity, improved means of communication. It is the last-named which has mainly created the fact of credit—phenomena such as a synchronized bank-rate the world over, and re-acting bourses. Now, credit[1] is merely an extension of the use of money, and we can no more shake off the domination of the one than of the other.   We have seen that the bloodiest despot is himself the slave of money, in the sense that he is compelled to employ it.   In the same way no physical force can in the modern world set at nought the force of credit. It is no more possible for a great people of the modern world to live without credit than without money, of which it is a part.   Do we not here get the same fact that intangible economic forces are setting at nought the force of arms?

One of the curiosities of this mechanical development, with its deep-seated psychological results, is the general failure to realize the real bearings

[1] I mean by credit all the mechanism of exchange which replaces the actual use of metal or notes.

of each step therein. Printing was regarded, in the first instance, as merely a new-fangled process which threw a great many copying scribes and monks out of employment. But who realized that in the simple invention of printing there was the liberation of a force greater than the power of kings? It is only here and there that we find an isolated thinker having a glimmering of the political bearing of such inventions; of the conception of the great truth that the more man succeeds with his struggle with nature, the less must be the rôle of physical force between men, for the reason that human society has become with each success in the struggle against nature a completer organism. That is to say, that the interdependence of the parts has been increased, and that the possibility of one part injuring another without injury to itself has been diminished. Each part is more dependent on the other parts, and the impulses to injury therefore must in the nature of things be diminished. And that fact must, and is, daily redirecting human pugnacity. Our struggle is with our environment, not with one another; and those who talk as though struggle between the parts of the same organism must necessarily go on, and that impulses which are redirected every day can never receive the particular redirection involved in abandoning the struggle between States, ignorantly adopt the formula of science, but leave half the facts out of consideration. And just as the direction of the impulses will be changed, so will the instruments used in the struggle be changed; the force which we shall use for our needs will be the force of intelligence, of hard work, of character, of patience, self-control, and a developed brain, and the pugnacity and combativeness, which, instead of being used up and wasted in world conflicts of futile destructiveness, will be, and are being, diverted into the steady stream of rationally-directed effort. The virile impulses become, not the tyrant and the master, but the tool and servant of the controlling brain.

The conception of abstract imponderable forces by the human mind is a very slow process. All man's history reveals this. The theologian has always felt this difficulty. For thousands of years men could only conceive of evil as an animal with horns and a tail, going about the world devouring folk; abstract conceptions had to be made understandable by a crude anthropomorphism. Perhaps it is better that humanity should have some glimmering of the great facts of the universe, even though interpreted by legends of demons and goblins, and fairies, and the rest; but we cannot overlook the truth that the facts *are* distorted in the process, and our advance in the conception of morals is marked largely by the extent to which we can form an abstract conception of the fact of evil—none the less a fact because unembodied—without having to translate it into a non-existent person or animal with a forked tail.

As our advance in the understanding of morality is marked by our dropping these crude physical conceptions, is it not likely that our advance in the understanding of those problems, which so nearly affect our general well-being, will be marked in like manner?

Is it not somewhat childish and elementary to conceive of force only as the firing off of guns and the launching of *Dreadnoughts?* of struggle, as the physical struggle between men, instead of the application of man's energies to his contest with the planet? Is not the time coming when the real struggle will inspire us with the same respect and even the same thrill as that now inspired by a charge in battle; especially as the charges in battle are getting very out of date, and are shortly to disappear from our warfare? The mind which can only conceive of struggle as bombardment and charges is, of course, the Dervish mind. Not that Fuzzy Wuzzy is not a fine fellow. He is manly, sturdy, hardy, with a courage and warlike qualities generally which no European can equal. But the frail and spectacled English official is his master, and a few score of such will make themselves the masters of teeming thousands of Sudanese; the relatively unwarlike Englishman is doing the same thing all over Asia, and he is doing it by the simple virtue of superior brain and character, more thought, more rationalism, more steady and controlled hard work. It may be said that it is superior armament which does it. But what is the superior armament but the result of superior thought and work?—and even without the superior armament the larger intelligence would still do it; for what the Englishman does the Roman did of old, with the same arms as his vassal worlds. Force is indeed the master, but it is force of intelligence, character, and rationalism.

I can imagine the contempt with which the man of physical force greets the foregoing. To fight with words, to fight with talk! No, not words, but ideas. And something more than ideas. Their translation into practical effort, into organization, into the direction and administration of organization, into the strategy and tactics of human life.

And what, indeed, is modern warfare in its highest phases but this? Is it not an altogether out-of-date and ignorant view to picture soldiering as riding about on horseback, bivouacking in forests, sleeping in tents, and dashing gallantly at the head of shining regiments in plumes and breastplates, and pounding in serried ranks against the equally serried ranks of the cruel foe, storming breaches—"war," in short, of Mr. Henty's books for boys? How far does such conception correspond to the reality—to the

German conception? Even if the whole picture were not out of date, what proportion of the most military nation would ever be destined to witness it or to take part in it? Not one in ten thousand. What is the character even of military conflict but for the most part years of hard and steady work, somewhat mechanical, somewhat divorced from real life, but not a whit more exciting? That is true of all ranks; and in the higher ranks of the directing mind war has become an almost purely intellectual process. Was it not the late W. H. Stevens who painted Lord Kitchener as the sort of man who would have made an admirable manager of Harrod's Stores; who fought all his battles in his study, and regarded the actual fighting as the mere culminating incident in the whole process, the dirty and noisy part of it, which he would have been glad to get away from?

The real soldiers of our time—those who represent the brain of the armies—have a life not very different from that of men of any intellectual calling; much less of physical strife than is called for in many civil occupations; less than falls to the lot of engineers, ranchers, sailors, miners, and so on. Even with armies the pugnacity must be translated into intellectual and not into physical effort.[1]

[1] "Battles are no longer the spectacular heroics of the past. The army of to-day and to-morrow is a sombre gigantic machine devoid of melodramatic heroics . . . a machine that it requires

The very fact that war was for long an activity
which was in some sense a change and relaxation
from the more intellectual strife of peaceful life,
in which work was replaced by danger, thought
by adventure, accounted in no small part for its
attraction for us. But, as we have seen, war is
becoming as hopelessly intellectual and scientific
as any other form of work: officers are scientists,
the men are workmen, the army is a machine,
battles are "tactical operations," the charge is
becoming out of date; a little while and war will
become the least romantic of all professions.

In this domain, as in all others, intellectual
force is replacing sheer physical force, and we
are being pushed by the necessities even of this
struggle to be more rational in our attitude to war,
to rationalize our study of it; and as our attitude
generally becomes more scientific, so will the purely
impulsive element lose its empire over us. That
is one factor; but, of course, there is the greater
one. Our respect and admiration goes in the long
run, despite momentary setbacks, to those qualities
which achieve the results at which we are all in
common aiming. If those qualities are mainly
intellectual, it is the intellectual qualities that
will receive the tribute of our admiration. We
do not make a man Prime Minister because he

---

years to form in separate parts, years to assemble them together,
and other years to make them work smoothly and irresistibly"
(General Homer Lea in *The Valour of Ignorance*, p. 49).

holds the light-weight boxing championship, and
nobody knows or cares whether Mr. Balfour or
Mr. Asquith would be the better man at polo.
But in a condition of society in which physical
force was still the determining factor it would
matter all in the world, and even when other
factors had obtained considerable weight, as during the Middle Ages, physical combat went for
a great deal: the knight in his shining armour
established his prestige by his prowess in arms,
and the vestige of this still remains in those countries that retain the duel. To some small extent
—a very small extent—a man's dexterity with
sword and pistol will affect his political prestige
in Paris, Rome, Buda-Pesth, or Berlin. But these
are just interesting vestiges, and in the case of
Anglo-Saxon societies have disappeared entirely.
My commercial friend who declares that he works
fifteen hours a day mainly for the purpose of
going one better than his commercial rival across
the street, must beat that rival in commerce,
not in arms; it would satisfy no pride of either to
"have it out" in the back garden in their shirt-
sleeves. Nor is there the least danger that one
will stick a knife into the other.

Are all these factors to leave the national relationship unaffected? Have they left it unaffected?
Does the military prowess of Russia or of Turkey
inspire any particular satisfaction in the minds
of the individual Russian or of the individual

Turk? Does it inspire Europe with any especial
respect? Would not most of us just as soon be a
non-military American as a military Turk? Do
not, in short, all the factors show that sheer physical force is losing its prestige as much in the
national as in the personal relationship?

I am not overlooking the case of Germany.
Does the history of Germany during the last half-
century show the blind instinctive pugnacity
which is supposed to be so overpowering an element in international relationship as to outweigh
all question of material interest altogether?
Does the commonly accepted history of the trick-
ery and negotiation which preceded the 1870
conflict, the cool calculation of those who swayed
Germany's policy during those years, show that
subordination to the blind lust for fight which the
militarist would persuade us is always to be an
element in our international conflicts? Does it
not, on the contrary, show that German destinies
were swayed by very cool and calculating motives
of interest, though interest interpreted in terms
of political and economic doctrines which the
development of the last thirty years or so have
demonstrated to be obsolete? Nor am I overlooking the "Prussian tradition," the fact of a
firmly entrenched, aristocratic status, the inter-
lectual legacy of pagan knighthood and Heaven
knows what else. But even a Prussian Junker
becomes less of an energumen as he becomes more

of a scientist, and although German science has of late spent its energies in somewhat arid specialism, the influence of more enlightened conceptions in sociology and statecraft must sooner or later emerge from any thoroughgoing study of political and economical problems. Of course, there are survivals of the old temper, but can it seriously be argued that when the futility of physical force to accomplish those ends towards which we are all striving is fully demonstrated we shall go on maintaining war as a sort of theatrical entertainment? Has such a thing ever happened in the past, when our impulses and sporting instincts came into conflict with our larger social and economic interests?

All this, in other words, involves a great deal more than the mere change in the character of warfare. It involves a fundamental change in our psychological attitude thereto. Not only does it show that on every side, even the military side, conflict must become less impulsive and instinctive, more rational and sustained, less the blind strife of mutually hating men and more and more the calculated effort to a definite end; but it will affect the very well-springs of much of the present defence of war.

Why is it that the authorities I have quoted in the first chapter of this section—Mr. Roosevelt, Von Moltke, Renan, and the English clergymen— sing the praises of war as such a valuable school of morals? Do these war advocates urge that war of itself is desirable? Would they urge going to war unnecessarily or unjustly merely because it is good for us? Emphatically no. Their argument in the last analysis resolves itself into this: that war, though bad, has redeeming qualities, as teaching staunchness, courage, and the rest. Well, so has cutting our legs off, or an operation for appendicitis. But who ever composed epics on typhoid fever or cancer? Such advocates might object to the efficient policing of a town because, while it is full of cut-throats, the inhabitants would be taught courage. One can almost imagine this sort of teacher pouring scorn upon those weaklings who want to call upon the police for protection, and saying, "Police are for sentimentalists and cowards and men of slothful ease. What will become of the strenuous life if you introduce police?" [1]

[1] The following letter to the *Manchester Guardian* is worth reproduction in this connection:

"SIR,—I see that 'The Church's Duty in regard to War' is to be discussed at the Church Congress. This is right. For a year the heads of our Church have been telling us what war is and does—that it is a school of character; that it sobers men, cleans them, strengthens them, knits their hearts; makes them brave, patient, humble, tender, prone to self-sacrifice. Watered by 'war's red rain,' one Bishop tells us, virtue grows; a cannonade, he points out, is an 'oratorio'—almost a form of worship. True; and to the Church men look for help to save their souls from starving for lack of this good school, this kindly rain, this sacred music. Congresses are apt to lose themselves in wastes of words. This

The whole thing falls to the ground; and if we do not compose poems about typhoid it is because typhoid has no attraction for us and war has. That is the bottom of the whole matter, and it simplifies things a great deal to admit honestly that while no one is thrilled by the spectacle of disease, most of us are thrilled by the spectacle of war—that while none of us are fascinated by the spectacle of a man struggling with a disease, most

---

one must not, surely cannot, so straight is the way to the goal. It has simply to draft and submit a new Collect for war in our time, and to call for the reverent but firm emendation, in the spirit of the best modern thought, of those passages in Bible and Prayer-Book by which even the truest of Christians and the best of men have at times been blinded to the duty of seeking war and ensuing it. Still, man's moral nature cannot, I admit, live by war alone; nor do I say with some that peace is wholly bad. Even amid the horrors of peace you will find little shoots of character fed by the gentle and timely rains of plague and famine, tempest and fire; simple lessons of patience and courage conned in the schools of typhus, gout, and stone; not oratorios, perhaps, but homely anthems and rude hymns played on knife and gun in the long winter nights. Far from me to 'sin our mercies,' or to call mere twilight dark. Yet dark it may become; for remember that even these poor makeshift schools of character, these second-bests, these halting substitutes for war—remember that the efficiency of every one of them, be it hunger, accident, ignorance, sickness, or pain, is menaced by the intolerable strain of its struggles with secular doctors, plumbers, inventors, schoolmasters, and policemen. Every year thousands who would once have been braced and steeled by manly tussles with smallpox or diphtheria are robbed of that blessing by the great changes made in our drains. Every year thousands of women and children must go their way bereft of the rich spiritual experience of the widow and the orphan."

of us are fascinated by the spectacle of men struggling with one another in war. There is something in warfare, in its story, and in its paraphernalia, which profoundly stirs the emotions and sends the blood tingling through the veins of the most peaceable of us, and appeals to I know not what remote instincts, to say nothing of our natural admiration for courage, our love of adventure, of intense movement and action. But this romantic fascination resides to no small extent in that very spectacular quality of which modern conditions are depriving war.

As we become a little more educated we realize that human psychology is a complex and not a simple thing; that because we yield ourselves to the thrill of the battle spectacle we are not bound to conclude that the processes behind it and the nature behind it are necessarily all admirable; that the readiness to die is not the only test of virility or a fine or noble nature.

In the book to which I have just referred (Mr. Steevens' *With Kitchener to Khartoum*) I read the following:

And the Dervishes? The honour of the fight must still go with the men who died. Our men were perfect, but the Dervishes were superb—beyond perfection. It was their largest, best, and bravest army that ever fought against us for Mahdism, and it died worthily of the huge empire that Mahdism won and kept so long. Their riflemen, mangled by every kind of death and torment that man can devise, clung round the black flag and the green, emptying their poor rotten home-made cartridges dauntlessly. Their spearmen charged death every minute hopelessly. Their horsemen led each attack, riding into the bullets till nothing was left. . . . Not one rush, or two, or ten, but rush on rush, company on company never stopping, though all their view that was not unshaken enemy, was the bodies of the men who had rushed before them. A dusky line got up and stormed forward: it bent, broke up, fell apart, and disappeared. Before the smoke had cleared another line was bending and storming forward in the same track. . . . From the green army there now came only death-enamoured desperadoes, strolling one by one towards the rifles, pausing to shake a spear, turning aside to recognize a corpse, then, caught by a sudden jet of fury, bounding forward, checking, sinking limply to the ground. Now under the black flag in a ring of bodies stood only three men, facing the three thousand of the Third Brigade. They folded their arms about the staff and gazed steadily forward. Two fell. The last Dervish stood up and filled his chest; he shouted the name of his God and hurled his spear. Then he stood quite still, waiting. It took him full; he quivered, gave at the knees, and toppled with his head on his arms and his face towards the legions of his conquerors.

Let us be honest. Is there anything in European history—Cambronne, the Light Brigade, anything you like—more magnificent than this? If we are honest we shall say no.

But note what follows in Mr. Steevens' narrative. What sort of nature should we expect those savage heroes to display? Cruel, perhaps; but at least loyal. They will stand by their chief. Men who can die like that will not betray him for gain. They are uncorrupted by commercialism. Well, a few chapters after the scene just described, one may read this:

As a ruler the Khalifa finished when he rode out of Omdurman. His own pampered Baggara horsemen killed his men and looted the cattle that were to feed them. Somebody betrayed the position of the reserve camels. . . . His followers took to killing one another. . . . The whole population of the Khalifa's capital was now racing to pilfer the Khalifa's grain. . . . Wonderful workings of the savage mind! Six hours before they were dying in regiments for their master; now they were looting his corn. Six hours before they were slashing our wounded to pieces; now they were asking us for coppers.

This difficulty with the soldier's psychology is not special to Dervishes or to savages. An able and cultivated British officer writes:

Soldiers as a class are men who have disregarded the civil standard of morality altogether. They simply ignore it. It is no doubt why civilians fight shy of them. In the game of life they do not play the same rules, and the consequence is a good deal of misunderstanding, until finally the civilian says he will not play with Tommy any more. In soldiers' eyes lying, theft, drunkenness, bad language, etc., are not evils at all. They steal like jackdaws. As to language, I used to think the language of a merchant ship's forecastle pretty bad, but the language of Tommies, in point of profanity and in point of obscenity, beats it hollow. This department is a speciality of his. Lying he treats with the same large charity. To lie like a trooper is quite a sound metaphor. He invents all sorts of elaborate lies for the mere pleasure of inventing them. Looting, again, is one of his preferred joys, not merely looting for profit, but looting for the sheer fun of the destruction.[1]

(Please, please, dear reader, do not say that I am slandering the British soldier. I am quoting a British officer, and a British officer, moreover, who is keenly in sympathy with the person that he has just been describing.) He adds:

Are thieving, and lying, and looting, and bestial talk very bad things? If they are, Tommy is a bad man. But for some reason or other, since I got to know him I have thought rather less of the iniquity of these things than I did before.

I do not know which of the two passages that I have quoted is the more striking commentary on the moral influence of military training: that such training should have the effect which Captain March Phillips describes, or the fact that the

---

[1] Captain March Phillips, *With Remington.*

second judgment should be given by a man of sterling character and culture—the judgment, that is, that thieving, and lying, and looting, and bestial talk do not matter. Which fact constitutes the severer condemnation of the ethical atmosphere of militarism and military training? Which is the more convincing testimony to the corrupting influences of war? I leave it to the reader.

To do the soldiers justice, they very rarely raise this plea of war being a moral training school. "War itself," said on one occasion an officer, "is an infernally dirty business. But somebody has got to do the dirty work of the world, and I am glad to think that it is the business of the soldier to prevent rather than to make war."

Not that I am concerned to deny that we owe a great deal to the soldier. I do not know even why we should deny that we owe a great deal to the Viking. Neither the one nor the other were in every aspect despicable. Both have bequeathed a heritage of courage, sturdiness, hardihood, and a spirit of ordered adventure; the capacity to take hard knocks and to give them; comradeship and rough discipline—all this and much more. It is not true to say of any emotion that it is wholly and absolutely good, or wholly and absolutely bad. The same psychological force which made the Vikings destructive and cruel pillagers made their descendants sturdy and resolute pioneers and colonists; and the same emotional force

which turns so much of Africa into a sordid and
bloody shambles would, with a different direction
and distribution, turn it into a garden. Is it for
nothing that the splendid Scandinavian race,
who have converted their rugged and rock-strewn
peninsula into a group of prosperous and stable
States, which are an example to Europe, and have
infused the great Anglo-Saxon stock with something of their sane but noble idealism, have the
blood of Vikings in their veins? Is there no place
for the free play of all the best qualities of the
Viking and the soldier in a world still so sadly
in need of men with courage enough, for instance,
to face the truth, however difficult it may seem,
however unkind to our pet prejudices?

There is not the least necessity for the peace
advocate to ignore facts in this matter. The
race of man loves a soldier just as boys we used to
love the pirate, and many of us, perhaps to our
very great advantage, remain in part boys our
lives through. But just as growing out of boy-
hood we regretfully discover the sad fact that we
cannot be a pirate, that we cannot even hunt
Indians, nor be a scout, not even a trapper, so
surely the time has come to realize that we have
grown out of soldiering. The romantic appeal
of war was just as true of the ventures of the old
Vikings, and even later of piracy.[1] Yet we super-

[1] Professor William James says: "Greek history is a panorama
of war for war's sake and . . of the utter ruin of a civilization

seded the Viking and we hanged the pirate, though
I doubt not we loved him while we hanged him;
and I am not aware that those who urged the
suppression of piracy were vilified, except by the
pirates, as maudlin sentimentalists who ignored
human nature, or, as Mr. Lea's phrase has it, as
"half-educated, sick-brained visionaries, denying
the inexorability of the primordial law of struggle."
Piracy interfered seriously with the trade and
industry of those who desired to earn for themselves as good a living as they could get, and to
obtain from this imperfect world all that it had to
offer. Piracy was magnificent, doubtless, but it
was not business. We are prepared to sing about
the Viking, but not to tolerate him on the high
seas; and those of us who are quite prepared to
give the soldier his due place in poetry and legend
and romance, quite prepared to admit, with Mr.
Roosevelt and Von Moltke and the rest, the qualities which perhaps we owe to him, and without
which we should be poor folk indeed, are nevertheless inquiring whether the time has not come to
place him (or a good portion of him) gently on the
poetic shelf with the Viking; or at least to find
other field for those activities, which, however
much we may be attracted by them, have in

---

which in intellectual respects was perhaps the highest the earth
has ever seen. The wars were purely piratical. Pride, gold,
women, slaves, excitement, were their only motives." *McClure's
Magazine*, Aug., 1910.

their present form little place in a world in which,
though, as Bacon has said, men love danger better
than travail, travail is bound, alas!—despite ourselves, and whether we fight Germany or not, and
whether we win or lose—to be our lot.

CHAPTER VI

THE STATE AS A PERSON: A FALSE ANALOGY AND ITS CONSEQUENCES

Why aggression upon a State does not correspond to aggression upon an individual—Our changing conception of collective responsibility—Psychological progress in this connection—The factors breaking down the homogeneous personality of States are of very recent growth.

DESPITE the common idea to the contrary, we dearly love an abstraction—especially, apparently, an abstraction which is based on half the facts. Whatever the foregoing chapters may have proved, they have at least proved this, that the character of the modern State, by virtue of a multitude of new factors which are special to our age, differs essentially and fundamentally from the ancient. Yet even those who have great and justified authority in this matter will still appeal to Aristotle's conception of the State as final, with the implication that everything which has happened since Aristotle's time should be calmly disregarded.

What some of those things are the preceding

chapters have indicated: First, there is the fact of
the change in human nature itself, bound up with
the general drift away from the use of physical
force—a drift explained by the unromantic fact
that physical force does not give so much response
to effort expended as do other forms of energy.
There is an interconnection of psychological and
purely mechanical development in all this which
it is not necessary to disentangle here. The
results are evident enough. Very rarely, and to
an infinitesimal extent, do we now employ force
for the achievement of our ends. But, added to
all these factors, there is still a further one bound
up with them which remains to be considered,
and which has perhaps a directer bearing on the
question of continued conflict between nations than
any one of them.

Conflicts between nations and international
pugnacity generally imply a conception of a State
as a homogeneous whole, having the same sort
of responsibility that we attach to a person who,
hitting us, provokes us to hit back. Now only
to a very small and rapidly diminishing extent
can a State be regarded as such a person. There
may have been a time—Aristotle's time—when
this was the case. Yet the fine-spun theories
on which are based the necessity for the use
of force as between nations, and the propositions
that the relationship of nations can only be determined by force and that international pugnacity

will always be expressed by a physical struggle between nations, all arise from this fatal analogy, which in truth corresponds to very few of the facts.

Thus Professor Spenser Wilkinson, whose contributions to this subject have such a deserved weight, infers that what will permanently render the abandonment of force as between nations impossible is the principle that "the employment of force for the maintenance of right is the foundation of all civilized human life, for it is the fundamental function of the State, and apart from the State there is no civilization, no life worth living. . . . The mark of the State is sovereignty, or the identification of force and right, and the measure of the perfection of the State is furnished by the completeness of this identification."

All of which, whether true or not, is irrelevant to the matter in hand. Professor Spenser Wilkinson attempts to illustrate his thesis by quoting a case which would seem to imply that those who take their stand against the necessity of armaments do so on the ground that the employment of force is wicked. There may be such, but it is not necessary to introduce the question of right. If means other than force gave the same result more easily, with less effort to ourselves, why discuss the abstract right? And when he reinforces the appeal to this irrelevant abstract principle by a case which, while apparently relevant, is in truth irrelevant, he has successfully confused the whole

issue.   After quoting three verses from Matt. v.,
Professor Spenser Wilkinson says[1]:

There are those who believe, or fancy they believe,
that the words I have quoted involve the principle
that the use of force or violence between man and
man or between nation and nation is wicked.   To the
man who thinks it right to submit to any violence or
be killed rather than use violence in resistance I have
no reply to make; the world cannot conquer him, and
fear has no hold upon him.   But even he can carry
out his doctrine only to the extent of allowing himself to be ill-treated, as I will now convince him.
Many years ago the people of Lancashire were horri-
fied by the facts reported in a trial for murder.   In
a village on the outskirts of Bolton lived a young
woman, much liked and respected as a teacher in one
of the Board-schools.   On her way home from school
she was accustomed to follow a footpath through a
lonely wood, and here one evening her body was
found.   She had been strangled by a ruffian who had
thought in this lonely place to have his wicked will
of her.   She had resisted successfully, and he had
killed her in the struggle.   Fortunately the murderer
was caught, and the facts ascertained from circum-
stantial evidence were confirmed by his confession.
Now the question I have to ask the man who takes
his stand on the passage quoted from the Gospel is
this: "What would have been your duty had you been
walking through that wood and come upon the girl
struggling with the man who killed her?   This is

---

[1] *Britain at Bay.*

the crucial factor which, I submit, utterly destroys the doctrine that the use of violence is in itself wrong. The right or wrong is not in the employment of force, but simply in the purpose for which it is used. What the case establishes, I think, is that to use violence in resistance to violent wrong is not only right, but necessary.

The above presents very cleverly the utterly false analogy with which we are dealing. Professor Spenser Wilkinson's cleverness, indeed, is a little Machiavellian, because he approximates non-resisters of a very extreme type to those who advocate agreement among nations in the matter of armaments—a false approximation, for the proportion of those who advocate reduction of armaments on such grounds is so small that they can be disregarded in this discussion. A movement which is identified with some of the acutest minds in European affairs cannot be disposed of by associating it with such a theory. But the basis of the fallacy is in the approximation of a State to a person. Now a State is not a person, and is becoming less such every day, and the difficulty which Professor Spenser Wilkinson indicates is a doctrinaire difficulty, not a real one. Professor Wilkinson would have us infer that a State can be injured or killed in the same simple way in which it is possible to kill or injure a person, and that because there must be physical force to restrain aggression upon persons, there must be physical force to restrain aggression upon States; and because there must be physical force to execute the judgment of a court of law in the case of individuals, there must be physical force to execute the judgment rendered by a decision as to differences between States. All of which is false, and arrived at by approximating a person to a State, and disregarding the numberless facts which render a person different from a State.

How do we know that these difficulties are doctrinaire ones? It is the British Empire which supplies the answer. The British Empire is made up in large part of a congeries of practically independent States, over whose acts not only does Great Britain exercise no control, but concerning whom Great Britain has surrendered in advance any intention of employing force.[1] The British States have disagreements among themselves. They may or may not refer their differences to the British Government, but if they do, is Great Britain going to send an army to Canada, say, to enforce her judgment? Everyone knows that that is impossible. Even when one State commits what is in reality a serious breach of international comity on another, not only does Great Britain do nothing herself, but so far as she interferes at all, it is to prevent the employment of physical force. For years now British Indians have been subjected to most cruel and unjust treatment in

[1] See quotation from Sir C. P. Lucas, pp. 112–17.

the State of Natal.[1] The British Government
makes no secret of the fact that she regards this
treatment as unjust and cruel; were Natal a
foreign State, it is conceivable that she would
employ force, but, following the principle laid
down by Sir C. P. Lucas, "whether they are right
or whether they are wrong, more perhaps when
they are wrong than when they are right, they
cannot be made amenable by force," the two States
are left to adjust the difficulty as best they may
without resort to force. In the last resort the
British Empire reposes upon the expectation that
its colonies will behave as civilized communities,
and in the long-run the expectation is, of course,
a well-founded one, because if they do not so
behave, retribution will come more surely by the
ordinary operation of social and economic forces
than it could come by any force of arms.

The case of the British Empire is not an isolated
one. The fact is that most of the States of the
World maintain their relations one with another
without any possibility of a resort to force; half
the States of the world have no means of enforcing
by arms such wrongs as they may suffer at the
hands of other States. Thousands of Englishmen, for instance, make their homes in Switzerland, and it has happened that wrongs have been
suffered by Englishmen at the hands of the Swiss
Government. Would, however, the relations be-

[1] See details on this matter given in Chapter VII, Part I.

tween the two States, or the practical standard of protection of British subjects in Switzerland, be any the better were Switzerland the whole time threatened by the might of Great Britain? Switzerland knows herself practically free from the possibility of the exercise of armed force, but that has not prevented her behaving as a civilized community towards British subjects.

What is the real guarantee of the good behaviour of one State to another? It is the elaborate interdependence, which, not only in the economic sense, but in every sense, makes an unwarrantable aggression of one State upon another react upon the interests of the aggressor. Switzerland has every interest in affording an absolutely secure asylum to British subjects; that fact, and not the might of the British Empire, gives protection to British subjects in Switzerland. Where, indeed, the British subject has to depend upon the force of his Government for protection it is a very frail protection indeed, because in practice the use of that force is so cumbersome, so difficult, so costly, that any other means are to be preferred to it. When the traveller in Greece had to depend upon British arms, great as were relatively the force of those arms, it proved but a very frail protection. In the same way, when physical force was used to impose on the South American and Central American States the observance of their financial obligations, such an attempt failed

utterly and miserably—so miserably that Great
Britain finally surrendered any attempt at such
enforcement. What means have succeeded? The
bringing of those countries under the influence of
the great economic currents of our time, so that
now property is infinitely more secure in Mexico
and in Argentina than it was when British gun-
boats were bombarding their ports. More and
more in international relationship is the purely
economic motive—and the economic motive is
only one of several possible ones—being employed
to replace the use of physical force. Austria the
other day was untouched by any threat of the
employment of the Turkish army when the annexation of Bosnia and Herzegovina was con-
summated, but when the Turkish population
enforced a very successful commercial boycott of
Austrian goods and Austrian ships, Austrian
merchants and public opinion made it quickly
plain to the Austrian Government that pressure of
this nature was not one that could be disregarded.

I anticipate the plea that while the elaborate
interconnection of economic forces renders the
employment of force as between nations unnecessary in so far as their material interests are
concerned, those forces cannot cover a case of
aggression upon what may be termed the moral
property of nations. A critic of the first edition
of this book[1] writes:

[1] *Morning Post*, April 21, 1910. I pass over the fact that to

The State is the only complete form in which human society exists, and there are a multitude of phenomena which will be found only as manifestations of human life in the form of a society united by the political bond into a State. The products of such society are law, literature, art, and science, and it has yet to be shown that apart from that form of society known as the State, the family or education or development of character is possible. The State, in short, is an organism or living thing which can be wounded and can be killed, and like every other living thing requires protection against wounding and destruction. . . . Conscience and morals are products of social and not of individual life, and to say that the sole purpose of the State is to make possible a decent livelihood is as though a man should say that the sole object of human life is to satisfy the interests of existence. A man cannot live any kind of life without food, clothing, and shelter, but that condition does not abolish or diminish the value of the life industrial, the life intellectual, or the life artistic. The State is the condition of all these lives, and its purpose is to sustain them. That is why the State must defend itself. In the ideal the State represents and embodies the whole people's conception of what is true, of what is beautiful, and of what is right, and it is the sublime quality of human nature

---

cite all this as a reason for armaments is absurd. Does the *Morning Post* really suggest that the Germans are going to attack England because they don't like the English taste in art, or music, or cooking? The notion that preferences of this sort need the protection of " Dreadnoughts " is surely to bring the whole thing within the domain of the grotesque.

that every great nation has produced citizens ready to sacrifice themselves rather than submit to an external force attempting to dictate to them a conception other than their own of what is right.

One is, of course, surprised to see the foregoing in the *Morning Post;* the concluding phrase would justify the present agitation in India or in Egypt or Ireland against British rule. What is that agitation but an attempt on the part of the peoples of those States to resist "an external force attempting to dictate to them a conception other than their own of what is right"? Fortunately, however, for British Imperialism a people's conception of "what is true, of what is beautiful, and of what is right," and their maintenance of that conception need not necessarily have anything whatever to do with the particular administrative conditions under which they may live— the only thing that a conception of "State" predicates. The fallacy which runs through the whole passage just quoted, and which makes it, in fact, nonsense, is the same fallacy which dominates the quotation that I have made from Professor Spenser Wilkinson's book, *Britain at Bay*—namely, the approximation of a State to a person, the conception of a State as the embodiment of "the whole people's conception of what is true, etc." A State is nothing of the sort. Take the British Empire. This State embodies not a homogeneous conception, but a series of often absolutely contradictory conceptions of "what is true, etc."; it embodies the Mohammedan, the Buddhist, the Copt, the Catholic, the Protestant, the Pagan conceptions of right and truth. The fact which vitiates the whole of this conception of a State is that the frontiers which define the State do not coincide with the conception of any of those things which the *Morning Post* critic has enumerated; there is no such thing as British morality as opposed to French or German morality, or art, or industry. One may, indeed, talk of an English conception of life, because that is a conception of life peculiar to England, but it would be opposed to the conception of life in other parts of the same State in Ireland, in Scotland, in India, in Egypt, in Jamaica. And what is true of England is true of all the great modern States. Every one of them includes conceptions absolutely opposed to other conceptions in the same State, but many of them absolutely agreeing with conceptions in foreign States. The British State includes in Ireland a Catholic conception in cordial agreement with the Catholic conception in Italy, but in cordial disagreement with the Protestant conception in Scotland, or the Mohammedan conception in Bengal. The real and only divisions of all those ideals which the critic enumerates cut right across State divisions, disregard them entirely. And yet again it is only the

State divisions which military conflict has in view.

What was one of the reasons leading to the cessation of religious wars between States? It was that religious conceptions cut across the State frontiers, so that the State ceased to coincide with the religious divisions of Europe, and a condition of things was brought about in which a Protestant Sweden was allied with a Catholic France. This rendered the conflict absurd, and religious war became an anachronism.

But is not precisely the same thing taking place with reference to the conflicting conceptions of life which now separate men in Europe? Have we not in Great Britain now the same doctrinal struggle which is going on in France and Germany and in America? To take one instance—social conflict. On the one side in each case are all the interests bound up with order, authority, individual freedom without reference to the comfort of the weak, and on the other the reconstruction of human society along hitherto untried lines. These problems are for most men probably—are certainly coming to be, if they are not now—much more profound and fundamental than any conception which coincides with or can be identified with State divisions. Indeed, what are the conceptions the divisions in which coincide with the political frontiers of the British Empire, in view of the fact that that Empire includes nearly every race and nearly every religion under the sun? It may be said, of course, that in the case of Germany and Russia we have an autocratic conception of social organization as compared with a conception based on individual freedom in England and America.

Both Mr. Hyndman and Mr. Blatchford seem to take this view. "To me," says the former, "it is quite evident that if we Socialists were to achieve success we should at once be liable to attack from without by the military powers," which calmly overlooks the fact that Socialism and anti-militarism have gone much farther and are far better organized in the "military" States than they are in England, and that the military governments have all their work cut out as it is to keep those tendencies in check within their own borders without quixotically undertaking to perform the same service in other States.

This conception of the State as the political embodiment of homogeneous doctrine is due in large part not only to the distortion produced by false analogy, but to the survival of a terminology which has become obsolete, as, indeed, the whole of this subject is vitiated by those two things. The State in ancient times was much more such a personality than it is to-day, and it is mainly quite modern tendencies which have broken up its doctrinal homogeneity, and such break-up has results which are of the very first importance in their bearing upon international pugnacity. The matter deserves careful examination. Professor William McDougal, in his fascinating work, *An Introduction to Social Psychology*, says in the chapter on the instinct of pugnacity:

The replacement of individual by collective pugnacity is most clearly illustrated by barbarous peoples living in small, strongly organized communities. Within such communities individual combat and even expressions of personal anger may be almost completely suppressed, while the pugnacious instinct finds itself in perpetual warfare between communities whose relations remain subject to no law. As a rule no material benefit is gained, and often none is sought, in these tribal wars. . . . All are kept in constant fear of attack, whole villages are often exterminated, and the population is in this way kept down very far below the limit on which any pressure on the means of subsistence could arise. This perpetual warfare, like the squabbles of a roomful of quarrelsome children, seems to be almost wholly and directly due to the uncomplicated operation of the instinct of pugnacity. No material benefits are sought; a few heads and sometimes a slave or two are the only trophies gained, and if one asks an intelligent chief why he keeps up this senseless practice, the best reason he can give is that unless he does so his neighbours will not respect him and his people, and will fall upon them and exterminate them.

Now, how does such hostility as that indicated in this passage differ from the hostility which marks international differences in our day? In

certain very evident respects. It does not suffice
in our case that the foreigner should be merely
a foreigner for us to want to kill him: there must
be some conflict of interest. We are completely
indifferent to the Scandinavian, the Belgian, the
Dutchman, the Spaniard, the Austrian, and the
Italian, and we are supposed for the moment
to be greatly in love with the French. The German is the enemy. But ten years ago it was the
Frenchman who was the enemy, and Mr. Chamberlain was talking of an alliance with the Germans
—our natural allies, he called them—while it was
for France that he reserved his attacks.[1] It
cannot be, therefore, that there is any inherent
racial hostility in our national character, because
the Germans have not changed their nature
in ten years, nor the French theirs. If to-day
the French are quasi-allies of the English and
the Germans enemies it is simply because the
respective interests or apparent interests have
modified in the last ten years, and political
preferences have modified with them. In other
words, national hostilities follow the exigencies
of real or imagined political interests. Surely the
point need not be laboured, seeing that the English
have boxed the compass of the whole of Europe

---

[1] I refer to the remarkable speech in which Mr. Chamberlain
notified France that she must "mend her manners or take the
consequences" (see London daily papers between November 28
and December 5, 1899).

in their likes and dislikes, and poured their hatred upon the Spaniards, the Dutch, the Americans, the Danes, the Russians, the Germans, the French, and again the Germans, all in turn.

The thing is a commonplace of individual relationships. "I never noticed that his collars were dirty till he got in my way," said some one of a rival. The second point of difference with Professor McDougal's savage is that when we get to grips our conflict does not include the whole tribe; we do not, in the Biblical fashion, exterminate men, women, children, and cattle. Enough of the old Adam remains for us to detest the women and children, so that a British Poet Laureate could write of the "whelps and dams of murderous foes"; but at least we do not slaughter them.[1]

But there is a third fact which we must note—that Professor McDougal's nation was made up

[1] Not that a very great period separates us from such methods. Froude quotes Maltby's Report to Government as follows: "I burned all their corn and houses, and committed to the sword all that could be found. In like manner I assailed a castle. When the garrison surrendered, I put them to the misericordia of my soldiers. They were all slain. Thence I went on, sparing none which came in my way, which cruelty did so amaze their fellows that they could not tell where to bestow themselves." Of the commander of the English forces at Munster we read: "He diverted his forces into East Clanwilliam, and harassed the country; killed all mankind that were found therein . . . not leaving behind us man or beast, corn or cattle . . . sparing none of what quality, age, or sex soever. Besides many burned to death, we killed man, woman, child, horse, or beast, or whatever we could find."

of a single tribe entirely homogeneous. Even the
fact of living across a river was sufficient to turn
another tribe into foreigners and to involve a
desire to kill them. The development from that
stage to the present has included, in addition to the
two factors just enumerated, this: we now include
as fellow-countrymen many who would under the
old conception necessarily be foreigners, and the
process of our development, economic and otherwise, has made of foreigners, between whom, in
General Lea's philosophy, there should exist this
"primordial hostility leading inevitably to war,"
one State from which all conflict of interest has
disappeared entirely. The modern State of France
includes what were, even in historical times,
eighty separate and warring States, since each of
the old Gallic cities represented a different State.
In England we have come to regard as fellow-
citizens between whom there can be no sort of
conflict of interest scores of tribes that spent
their time mutually throat-cutting at no very
distant period, as history goes. We recognize,
indeed, that profound national differences like
those which exist between the Welshman and
the Englishman, or the Scotchman and the Irish-
man, not only need involve no conflict of interest, but need involve even no separate political
existence.

One has heard in recent times of the gradual
revival of nationalism, and it is commonly argued

that the principle of nationality must stand in the way of co-operation between States. But the facts do not justify such conclusion for a moment. The formation of States has disregarded national divisions altogether. If conflicts are to coincide with national divisions, Wales should co-operate with Brittany and Ireland as against Normandy and England; Provence and Savoy with Sardinia as against— I do not know what French province, because in the final rearrangement of European frontiers races and provinces have become so inextricably mixed, and have paid so little regard to "natural" and "inherent" divisions, that it is no longer possible to disentangle them.

In the beginning the State is a homogeneous tribe or family, and in the process of economic and social development these divisions so far break down that a State may include, as the British State does, not only half a dozen different races in the Mother Country, but a thousand different races scattered over various parts of the earth— white, black, yellow, brown, copper-coloured. This, surely, is one of the great sweeping tendencies of history—a tendency which operates immediately any complicated economic life is set up. What justification have we, therefore, for saying dogmatically that a tendency to co-operation which has swept before it profound ethnic differences, social and political divisions, a process which has been constant from the dawn of men's attempts to live and labour together, is to stop at the wall of modern State divisions, which represent none of the profound divisions of the human race, but mainly mere administrative convenience, and embody a conception which is being every day profoundly modified?

Some indication of the processes involved in this development has already been given in the outline sketch in Chapter II. of this section, to which the reader may be referred (p. 162). I have there attempted to make plain that *pari passu* with the drift from physical force towards economic inducement goes a corresponding diminution of pugnacity, until the psychological factor which is the exact reverse of pugnacity comes to have more force even than the economic one. Quite apart from any economic question, it is no longer possible for the British Government to order the extermination of a whole population, of the women and children, in the old Biblical style. In the same way, the greater economic interdependence which improved means of communication have provoked must carry with it a greater moral interdependence, and a tendency which has broken down profound national divisions, like those which separated the Celt and the Saxon, will certainly break down on the psychological side divisions which are obviously more artificial.

Among the multiple factors which have entered into the great sweeping tendency just sketched are one or two which stand out as most likely to have immediate effect on the breakdown of a purely psychological hostility embodied by merely State divisions. One is that lessening of the reciprocal sentiment of collective responsibility which the complex heterogeneity of the modern State involves. What do I mean by this sense of collective responsibility? To the Chinese Boxer all Europeans are "foreign devils"; between Germans, English, Russians there is little distinction, just as to the black in Africa there is little differentiation between the various white races. Even the yokel in England talks of "them foreigners." If a Chinese Boxer is injured by a Frenchman, he kills a German, and feels himself avenged—they are all "foreign devils." When an African tribe suffers from the depredations of a Belgian trader, the next white man who comes into its territory, whether he happens to be an Englishman or a Frenchman, loses his life; the tribesmen also feel themselves avenged. But if the Chinese Boxer had our clear conception of the different European nations, he would feel no psychological satisfaction in killing a German because a Frenchman had injured him. There must be in the Boxer's mind some collective responsibility between the two Europeans, or in the negro's mind between the two white men, in order to obtain this psychological satisfaction. If that collective responsibility does not exist, the hostility to the second white man in each case is not even raised.

Now, our international hostilities are largely based on the notion of a collective responsibility in each of the various States against which our hostility is directed, which does not, in fact, exist. There is at the present moment great ill-feeling in England against the "German." Now, "German" is a non-existent abstraction. We are angry with the German because he is building warships, conceivably directed against us; but a great many Germans are as much opposed to that increase of armament as are we, and the desire of the yokel to "have a go at them Germans" depends absolutely upon a confusion just as great as—indeed, it is greater than—that which exists in the mind of the Boxer, who cannot differentiate between the various European peoples. Mr. Blatchford commenced the series of articles which have done so much to accentuate ill-feeling with this phrase:

Germany is deliberately preparing to destroy the British Empire;

and later in the articles he added:

The German nation is homogeneous, organized. Their Imperial policy is continuous, their rulers work strenuously, sleeplessly, silently. Their principle is the theory of blood and iron.

It would be difficult to pack a more dangerous untruth into so few lines. What are the facts? If "Germany" means the bulk of the German people, Mr. Blatchford is perfectly aware that he is not telling the truth. It is not true to say of the bulk of the German people that they are deliberately preparing to destroy the British Empire. The bulk of the German people, if they are represented in any one party at all, are represented by the Social Democrats, who have stood from the first resolutely against any such intention. Now the facts have to be misstated in this way in order to produce that temper which makes for war. If the facts are correctly stated, no such temper arises.

What has a particularly competent German to say to Mr. Blatchford's generalization? Mr. Fried, the editor of *Die Friedenswarte*, writes:

There is no one German people, no single Germany. . . . There are more abrupt contrasts between Germans and Germans than between Germans and Indians. Nay, the contradistinctions within Germany are greater than those between Germans and the units of any other foreign nation whatever. It might be possible to make efforts to promote good understanding between Germans and Englishmen, between Germans and Frenchmen, to organize visits between nation and nation; but it will be for ever impossible to set on foot any such efforts at an understanding between German Social Democrats and Prussian

Junkers, between German Anti-Semites and German Jews.[1]

The disappearance of most international hostility depends upon nothing more complicated than the realization of facts which are little more complex than the geographical knowledge which enables us to see that the anger of the yokel (to whom all "furriners" are one) is absurd when he pummels a Frenchman because an Italian has swindled him

It may be argued that there never has existed in the past this identification between a people and the acts of its Government which rendered the hatred of one country for another logical, yet that the hatred has arisen. That is true; but certain new factors have entered recently to modify this problem. One is that never in the history of the world have nations been so complex as they are to-day; and the second is that never before have the dominating interests of mankind so completely cut across State divisions as they do to-day. The third factor is that never before has it been possible, as it is possible by our means of com-

[1] In *The Evolution of Modern Germany* the author says: "Germany implies not one people but many people . . . of different cultures, different social and political institutions . . . diversities of intellectual and economic life. When most foreigners speak of Germany they generally have in mind Prussia. . . . in but few things can Prussia be regarded as typical of the whole Empire."

munication to-day, to offset a solidarity of classes
and ideas as against a presumed State solidarity.

Take an actual instance. When the Russian
fleet sunk the Hull fishing-smacks, not long since,
England could have gone to war with Russia—
to the great satisfaction, probably, of the Russian
Government, at that time at grips with a budding
Liberal movement in its own country. In so far as
Liberal opinion can obtain expression in Russia,
that opinion was as condemnatory of the action
of the Admiral as was opinion in England.
Imagine for a moment that Liberalism had made
a little more progress, as it has lately, in Russia, and was a little more articulate, and that
the Russian Liberals were using this incident to
discredit autocracy in Russia, and to advance a
cause animated by English ideas. England would,
in declaring war upon the Russian Government,
be declaring war, in fact, upon the Liberals, upon
English ideas. (For a state of war would be
used by the Russian Government as excuse for
crushing Russian Liberalism.) Would the killing of Russian peasants bring to any Englishman
understanding the facts of the case any satisfaction to his just anger against the Russian Admiral?
Might the Englishman not as soon kill a number
of Chinamen? And in killing Russian Liberals
could he overlook the fact that he was killing
those as keenly desirous of the punishment of the
Russian Admiral as Englishmen could be?

Never at any stage of the world's development has there existed as to-day the machinery for embodying these interests and class ideas and ideals which cut across frontiers. It is not generally understood how many of our activities have become international. Two great forces have become internationalized: Capital on the one hand, Labour, or Socialism, on the other.

The Labour and Socialist movements have always been international, and become more so every year. Few considerable strikes take place in any one country without the labour organizations of other countries furnishing help, and very large sums have been contributed by the labour organizations of various countries in this way. The International Socialist Bureau was created in 1900, having its permanent secretariat at Brussels. Each year, at the International Congress, the delegates from the various countries get nearer to common action. At the Stuttgart Congress of 1907 one of the subjects of discussion was the practical means of stopping war by International Trades Union intervention, and the principle of such intervention was voted unanimously by the Congress. Such international co-operation between the Socialist parties has been much more effective than is generally realized. During the Fashoda crisis the French and German Socialists were in daily communication, and the line taken by the Socialist party in the French

Parliament and the Social Democrats in the Reichstag was predetermined by a conference between
the two. In the same way there was a conference
between the Austrian and Italian Socialists at
Trieste when Austro-Italian relations became
strained. Again, there was the same co-operation
between the Swedish and Norwegian Socialists
when war was threatened between those two
countries. But international Socialism has gone
farther: it is notorious that ministerial tactics
in France were directly modified as the result of
the decision taken by the International Socialist
Congress at Amsterdam, in which the line to be
taken by the French Socialists was there laid down.
In other words, the policy of the French Ministry
was being dictated as much by Socialists in Germany and in Belgium as by its own supporters in
France.

The progress of the International Trades Union,
as distinct from the Socialist bodies, may be
indicated by the fact that in 1904 something over
two millions, representing twelve countries, were
affiliated, whereas in 1908 nineteen countries were
represented in a total membership of nearly six
millions. Although this international body works
on the principle of being non-political, at the Paris
Conference it voted a motion of sympathy unanimously in favour of "the plucky Spanish com-
rades who opposed the order of mobilization by a
general strike," which motion also gave expression

to the hope that the workers of all countries would shortly be sufficiently organized internationally to prevent war by their influence and the employment of all the means in their power. At the last general strike in Sweden, 1909, the German Trades Unionists contributed fifty thousand pounds, the English Trades Unionists nearly two thousand, and so on.[1]

So much for the labour side. What for the side of capital? With reference to capital, it may almost be said that it is organized so naturally internationally that formal organization is not necessary. When the Bank of England is in

[1] The last Congress at Copenhagen dealt with such practical questions as the general line to be taken by Socialists and advanced political parties with reference to the co-operative movement; measures were taken for unifying working-class legislation throughout Europe, for insuring common action in the matter of international arbitration and disarmament, and practical means were again discussed for giving effect to the resolution of the International Congress. For the International Trades Union movement there is an international secretariat at Berlin, and each of the adhering bodies pays a due of 1.50 marks a year for each thousand Trades Unionists. Common action in the matter of "blacklegs" resulted from the Congress held by the International Trades Union at Christiania, and was confirmed by the Paris Conference of 1909; and common action was also decided in this last Congress on the question of "sweating." A beginning was made also in arriving at a common minimum European eight-hour day. The International Trades Union body publishes a yearly report in German, French, and English, and the total number of Trades Unionists is there given as very nearly ten millions, of whom rather more than half are affiliated internationally.

danger, it is the Bank of France which comes automatically to its aid, even in a time of acute political hostility. It has been my good fortune in the last ten years to discuss these matters with financiers on one side and labour leaders on the other, and I have always been particularly struck by the fact that I have found in these two classes precisely the same attitude of internationalization. In no department of human activity is internationalization so complete as in finance. The capitalist has no country, and he knows, if he be of the modern type, that arms and conquests and jugglery with frontiers serve no ends of his, and may very well defeat them. But employers, as apart from capitalists, are also developing a strong international cohesive organization. Among the Berlin despatches in the *Times* of April 18, 1910, I find the following concerning a big strike in the building trade, in which nearly a quarter of a million men went out. Quoting a writer in the *North German Gazette*, the correspondent says:

The writer lays stress upon the efficiency of the employers' arrangements. He says, in particular, that it will probably be possible to extend the lock-out to industries associated with the building industry, especially the cement industry, and that the employers are completing a ring of cartel treaties, which will prevent German workmen from finding employment in neighbouring countries, and will insure for German employers all possible support from abroad.

It is said that Switzerland and Austria were to conclude treaties yesterday on the same conditions as
Sweden, Norway, Denmark, Holland, and France, and
that Belgium and Italy would come in, so that there
will be complete co-operation on the part of all Germany's neighbours except Russia. In the circumstances the men's organs rather over-labour the point
when they produce elaborate evidence of premedita-
tion. The *Vorwarts* proves that the employers
have long been preparing for "a trial of strength,"
but that is admitted. The official organ of the
employers says, in so many words, that any intervention is useless until "the forces have been measured
in open battle."

And have not these forces begun already to
affect the psychological domain with which we are
now especially dealing? Do we place national
vanity, for instance, on the same plane as the
individual? Have we not already realized the
absurdity involved?

I have quoted Admiral Mahan as follows:

That extension of national authority over alien
communities, which is the dominant note in the world
politics of to-day, dignifies and enlarges each State
and each citizen that enters its fold. . . . Sentiment,
imagination, aspiration, the satisfaction of the rational and moral faculties in some object better than
bread alone, all must find a part in a worthy motive.
Like individuals, nations and empires have souls as
well as bodies. Great and beneficent achievement

ministers to worthier contentment than the filling of the pocket.

Have we not come to realize that this is all moonshine, and very mischievous moonshine? Let us examine it a little.

A man who boasts of his possessions is not a very pleasant, admirable type, but at least his possessions are for his own use and do bring a tangible satisfaction, materially as well as sentimentally. He is the object of a certain social deference by reason of his wealth—a deference which has not a very high motive, if you will, but the outward and visible signs of which are pleasing to a vain man. But is the same in any sense true, despite Admiral Mahan, of the individual citizen of a big State as compared with the individual citizen of a small one? Does any one think of paying deference to the Russian *moujik* because he happens to belong to one of the biggest empires territorially? Does any one think of despising an Ibsen or a Björnsen, or any educated Scandinavian or Belgian or Hollander, because they happen to belong to the smallest nations in Europe? The thing is absurd, and the notion is simply due to inattention. Just as we commonly overlook the fact that the individual citizen is quite unaffected materially by the extent of his nation's territory, that the material position of the individual Dutchman as a citizen of a small State will not be improved by the mere fact of the absorption of his State by the German Empire, in which case he will become the citizen of a great nation, so in the same way his moral position remains unchanged; and the notion that an individual Russian is "dignified and enlarged" each time that Russia conquers some new Asiatic outpost, or Russifies a State like Finland, or that the Norwegian would be "dignified" were his State conquered by Russia and he became a Russian, is, of course, sheer sentimental fustian of a very mischievous order. This is the more emphasized when we remember that the best men of Russia are looking forward wistfully, not to the enlargement, but to the dissolution of the unwieldy giant—"stupid with the stupidity of giants, ferocious with their ferocity" —and the rise in its stead of a multiplicity of self-contained, self-knowing communities, "whose members will be united together by organic and vital sympathies, and not by their common submission to a common policeman."

How small and thin a pretence is all the talk of national prestige when the matter is tested by its relation to the individual is shown by the commonplaces of our everyday social intercourse. In social consideration everything else takes precedence of nationality, even in those circles where Chauvinism is the cult. British Royalty is so impressed with the dignity which attaches to membership in the British Empire that its Princes

will marry into the royal houses of the smallest
and meanest States in Europe, while they would
regard marriage with a British commoner as an
unheard-of *mésalliance*. This standard of social
judgment so marks all the European royalties
that at the present time not one ruler in Europe
belongs, properly speaking, to the race which he
rules. In all social associations an analogous
rule is followed. In our "selectest" circles an
Italian, Roumanian, Portuguese, or even Turkish
noble, is received where an English tradesman
would be taboo.

This tendency has struck almost all authorities
who have investigated scientifically modern international relations. Thus Mr. T. Baty, the well-
known authority on international law, writes as
follows:

All over the world society is organizing itself by
strata. The English merchant goes on business to
Warsaw, Hamburg, or Leghorn; he finds in the merchants of Italy, Germany, and Russia the ideas, the
standard of living, the sympathies, and the aversions
which are familiar to him at home. Printing and the
locomotive have enormously reduced the importance
of locality. It is the mental atmosphere of its fellows,
and not of its neighbourhood, which the child of the
younger generation is beginning to breathe. Whether
he reads the *Revue des Deux Mondes* or *Tit-Bits*,
the modern citizen is becoming at once cosmopolitan
and class-centred. Let the process work for a few

more years; we shall see the common interests of cosmopolitan classes revealing themselves as far more potent factors than the shadowy common interests of the subjects of States. The Argentine merchant and the British capitalist alike regard the Trades Union as a possible enemy—whether British or Argentine matters to them less than nothing. The Hamburg docker and his brother of London do not put national interests before the primary claims of caste. International class feeling is a reality, and not even a nebulous reality; the nebula has developed centres of condensation. Only the other day Sir W. Runciman, who is certainly not a Conservative, presided over a meeting at which there were laid the foundations of an International Shipping Union, which is intended to unite shipowners of whatever country in a common organization. When it is once recognized that the real interests of modern people are not national, but social, the results may be surprising.[1]

As Mr. Baty points out, this tendency, which he calls "stratification," extends to all classes:

It is impossible to ignore the significance of the International Congresses, not only of Socialism, but of pacificism, of Esperantism, of feminism, of every kind of art and science, that so conspicuously set the seal upon the holiday season. Nationality as a limiting force is breaking down before cosmopolitanism. In directing its forces into an international channel, Socialism will have no difficulty whatever. . . . We are, therefore, confronted with a coming condition of

[1] *International Law.*

affairs in which the force of nationality will be distinctly inferior to the force of class-cohesion, and in which classes will be internationally organized so as to wield their force with effect. The prospect induces some curious reflections.

We have here, at present in merely embryonic form, a group of motives otherwise opposed, but meeting and agreeing upon one point: the organization of society on other than territorial and national divisions. When motives of such breadth as these give force to a tendency, it may be said that the very stars in their courses are working to the same end.

PART III

The Practical Outcome

CHAPTER I

ARMAMENT, BUT NOT ALONE ARMAMENT

Why we cannot abandon armament irrespective of others—The
human nature of this part of the problem—Why armaments
alone are likely to lead to war—Why agreements between
Governments are likely to fail, and must in any case be of
limited effect.

IN the first edition of this book I wrote:

Are we immediately to cease preparation for war,
since our defeat cannot advantage our enemy nor
do us in the long run much harm? No such conclusion results from a study of the considerations
elaborated here. It is evident that so long as the
misconception we are dealing with is all but universal
in Europe, so long as the nations believe that in
some way the military and political subjugation of
others will bring with it a tangible material advantage
to the conqueror, we all do, in fact, stand in danger
from such aggression. Not his interest, but what he
deems to be his interest, will furnish the real motive
of our prospective enemy's action. And as the
illusion with which we are dealing does, indeed,
dominate all those minds most active in European
politics, we must, while this remains the case, regard

an aggression, even such as that which Mr. Harrison foresees, as within the bounds of practical politics. (What is not within the bounds of possibility is the extent of devastation which he foresees as the result of such attack, which, I think, the foregoing pages sufficiently demonstrate.)

On this ground alone I deem that we or any other nation are justified in taking means of self-defence to prevent such aggression. This is not, therefore, a plea for disarmament irrespective of the action of other nations. So long as current political philosophy in Europe remains what it is, I would not urge the reduction of our war budget by a single sovereign or a single dollar.

I see no reason to alter a word of this, but I would add one or two, as some of my critics seem to have overlooked a part of the conclusion which goes with the foregoing—namely, that so long as the production of war material and the training for war are our only preparation for peace, we shall almost certainly prepare not for peace but for war, and every ship that we add does but add to the wealth which we throw into the gulf, and, by increasing the suspicion and distrust that go with the ever-increasing weight of material, does but render a solution of the matter more difficult.

What is the situation as exemplified for instance in the present Anglo-German rivalry?

At present there is only one policy that holds the field—to go on building ships. The other

policy—looking to an agreement for the limitation
of armaments—Germany has rejected for reasons
which are sufficiently clear. While Great Britain
at the present moment is predominant, Germany,
in the terms of current diplomacy, exists on the
sufferance of Great Britain. That is to say, a
nation of sixty million people, constituting the
greatest military Power in Europe, is, in so far as
the field of activity covered by naval force is concerned—a field of activity which our own philosophy, as voiced by Admiral Mahan, represents
as the very key of political influence in the world
at large, and all the advantages that are supposed
to go therewith—at the mercy of forty millions.
Can we expect a proud people, as political doctrines go at present, to accept such a situation?
England would not, and does not, accept it.
Germany, like England, is determined to base
her national security, not on the good-will of
foreigners, but on her own strength. English
statesmanship takes exactly the same view.

I am aware that, according to the English view,
the situation of the two countries is not exactly
identical, in that while England's very existence
reposes on sea power, the existence of Germany
reposes on land power. (I am talking always
now in the terms of currently accepted political
doctrine.) But our highly organized modern
State exists not only for the protection of its
people, but for their advantage. Now, quite

apart from all question of defence, the English have always urged that great advantage[1] in world politics goes with the possession of sea power, and that no statesman can be properly armed in his diplomatic struggle with another Power while that other Power has all the advantage of sea force. Admiral Mahan himself says[2]:

Observant men know that there have been at least three wars in this so-called period of peace (during the last decade)—wars none the less because no blows were exchanged, for force determined the issues. The common phrase for such transactions is "the risk of war has been averted." The expression is dangerously misleading, because it is supposed that the

[1] Professor Hans Delbruck, in the *Contemporary Review*, September, 1909, says: "The definite aim which Germany sets herself is not to acquire vast colonies. . . . The German Navy is not, and never will be, sufficiently strong directly to menace England. . . . A German invasion of England is out of the question, even under the most favourable circumstances. . . . In Germany these English ideas are considered either vain illusions or party politics. It will be remembered that, during the whole of the nineteenth century, the British public were continually scared by a threatened invasion either from France or Russia. . . . What Germany has set herself to do is to enforce such a position that German influence, German capital, German commerce, German engineering, and German intelligence, can compete on equal terms with other nations." The more we urge that a great navy is wrapped up with commercial success, the more we urge that a powerful navy can impose favourable conditions, the more reason has Germany to oppose the growth of the British Navy, and get a large one of her own.

[2] *Daily Mail*, July 16, 1910.

controlling element in this conclusion has been the adroitness of statesmen, whereas the existence and calculation of force have been really determinative. Force, too, not merely in the raw material, but the organized force of armies and navies ready—or unready—to move.

His commentator, *The Daily Mail*, adds:

Without sufficient armaments a Power can be beaten in diplomacy or battle, or in both. . . . What happens when the interests of two Powers conflict? The statesman of the first Power says to the second Power, "We must beg you to give way." The second Power replies, "We really cannot." The first Power rejoins, "If so, we are sorry, but it will be very unpleasant for you." The second Power then calculates its battleships and army corps. It calls upon its General Staff for a statement as to whether it has a chance of winning. If it learns that it has no chance—that it has only twenty *Dreadnoughts* to the other Power's thirty—then it will give way rather than meet disaster. It has suffered defeat, if a bloodless one. It has surrendered its interests, and those interests may be vital. From start to finish this process, which is known as diplomacy, depends on estimates of force and on the existence of force. But because force all the time remains in the background, the ignorant misconceive its real nature. They do not see that Russia, for example, by her surrender to the German ultimatum of last year, lost as much as by her defeat at the hands of Japan in the actual war in the Far East. Indeed, she lost more, for her interests in the Far East were less vital than those in the Balkans.

But if the foregoing reasoning appeals with force to Englishmen, who already have the predominance of sea power, how is it likely to appeal to Germans, whose sea power is so greatly inferior? They are asking of Germany very much more than she asks of them. She says, "We want equality of force, an equilibrium." England says: "We don't want equilibrium, we want domination." The German Admiral Rosendahl, discussing the British and German navies and the proposals for disarmament, wrote in the *Deutsche Revue* for June, 1909:

If England claims, and it is permanently necessary for her, an absolute supremacy at sea, that is her affair, and no sensible man will reproach her for it; but it is quite a different thing for a great Power like the German Empire, by an international treaty, supposed to be binding for all time, expressly to recognize and accept this in principle. Assuredly we do not wish to enter into a building competition with England on a footing of equality . . . but a political agreement on the basis of the unconditional superiority of the British fleet would be the equivalent of an abandonment of our national dignity; and though we do not, speaking broadly, wish to dispute England's predominance at sea, yet we do mean, in case of war, to be, or to become, the masters of our own coasts.

Professor Spenser Wilkinson, who quotes this passage,[1] adds: "There is not a word in this which can give just cause of offence to England or Englishmen." The redoubtable Mr. Blatchford himself, completely recognizes the reasonableness of the German view in this matter. He says[2]:

It does not require a very great effort of the imagination to enable us to see that proposal with German eyes. Were I a German I should say, "These islanders are cool customers. They have fenced in all the best parts of the globe, they have bought or captured fortresses and ports in five continents, they have gained the lead in commerce they have a virtual monopoly of the carrying trade of the world, they hold command of the seas, and now they propose that we shall all be brothers, and that nobody shall fight or steal any more.

We are therefore at an *impasse*, or rather at a mere battle of purses: both sides must go on building—if necessary, to the limit of their national resources.

But has this no danger?

We, all of us, Big Navy men and Little Navy men alike, know that it has very grave danger. There is first the danger arising from that human nature to which the war advocates are so

[1] *Britain at Bay.*
[2] *Germany and England*, p. 13.

fond of appealing.   An acute American observer[1]
writes:

Talk of war, however causeless, tends to beget
war. Familiarize two nations with the daily thought
of fighting, and it will be a miracle if they fail to
fight. Let them occupy themselves daily for two
or three years with discussing, even when utterly
denying the possibility of the thing, and that thing
becomes more possible. Discuss causes of war, deny
that they exist, and you provoke them. I mean to
say that it is of no consequence that you are all
the time protesting that war is impossible; you are
all the time talking of it. It does not matter what
is said on a subject; the matter is that the subject is
kept constantly in mind. It becomes an obsession.
A subconscious process is set up tending to a conclusion with which rational thought has nothing to
do. Every incident takes on special significance.
Events are scrutinized with a purpose which, though
unconscious, becomes fixed. Everybody is uncon-
sciously on the look-out for an offence. . . . The
national mind is prepared for an emotional crisis
which any trivial incident may release, for a national
"brain storm" in the passion of which the murderous
deed will be swiftly done. There is nothing far-
fetched nor fanciful in this; it is precisely what most
often happens with nations. . . . At the Aldershot
practice manœuvres this year the combatants
referred to each other as "the Germans." "Is n't
that rather an ill-considered custom?" an officer was

[1] Dr. Bayard Hale in *World's Work*, Feb., 1910.

asked. "Is n't it calculated to encourage hatred and stir up bad blood?" "I don't know as to that," he replied, "but it certainly is calculated to get the keenest sort of work out of them. They 're lazy beggars unless we set 'em on the Germans; then you should see them."

I do not want to labour the importance of this, but it is there, and has to be reckoned with. But there is a much more serious point.

To Englishmen it seems ridiculous, of course, that the Germans should think England has any intention of attacking them. But then, most Germans think it just as ridiculous that Englishmen should think that Germans have any intention of attacking them. Putting ourselves for a moment in their [*i.e.*, the Germans] place, does not the present English attitude justify a certain suspicion in the minds of Germans?

A few years ago the Germans were in a position of manifest inferiority; in that which relates to world policy they were absolutely at England's mercy. As one German public man said, "Our ships sailed the seas on sufferance." Even the *Spectator* some ten years ago pointed out the hopeless position that Germany would occupy in any conflict with England. From an article published in that journal, January 16, 1897, I take the following:

Let us consider quietly and without heat what would have happened had the State [England] . . . tried the experiment of war with Germany this time last year. . . . Our fleet is much stronger than the German fleet, so much stronger, indeed, that the Germans would not have risked its destruction, but would have kept it safely in port. The German Navy is a good one, and its sailors and officers are brave men, but even they do not consider that it would be possible to beat our ships when outnumbered three to one. . . . We may take it, then, that the Germans, having no need to show their courage in a hopeless engagement, would have kept their fleet in port. What would have been the result of such an action? In the first place, such German ships of war as are to be found in the Pacific or on the African coasts would have been either sunk or captured. . . . The next result would have been that an expedition despatched from India or Mauritius would have seized German East Africa, one from the Cape Angra Pequena and Damaraland, one from England the Cameroons, and one from Australia German New Guinea. But, it may be said, so far Germany would have suffered very little. No doubt, but this is by no means all the harm we could have inflicted on Germany. . . . Germany has a mercantile marine of vast proportions. The German flag is everywhere. But on the declaration of war the whole of Germany's trading ships would be at our mercy. Throughout the seas of the world our cruisers would seize and confiscate German ships. Within the first week of the declaration of war Germany would have suffered a loss of many million pounds by the capture of her ships. Nor is that all. Our Colonies are dotted with German trading-houses, which, in spite of a keen competition, do a great deal of business. . . . We should not, of course, want to treat them harshly, but war must mean for them the selling of their businesses for what they would fetch and going home to Germany. In this way Germany would lose a hold upon the trade of the world which it has taken her many years of toil to create. Think, too, of what Germany has spent upon subsidized steamship lines like the North German Lloyd. War with England must mean the utter ruin of this great carrying corporation. Again, think of the effect upon Germany's trade of the closing of all her ports. Hamburg is one of the greatest ports of the world. What would be its condition if practically not a single ship could leave or enter it? Blockades are no doubt very difficult things to maintain strictly, but Hamburg is so placed that the operation would be comparatively easy. In truth the blockade of all the German ports on the Baltic or the North Sea would present little difficulty. . . . Consider the effect on Germany if her flag were swept from the high seas and her ports blockaded. She might not miss her colonies, for they are only a burden, but the loss of her sea-borne trade would be an equivalent to an immediate fine of at least a hundred million sterling. In plain words, a war with Germany, even when conducted by her, with the utmost wisdom and prudence must mean for her a direct loss of a terribly heavy kind, and for us virtually no loss at all.[1]

[1] This article was written in reply to a German allegation of our helplessness. But that does not alter the facts.

This, an it please you, is not from some pamphlet of the German Navy League, but from the organ which is now apt to resent the increased German Navy as implying aggression upon England!

Supposing that in the foregoing the rôles were reversed, and the passages were to be read by an Englishman in a German paper. Is there a single Englishman animated by the axioms of our present-day statecraft who would not say that it was his country's first duty to alter so humiliating and so intolerable a situation by an increase of naval armament? Very well, Germans have done it, and are doing it, and what is the result? That our great popular papers represent this fact as an aggression upon England. Is there not at least some justification for the view held by some parties in Germany that Englishmen demand the overpowering predominance of the British Navy, not for purposes of defence, but for the purpose of keeping Germany in perpetual tutelage, and for the purpose of continuing to beat her in those diplomatic world battles which take place without the actual exercise of force, but with only the threat of force, about which Admiral Mahan has written in the passage that I have quoted? Take the foregoing passage from the *Spectator*, showing the utter helplessness of Germany ten years ago, together with the sort of boast which, like the following, one may find in at least some English papers:

Thanks to the Navy we are the most hardened invaders the world has ever seen. Take a single British regiment at random, the 50th Queen's Own. Its records show that during the period of only 130 years it has fought in Canada, Germany, Corsica, Egypt, Denmark, Spain, France, Holland, India, Russia, and New Zealand. Pretty well, is it not?

The British Army has fought in every land, from China to the Argentine Republic, and from the Himalayas to the Cape and New Zealand. The only service that the British Army has never been called on to render is the defence of England against invasion.[1]

Speaking in practical terms, there is not an Englishman living who would have accepted the situation in which Germany found herself ten years ago, yet immediately Germany proceeds to alter it we get accusations of a violent and clamorous order that Germany is bent upon aggression, and an agitation which the Government is unable to resist for maintaining the ratio of inequality between the power of the two States at somewhere near what it was ten years ago.

The result, therefore, is this: England is asking that Germany shall accept normally a position of manifest inferiority. Is she likely to? Would Englishmen, especially if they had the larger population and the prospective amalgamation with another country (I am thinking of Austria)

[1] *Referee.*

which would give Englishmen a superiority of two to one in numbers—even if we include the white Colonies? Again, there is no Englishman living who, in the terms of the present political philosophy, would accept such a solution.

Why then, are Englishmen asking it of Germany?

But the fact of England's insistence on this solution carries with it a still graver danger. Since time is on the side of the German and is against England, that fact places the advantage of aggression on the English side. Germans who discuss this matter thoroughly realize the fact. In the February number of the *Deutsche Revue* for the present year, Professor Bernard Harms, of Kiel University, in deriding the idea that Germany is preparing a surprise attack on England, disposes of such an accusation by pointing out that Germans are winning the war of peace competition so unmistakably, that it would be folly for them to translate the struggle from the arena of Germany's attested superiority to an arena where the conflict must, at any rate, be doubtful. He urges that England, on the other hand, is far more likely to break the peace as soon as she finds her economic rival to be striding past her in trade. He urges that the past history of British rivalry with the maritime Powers of the Continent all tends to establish the same theory. The Professor concludes with this advice to his countrymen:

"Germany should seek to establish the same state of peace as the United States has succeeded in imposing. There has been no war between the two countries because the British have feared America, have believed that they could not hold Canada except by American forbearance and have no desire to quarrel with the great Republic under any circumstances."

The view of Professor Harms finds confirmation in that expressed by Professor Delbruck in the article from which I have already quoted.[1] Professor Delbruck says:

The English population is disturbed by German industrial progress . . . English industry is being pressed on all sides by German competition. From these facts the feeling has arisen in England that it is not desirable to wait until her maritime as well as her industrial supremacy is lost, but that while she is still mistress of the seas and is in alliance with France the opportunity should be taken to suppress Germany.

Do we, on the English side, find any confirmation of the foregoing suspicion? Unfortunately, we find a great deal. Sir Edmund C. Cox writes in the premier English review, the *Nineteenth Century*, for April, 1910:

Is there an alternative to this endless yet futile competition in shipbuilding? Yes, there is. It is one

[1] *Contemporary Review*, Oct., 1909.

which a Cromwell, a William Pitt, a Palmerston, a Disraeli, would have adopted long ago. This is that alternative—the only possible conclusion. It is to say to Germany: "All that you have been doing constitutes a series of unfriendly acts. Your fair words go for nothing. Once for all, you must put an end to your warlike preparations. If we are not satisfied that you do so we shall forthwith sink every battleship and cruiser which you possess. The situation which you have created is intolerable. If you determine to fight us, if you insist upon war, war you shall have; but the time shall be of our choosing and not of yours, and that time shall be now."

Even Professor Wilkinson admits that a party in favour of the policy outlined by Sir E. C. Cox does exist.[1] The American observer, Dr. Hale, whom I have already quoted, carries away the same impression. He says[2]:

The immediate dangers of the situation are primarily from the English side, and may be scientifically stated as consisting in . . . the more rational realization by a deteriorating people of the necessity of an early and swift effort to regain a prestige which is slipping from them. . . . England does not in its heart of hearts believe its own talk of Germany's warlike intentions, but it shivers with awakening consciousness of its own . . . for an immense advantage will lie with the Power which launches the first blow. It is the knowledge of this fact that multiplies

[1] *Britain at Bay*, p. 101.
[2] *World's Work*, Feb., 1910.

many times the likelihood of hostilities: mutual suspicion, which cannot afford to await verification,
will urge to prior action. England and Germany
will each be impelled to strife, even without cause, by
the conviction that the other is preparing to strike.

In view of the foregoing, can anyone honestly
say that the sheer savage bulldog piling up of the
machinery of war carries no danger? Is it not,
on the contrary, full of danger?

It is noteworthy that the war advocate who
flings so readily at the head of the pacifist the
charge of ignoring human nature does so himself
habitually; he expects other people to be guided
by a motive which he would never allow to affect
his own conduct. He knows perfectly well that
if he were a German, in the circumstances of the
case he would not surrender the contest merely
because of the tenacity of the opposing nation;
yet he expects the German to do what he would
never do. Even Admiral Fisher, whom I do not
place among the Jingoes, can speak as follows[1]:

I am not for war, I am for peace. That is why I
am for a supreme Navy. Did I not write in your
autograph book at The Hague: "The supremacy
of the British Navy is the best security for the peace
of the world"? My sole object is peace. What you
call my truculence is all for peace. If you rub it in
both at home and abroad that you are ready for

[1] *Review of Reviews*, Feb., 1910.

Lightning Source UK Ltd.
Milton Keynes UK
UKOW06f0003301014

240840UK00004B/141/P